DEAN'S LIST

REFERENCE

DEAN'S LIST

Eleven Habits of
Highly Successful College Students

JOHN B. BADER

The Johns Hopkins University Press
Baltimore

© 2011 John B. Bader
All rights reserved. Published 2011
Printed in the United States of America on acid-free paper
9 8 7 6 5 4 3 2 1

The Johns Hopkins University Press
2715 North Charles Street
Baltimore, Maryland 21218-4363
www.press.jhu.edu

Library of Congress Cataloging-in-Publication Data

Bader, John B.
    Dean's list : eleven habits of highly successful college students / John B. Bader.
        p.   cm.
    Includes bibliographical references and index.
    ISBN-13: 978-1-4214-0080-8 (hardcover : alk. paper)
    ISBN-13: 978-1-4214-0081-5 (pbk. : alk. paper)
    ISBN-10: 1-4214-0080-4 (hardcover : alk. paper)
    ISBN-10: 1-4214-0081-2 (pbk. : alk. paper)
    1. Study skills. 2. College student orientation. I. Title.
    LB2395.B28 2011
    378.1'98—dc22   2010046743

A catalog record for this book is available from the British Library.

Special discounts are available for bulk purchases of this book. For more information,
please contact Special Sales at 410-516-6936 or specialsales@press.jhu.edu.

The Johns Hopkins University Press uses environmentally friendly book materials,
including recycled text paper that is composed of at least 30 percent post-consumer waste,
whenever possible. All of our book papers are acid-free, and our jackets and covers are
printed on paper with recycled content.

To Calvin and Eli

CONTENTS

JOHN T. O'KEEFE, Ph.D., Director of Advising and Academic Support Services and Class Dean, Wellesley College

ACKNOWLEDGMENTS

This book is a project many years in the making, only becoming reality with the help of many supporters. I am grateful for the encouragement, frank feedback, and support of Ashleigh McKown at the Johns Hopkins University Press. She saw real promise in the project, but that promise could not have been realized without her honesty. I also appreciate the exacting pen of copyeditor Carolyn Moser.

The project became a communal effort, an attempt at capturing collective wisdom, thanks to the advice and contributing essays of many colleagues at peer institutions. We started a yearly conference of these advising deans in 2007; and in 2008, many of them accepted my invitation to contribute to this book. I am most grateful to them all. Their names and biographies appear in the book's list of contributors.

I want to thank my senior colleagues at the Johns Hopkins University: Paula Burger, Dan Weiss, Steven David, Adam Falk, Richard Sanders, Karen Desser, Kathie Sindt, Ruth Aranow, Adriene Breckenridge, Jim Fry, Michelle Rodriguez, Janet Weise, Andrew Douglas, John Latting, Lori Citti, Ken Romaine, Steve Pomper, Jessica Madrigal, Liza Thompson, Bill Conley, Michael Mond, and Susan Boswell. Their wisdom, experiences, stories, and support run through every sentence I have written. I would have been helpless without my assistants at Hopkins, first Sydney Green and then Vicki Fitzgerald, who have proven that no man can succeed without strong women.

My family has always supported this project. I am grateful, as always, to my wife, Amy. And I happily dedicate this book to our sons, Calvin and Eli, with the hope that they will lead lives of adventure and exploration.

Finally, I am deeply grateful to the hundreds of students at UCLA and especially at Johns Hopkins who have been a joyous source of inspiration, wisdom, and hope for our future.

DEAN'S LIST

Introduction
Facing Freshman Year

Congratulations! You did it. You got into college! Maybe you're going to Princeton, Michigan, Duke, Berkeley, Stanford, or another of the best research universities in the world. Or perhaps you're bound for a great liberal arts college like Swarthmore, Davidson, Pomona, or Kenyon. Maybe it's a private college in New England or the flagship campus of your state university system. That is wonderful and, I'm sure, well deserved.

You've worked hard the past few years, building an amazing record of academic achievements, community service, and activities that have kept you busy and challenged. You sweated through exams like the SAT, filled out countless applications and forms, and waited in agony to get word from your dream schools. And now you're in.

Now what?

It sounds strange, but a lot of incoming freshmen have no good answer to that question. They might have a plan for a major or even a career, but if pressed, they'll confess that they're not sure what that means. They have worked incredibly hard, to the point of exhaustion, to start an experience that they don't really understand. They know college is important. (Why go to all that trouble and expense if it weren't?) But it's not quite clear what college will be like or how to succeed, especially if they are the first in their family to go to college.

This book will answer your questions, helping you to find real and lasting success in college. I have gathered the wisdom of dozens of deans from the best colleges in America, including the entire Ivy League, to combine with my observations so that you can enjoy the success you want and deserve. Together, we offer a list of 11 habits of highly successfully college students, 11 strategic choices to help you navigate the next four years.

We'll do this in a way that's a bit unconventional, because you're too smart and savvy to be offered a laundry list of tips.[1] You want to drink deeply from this fountain, not just find shortcuts. So we're going to push you to be strategic in your thinking, to reevaluate why you're going to college, to learn more about colleges as institutions, and to prepare for the possibility of failure. As you learn the habits on the Dean's List, you will learn how to find your own path and, if you embrace the mission of learning, enjoy great success.[2]

Going to College

If you're reading this in April of your senior year, you may be considering several acceptance offers. Maybe it's June, and you're celebrating high school graduation with just a hint of wistfulness. By July, you've made a decision and are looking at lots of documents from your college, filling out endless forms online. In August, the uncertainties and anxieties of moving away from home and onto a strange campus are upon you. Or maybe it's September, the academic year has started, and you're working to find your legs as a college freshman.

Whatever the moment in time, you need to think about the differences between your life in high school and the one you are starting in college, particularly the academic differences. Of course, if you don't, you'll probably be just fine. Most freshmen are. But you may miss the chance to take the campus at a faster speed, to jump onto the fast-moving train that is college life without stumbling. You want to do much better than "fine." So let's look at some of the key differences you will find, some of which we'll examine at length in the chapters that follow, and what they mean to your success.

❡ *There are no teachers in college!* A college professor is not a teacher, as strange as that sounds. Not only does she have a full professional life outside your classes—with research, university service, national conferences, and so on—but she probably doesn't think of herself as a "teacher," even when teaching in the classroom. Professors' idea of teaching is to make you more of a partner in learning. In fact, they want you to take charge of your education, to prepare independently, to ask bold questions, and to examine assigned materials with your own eyes. They may not be clear on what they want, and you won't see them enough to figure that out—but you don't have to learn alone. There are classmates, tutors, teaching assistants, and your professor, of course. But learning is now *your* job, without the direction and constant supervision your high school teachers may have given you.

❡ *The professors don't know me.* Most freshmen take introductory courses taught primarily through lectures. These classes can be huge, sometimes with over a thousand students. Even when the class size goes over as few as 30, the professor loses the ability, if not the desire, to get to know you, your name, or your needs. This anonymity can be pretty shocking when you're used to seeing your high school teachers every day, and they know you so well. As a successful high school student, you were probably a favorite of your teachers. And now none of the faculty knows you. To a degree, this is a reality of your first year, but it is also a matter of the class choices you make. You do not have to choose only large lectures; you can match them with seminars or language courses. Writing courses are usually small, as are most courses offered by smaller departments, such as classics, earth sciences, or philosophy. You can also find ways to get to know professors by asking questions or visiting them during office hours. So, if you don't like being anonymous, do something about it.[3]

❡ *Lectures are collegiate, but what do I do in them?* Let's say that you take a few of the large lecture courses I just mentioned. Despite their size and your anonymity, they can be interesting, entertaining, and provocative. And they're nothing like anything you've seen in high school; instead, lectures are a very collegiate phenomenon with lots of students furiously scribbling notes. When you're faced with something as important and unfamiliar as a lecture, try to avoid following everyone else's lead. First, you can't be sure what other students are writing in their notes. But second, you want to be strategic about what you are hearing and what you want to remember. That means engaging in a mental conversation with the lecture. Does this make sense? How does this connect with the readings? Why does that seem important? Just as critically, take note of things you do not understand, and be sure to ask the professor during office hours. Professors love it when you come to them with specific questions.

❡ *I've got a lot of time, right?* Not quite, but it sure looks that way. Do the math for a minute. In high school, you're in class for six to seven hours a day, five days a week. And you study another two hours a night, five nights a week. That's about 42 hours total, with nearly 75 percent of that in school. In college, you're in class about 15 hours a week, with 30 hours of studying outside of class. So now more than 65 percent of your academic time is unsupervised work, often in a library. College has turned your academic world almost exactly upside down. While 30 hours seems like a lot, you have to be really organized about using it or it will just float away. And it's not just about resisting the television, staying off Facebook, or turning off your cell phone. It's about finding ways to be thoughtful, analytic, and insightful while you're reading, writing, and working on problems. That will require experimentation to figure out when and where you're most productive, and how to engage the material even when you are alone.

❡ *My parents aren't here!* This is the best difference of all, for some students. There's no one to nag you about homework, to make you get to bed on time, or to be sure you take care of your body. But guess what? Now there's *no one to nag you about homework, to make you get to bed on time, or to be sure you take care of your body*! Now it's all up to you, or you won't be prepared for class or exams, you'll get exhausted and unable to learn, and you'll fall apart physically. The upside is that you can begin to take personal ownership of your education. The best part of that is learning what most interests you, rather than what people are expecting you to learn.

❡ *What is sociology?* One of the most important goals you can have in this transition is to sample widely from the academic offerings at your college. Even the most elite prep schools do not have the range of departments found at most colleges. Your high school probably didn't have a sociologist or an anthropologist on the faculty. But your ignorance about their disciplines, just from lack of exposure to them, could cost you. For all you know, you'd be a happy and successful anthropology major, but since you don't know what that means, you don't bother exploring it. So, when you arrive on campus, make it a point to learn about unfamiliar areas and disciplines, perhaps through open houses. You might find an academic home you never knew was there.

❡ *College is a big place.* While it is possible that your high school is bigger than your college, you're probably going to a college or university that is *much* bigger. It might have multiple campuses, professional schools (like a law school), research centers, and large libraries. Your high school might have a few thousand books. Yale's Sterling Library has *13 million* volumes. It's easy to get lost or intimidated, so remember to think small by focusing on your roommates, your instructors, your advisors, your classes, and your assignments first. You can build from there, once you know your way around.

❡ *Who are all these people?* Part of being in a bigger place is adjusting to the many kinds of people you now have around you. Remember that you're not the only kind of student. While traditional colleges have only undergraduates, universities have graduate students, professional students, and a large number of part-time students. The faculty is going to be much larger and more diverse intellectually. The student body will come from all over the world. Learn from this diversity and celebrate it by exploring and getting involved.

❡ *I can't get involved. I'm adjusting.* If you're typical of students who get into good colleges, you have been very busy outside of your high school classes: band, orchestra, drama, environmental club, community service, varsity soccer, on and on. You may be tempted to reduce your level of involvement as a freshman, thinking that it's good to not become overcommitted while you adjust to college. This is a mistake. The place may be big, with lots of people, but the only way you will have a rich experience is to be active and engaged. Joining a few clubs, writing for the school paper, playing on intramurals, or trying out for a singing group will connect you to new friends, skills, and ideas. Don't overdo it, but don't make excuses. Get out there!

If you understand the differences between high school and college, you can stop being surprised and start being curious. You can ask deeper questions about the experience you're having and the institution you've joined. Rather than simply thinking, "I'd better get some studying done this afternoon because I did nothing last night," you can start thinking more strategically: "How do I read this novel in a way to craft a well-argued essay?" "How do I find the connection between yesterday's lecture on military strategy and this book on the development of a railway system in France?" "What do I want to learn this year, and how do I do that?"

By appreciating and understanding where you are, and how different it is from where you've been, you'll be ready to develop the habits that are on the Dean's List.

The Habits of Successful Students

This book outlines the Dean's List of habits of successful college students. These habits are 11 ways to approach your education thoughtfully. Learning and adopting these habits won't be mechanical—do X, and Y grades pop out—because your education is complex and so are the ideas and actions that drive it forward. These habits are equally complex and deserve a full treatment.

Habit #1: **Focus on Learning, Not on Grades.** As a freshman, you can have the biggest impact on your college experience if you take the time to think deeply about *why* you're going to college.[4] We urge you to put your grades into perspective as a crude measurement of a professor's assessment. A more important way to think of success is whether you have become a *learned person,* whether you value the education you now own, whether you have learned what you want, and how well-prepared you will be to move on.

Habit #2: **Build an Adult Relationship with Your Parents.** Your parents have been your guides, guardians, and advocates. But now you are in college without them. It is time to develop a relationship with your parents that gives you more freedom and responsibility.[5] Having a new, adult relationship with a parent is not easy, but it is important. This book will help you find ways to do that.

Habit #3: **Work the System by** *Understanding* **the System.** You may know something about your college, but you probably don't understand how the tenure system affects you, what a dean can (and cannot) do for you, and what a president does.[6] (Preview: raise money.) You may be surprised at how your college's institutional qualities will influence your experience.

Habit #4: **Approach the Curriculum Like a Great Feast.** You've been invited to be an academic glutton at a huge intellectual buffet. But it's hard to take advantage of these choices without the right attitude, a knowledge about disciplines, and other tools for open exploration. Those tools can help you find a "home" where you will enjoy learning and thrive.

Habit #5: **Understand That Majors and Careers Are Not the Same Thing.** Choosing a major may be your biggest academic decision, but too many students believe it will affect their careers forever. In fact, the connection between majors and careers is very weak, and I'll explain why.[7] (Preview: it's a way to teach how to think seriously, not a way to give you expertise.) Once you disconnect them, you'll rediscover the freedom that the college wanted you to have in the beginning.

Habit #6: **Don't Just Work Hard—Work** *Smart*. As a successful applicant to college, you have shown your capacity for hard work. Maybe you know how to study, but maybe you don't. Worse, you **think** you know, but you don't. This discussion invites you to be a strategic student, consciously choosing study techniques that suit your learning style.[8]

Habit #7: **Build Integrity to Get into Professional or Graduate School.** Getting into a professional or graduate school is not so simple as earning a high GPA and acing the standardized tests (though those help, of course). Here, I'll talk about how you can reach that dream most effectively by building integrity through academic honesty and becoming distinctive.[9] Finding your own way is especially important, as your unique blend of skills and experience is your best selling point.

Habit #8: **Learn from Diversity at Home and Abroad.** College should challenge your worldview, but for you to succeed in that goal, you're going to need to face diversity issues. On campus, that will mean engaging in meaningful conversations with people who do not see the world as you do.[10] While studying abroad, it means overcoming the barriers to world travel for a chance at real immersion.[11]

Habit #9: **When You Are Failing, Understand Why.** No one goes to college expecting to fail. But the reality is that academic struggles are common. This would be hard for you, since, as a strong student, you may define yourself in part by real success. But it is important to talk about this possibility and its causes, if only to make it less frightening and easier to address.[12]

Habit #10: **Cope with Failure by Rebuilding and Forgiving.** Once you have identified the problems contributing to failure, it can be hard to do something about them. Here, we'll look at solutions to issues like lack of motivation and poor time management.[13] But the most important lesson in this case is the power of forgiveness. We all make mistakes, and we are strongest when we acknowledge them, forgive ourselves, and move on.

Habit #11: **Plan Boldly for Life after College.** College life ends quickly. This is sad and a little terrifying, as an uncertain future rushes toward you. You might have that feeling even as a freshman, and so you're likely to be planning for the future already. This discussion takes on issues that are years away but require thought—though not necessarily action—now. Building a practical supplement to your studies is sensible, as is the possibility of short-term work or public service post-graduation.[14] Better to build slowly than to panic late.

Cross-Cutting Themes

Now that you have a sense of the strategic offerings in this book, below are some of the themes that run through all 11 habits of highly successful college students. They are the "big picture"[15] ideas that should help you become a sophisticated consumer of your education. If you can embrace some of these ideas, you will truly appreciate that your four years in college form a precious, unrepeatable experience that should be respected, savored, and exploited. And that is a very good way to think of success.

❡ *Finding the right fit is a tough challenge.* These next years will be filled with questions, many of which can be answered only by you because they are about your path. Where should you go? What should you do? What can you learn? These choices are as unique as your DNA, which means you cannot follow what other people, including your friends and parents, have done. Indeed, finding a path is life's hardest challenge, requiring experimentation and exploration, heartbreak, and error. But finding that "fit" will bring peace and contentment.

❡ *Your family and friends should be your partners.* Finding a path may be very personal and at times lonely, but it is difficult to do without support. Friends and family may have a vision at odds with yours, but that is a discussion worth having. Ultimately, the choice belongs to you, but it would be better to bring those supporters along. That requires engagement, education, and mutual respect.

❡ *Enjoyment and success require self-awareness.* Stumbling from one mistake to another is not a healthy way to learn. It is also a waste of time. Being aware of how to make decisions and seriously consider alternatives is more prudent and mature. That means taking the time to reflect on what you are doing and the mistakes you make. Again, you can get help with this, perhaps this time from academic advisors and therapists.

❡ *Success should be measured internally.* While the support of family and professors is important, try not to depend on the approval of others to find satisfaction and a sense of accomplishment. Learning something useful and interesting is more important than earning a good grade. As Habit #1 suggests, setting intellectual goals —to become *learned* in some way—is healthier than setting numerical goals, if only because you can be satisfied on your own terms.

❡ *Body and mind are not separate.* It is a sad irony that when a student's mind is most capable of learning, he is statistically most likely to abuse it with by drugs, alcohol, and sleep deprivation.[16] You are strong and young, but not immortal. Your brain functions better when you're healthy, happy, and engaged. (Now try to remember that late at night and on Fridays.)

❡ *Any plan (even a good one) is a plan worth questioning.* Many students come to college with a plan for a predetermined major and a clear picture of a career. Try to be among those who are ready to test this plan. You may find that your goals are the result of parental and peer pressure. Or you may have hatched this plan without the amount of thinking, research, and testing that you spent on choosing colleges. That's really okay; maybe you're not ready. But don't let it trap you into obligations before questioning it. To paraphrase Socrates, an unexamined plan is not worth having.[17]

❡ *Don't forget the "small" stuff.* You might think that the biggest decision you'll make is your major. Actually, the real decisions come every term, as you choose classes. You'll build a major from class choices, naturally, but you're also building your education from them. So pay as much attention to your electives as your major courses. Consider that most alumni regret not taking "fun" classes like studio art or an acting course. Maybe they thought college was a pre-career boot camp, so they took practical or conventional courses. Or they followed the pack, taking large lecture classes. Or they simply failed to look around. Taking a small philosophy seminar or a course on modern art may reshape your worldview forever. So, find courses each term that you can celebrate and enjoy.

❡ *College students gain skills, not expertise.* Ten minutes after your last college final, you will forget most of the facts you crammed into your head. Like anything you learn, if you do not use it, you lose it. So what do you have left? The ability you gained or refined to gather, digest, and analyze complex ideas. The skills you practiced to write a crisp sentence or to give a clear presentation. The methods you learned from clubs and teams to lead and inspire. The sophistication and confidence you built with travel and cultural exchange. The network of friends and alumni who can help you professionally. The list goes on and on, but it does not include expertise.

❡ *Studying is not the same as memorizing.* A lot of students wish that they could simply open their brains and dump everything into it. The perfect student, they think, has an unlimited memory with perfect recall. So they read and take notes in a vain attempt to remember everything. This is a misunderstanding of both the process of learning and the purpose of higher education. An educated person is not a phone book, but someone who can make sense of information.[18] She looks at data, extracts what seems important, discerns meaningful patterns, builds principles on those patterns, and then applies the principles to a new situation or problem. None of those skills requires memorization.

❡ *We all fail sometimes, so we must forgive each other.* This book is written primarily for incoming freshmen, but I hope parents will read it, too. Communication between you and your parents is important to enjoying success, but it is *critical* when suffering failure. My colleagues and I spend a lot of time discussing the causes of and remedies for academic failure, a challenge far more common than one might expect, even at elite institutions like Duke and Brown. At the heart of the challenge is the need to forgive ourselves and those we love. Forgiveness is difficult for everyone, but without it, the smallest of missteps can cascade to disaster.

❡ *Uncertainty and freedom are intertwined.* College students cannot decide whether they appreciate the freedom they have or resent it. You may be free from daily supervision by parents, free to pick classes and a major, and free to set a professional course. But those choices seem so numerous and important that you may be frozen with fear. You might quickly retreat to conventional choices (like medical school) or defer to influential advisors (like your parents) before giving yourself a chance to figure it out. Try not to confuse the joys and privilege of free choice with the fears of uncertainty. It may be scary to look at an open landscape, but it can and should be a thrilling moment of possibility.

A Final Thought

I hope you find the lessons in this book to be helpful and provocative. The 11 habits on the Dean's List are meant to be as practical as they are to be challenging. As you read, think about how they connect or refute your own expectations or conceptions of college. At the very least, take from us deans one piece of advice: become a better-educated consumer of your college education. You and your family are spending a lot of money and deserve your money's worth. That will not happen unless you pause to think consciously and seriously about why you should go to college at all, what it will be like, and what can be done to make it worthwhile. This book should prompt some of that thinking. But there are other sources of inspiration for this thinking: visiting campuses; asking current students savvy questions (What are the lectures like here? How do you get to know faculty? What's the best choice you've made academically? The worst? What do you regret? Celebrate?); exploring Web sites more deeply (for example, look at what the faculty research vs. what they teach); talking openly with family and friends; and just taking a personal moment from the bustle of the college entrance process or the busy summer before college.

At this moment of reflection, you also can put the enterprise of higher education in some historic perspective.[19] Today, a college education is less a rite of passage for the privileged and more a universal experience for the middle class. Consider how profound and important a change this is. It represents a sea change of historic proportions, just as it represents a triumph by civil rights leaders, feminist activists, and families who overcame poverty and prejudice.

In a way, the choices and opportunities that lay before you are gifts from these people, just as they are gifts from your immediate family. Yet a true gift does not obligate the recipient to do anything but enjoy it and appreciate the love it represents. This is an important point that animates this entire book: a college education should be enjoyed for its own pleasures, and it should be appreciated as a selfless act of generosity from those who made it possible.

The gift of a college education—or access to higher education—also represents an act of liberation. To your ancestors, going to college would mean access to new opportunities, greater economic potential, and a higher social class. And they worked hard to get you to this point. So, consider college the gift of freedom and choice.

All students deserve a great, liberating college education and a memorable experience that they can celebrate for the rest of their lives. Do whatever you must to make that happen for you. I hope this book helps.

Focus on Learning, Not on Grades

To begin a college life filled with success, you can start by imagining the last day you will be in college. Looking backwards from the future always puts any experience in perspective. That day will be a university commencement—a profound event, the zenith of academic tradition and spectacle. Even the most reserved of campuses blossoms each spring as everyone proudly wears academic garb. Faculty who might wear sandals and jeans to teach will hide the casual under robes of black and of many colors: rich royal blues, crimson velvet, and vivid gold. On their heads might be the same mortar boards worn by their medieval predecessors or a cap that Sir Thomas More would have found familiar.[1] Faculty members who earned doctorates at foreign universities are even more spectacular, with hats and robes Americans might consider outrageous and flamboyant. They grin broadly, thanks to the unusual attention they get that day.

The graduates beam with satisfaction, under black robes that unite them in common achievement. Doctoral and medical students show off new academic hoods or striped gowns they may have rented but have earned with extraordinary effort. Families crowd for a view, watching those of us in the procession with happy awe, and waiting for a celebrity or a respected academic to intone about the future or the challenges of the now. Student leaders stand to read the same lines year after year, observing "how far we have come." They all think the thought is original, unwittingly creating an unbroken line of glorious, consistent tradition.

I love commencement for many reasons, but there is one reason that is special. On that day, all students are successful. They may have taken a thousand paths to get to that moment, but they are united by ritual, celebration, and uniform. There are no real distinctions among the undergraduates on that day. Despite the occasional effort to look different, thanks to a Hawaiian lei around someone's neck, or "Love You Mom" on a mortar board, or a large beach ball under an arm, they are one in success and achievement that day. For those brief hours, everyone—graduates, parents, faculty, friends, family—all agree on a healthy definition of success. They agree to celebrate the perpetuation of a new generation of learned people. They agree that a student who has grown, has challenged herself, appreciates the world's complexity anew, and is eager to learn more in the years ahead—*that* is a successful student.

Unfortunately, the values and successes celebrated on graduation are not easy to see in the years leading up to that moment, especially freshman year. There, the definition of "success" can be too narrow, describing a "successful" student as one who has secured admission to the highest-ranked college possible, preferably an Ivy League school, and is earning high grades. While I disagree with this definition, I cannot blame those who hold it tightly. Many believe that this two-step process of attending a prestigious college and achieving a high GPA will bring financial security and professional prestige.

For many parents, this vision influences the way that they do a lot of things: what and how much they read to their children, whether they send them to an independent or a public school, how involved (or interfering) they are with teachers and principals, and whether and how much they enhance that education with after-school activities such as violin lessons, SAT prep, or an engineering club. Both child and parent seem to agree that they are on a mission: get into a great college and then get strong grades.

Most people think that a "great" college is one of the Ivy League schools or the famous private universities in their company: Stanford, Williams, Pomona, the University of Chicago, and Johns Hopkins University. There is really nothing wrong with that. The Ivy League schools, such as Harvard, Brown, and Princeton, hold historic and deserved reputations of excellence in every aspect of undergraduate life.

Success and Failure
Creating Conversations on Campus

ARIEL PHILLIPS, Ed.D., COUNSELOR

ABIGAIL LIPSON, Ph.D., DIRECTOR

BUREAU OF STUDY COUNSEL

HARVARD UNIVERSITY

Success is the ability to go from failure to failure with no loss of enthusiasm.
—Winston Churchill

Many students have heard all their lives that if they follow the right path—that is, if they work hard, keep their GPAs up, and take part in plenty of extracurricular activities—they will succeed and get into a good college. So, they conscientiously do all that, and then they arrive at college expecting to continue on the same trajectory toward further success.

It turns out, however, that the "real world" (whether business, science, or the arts—not to mention college itself) operates according to a different sensibility. In the real world, the path to success is often a twisted path of dead ends and detours that leads to the most creative exploration, the deepest learning, and thus to *real* success—success both in the traditional sense and in the sense of meaningful personal development. Many students come to college unprepared to navigate this new kind of path.

The dilemma arises almost immediately, in the contexts of choices about courses, paper topics, extracurricular options, career plans, and so on. Consider the case of college grades:

Student: So, I got my test back today. I got an A.

Advisor: Hey, congratulations!

Student: No—it's actually really frustrating! I could have taken the more advanced class, but I knew this one would help my GPA. So now I'm getting a perfect grade, but I'm so bored—I hate the class! But still . . . I do really want to get into a good grad school, so maybe I do need that A . . .

Sometimes a failure isn't simply a failure and a success isn't simply a success. For most of us, this represents a significant, deeply

continued

felt, ongoing challenge, whether related to grades, professional advancement, or financial status. For students, one of the most transformative qualities of the liberal arts college experience is that it challenges them to reexamine their assumptions about themselves and the world, including assumptions about what it means to succeed and what it means to fail.

In recognition of these challenges, the Bureau of Study Counsel at Harvard University formed the Success/Failure Project (see www .bsc.harvard.edu/successfailure). Its mission is to create opportunities for discussion, reflection, understanding, and creative engagement regarding the meanings of success and failure in our lives and work. The Success/Failure Project is an invitation for students and other members of the university community to consider what really matters to them. Students have told us it was the project's Web site that prompted them to speak with a counselor or someone else they trusted about the meaning of their lives before, during, and after college and about the meanings of success, failure, learning, ambition, and integrity.

There seems to be something powerful about simply making space for these conversations. And maybe that's not so surprising. Conversation about the "big questions"—questions of values, life direction, and the essential meaning of one's endeavors—can happen in the classroom, in dining halls, in dorm rooms, in offices, on the Internet, in hallways. The most powerful conversations take place not only among students: these questions affect everyone in the college community, including faculty, deans, staff, and parents.

The missions of most liberal arts universities reflect these very ideals. They express commitments to values such as open intellectual questioning and exchange; the development of perspective-taking and contextual reasoning; ethics, citizenship, and character development; and the relevance of the academic endeavor to the betterment of the world. In fact, it may be that the greatest value of a college environment is precisely that it is a context for encountering and addressing these big questions.

From Ariel Phillips and Abigail Lipson, *Success and Failure: Creating Conversations on Campus.* © 2009 President and Fellows of Harvard College. Reprinted with permission.

Professors are world-class; facilities are superb; programming is interesting and provocative; and above all, these schools offer the opportunity to be with other extraordinary students from around the country and around the world. As a Yale graduate, I do not need to argue about the advantages of going to a top college.

But there are those who believe that the value of an Ivy League education is completely overrated. Loren Pope, in his widely read *Colleges That Change Lives*, argues that many colleges offer a superb, fulfilling experience.[2] There is a lot of truth to that. One does not need to be an Ivy League graduate to be happy—and, of course, there are many Ivy League graduates who are completely miserable.

Whether a college is in the Ivies or not is beside the point. *How you approach a college education matters, not where the college is located.* The key to a great education is not a famous institution but the right institution for you, coupled with a healthy attitude about your personal, intellectual, and professional goals. Consider focusing on the process, not outcomes, more on learning than on GPA. If you focus on the immediate future of deeply enriching education, your distant future will be bright—though not predictable. And that is why Habit #1 on the Dean's List—perhaps the most important habit of successful college students—is *Focus on Learning, Not on Grades.*

A traditional definition of college success, based on outcomes such as high GPAs or admission to medical school, has the virtue of being easy to measure, making it simpler to communicate and to take credit. Our friends and families may not want a textured argument of happiness; they will settle for hearing a college name they recognize and good grades as shortcuts to assessing the situation.

Given the cost of a top college education, having a ready way to measure success is understandable. If you are going to spend over $40,000 a year, there had better be some kind of payoff. For most students, that payoff is pretty obvious: a great-looking transcript. The better the GPA, the more successful the student's college experience has been. Then that GPA—along with all of the privileges and confidence that come with it—can be leveraged into entrance into something else, and so on into the future.

The problem with this model of success is that we do not know

Is This Jar Full?

THOMAS A. DINGMAN, Ed.M.

DEAN OF FRESHMEN

HARVARD UNIVERSITY

Years ago freelance writer Linda Weltner shared the following story, attributed to Norris Lee, in the *Boston Globe*:

> A lecturer stands in the front of a class of overachievers, holding a 1-gallon wide-mouth mason jar. He fills it with good-size rocks, then asks the group, "Is this jar full?" The audience agrees that it is.
>
> "Oh, really?" he asks. He pours in several handfuls of gravel. "Is the jar full now?" The audience is doubtful. Probably not. He pours a handful of sand into the jar, filling it to the brim. "How about now?" he asks. Not yet. He pours in a pitcher of water.
>
> "OK," he asks. "What's the lesson to be learned here?"
>
> "Well," says a man sitting near the front, "you've just demonstrated that no matter how full your schedule is, you can always fit more in."
>
> "You're absolutely wrong," says the teacher. "The point I'm making is that if you don't put the rocks in first, you'll never get them all in."

Part of an educator's job is to help students identify their "rocks"—the measures they use to assess their progress. Students want to be successful, but too often they define success narrowly (for instance, a nearly flawless transcript) or they don't really know what they are working toward. In high school, it is simpler. Success there can mean getting into top colleges. With tougher competition in college, it is more difficult to achieve the nearly flawless transcript. And, with many more postgraduate options, it is difficult to feel a clear sense of direction.

We do students a disservice if we don't help them set measures for success. When I ask students what markers of success they want to put in their jar, they have to think hard. Once they consider the question carefully, they often find that their answers give them a compass and a chance to reflect on the year with a sense of accomplishment and self-worth: I want to feel like I fit in and to have one or two really good friends. I want to make strong progress in identifying a major. I want to gain a starting position on the varsity team.

The student may already have a plan for achieving these goals; if not, strategizing together may lead to some very creative solutions and a rewarding sense of collaboration.

where it ends. Is there some point at which we stop trying to list accomplishments and start to be fulfilled, satisfied, and happy?

As an alternative, consider that the best measure of college success is how much you feel fulfilled and challenged by your education. College should be a starting point for a rich and full life, one in which you appreciate the human experience—culture, art, music, literature, religion, history—and the natural environment. A good college education introduces you to the broad canvas of life, here and around the world, past and present. And it gives you the tools to make sense of it. It is not enough to look at something and respect its beauty or complexity or scale. You need to *understand* it, using the skills that higher education offers.

As those skills grow, so does the world. When we do not understand something, we avoid bewilderment by turning away, letting the world shrink. You could dismiss something as unimportant and uninteresting. The better alternative is to acknowledge ignorance and embrace the mission to learn. Socrates may have thought this the prerequisite to wisdom, but that does not change how uncomfortable it is. Without facing this discomfort and building the tools for understanding, we cheat ourselves of a richer life and a larger world.

The Trouble with Grades

When most students get a graded assignment or exam back, they immediately turn to the last page, filled with hope and dread as they look for the letter grade. If that is an A, they are overwhelmed with feelings of relief and then of pride and validation. If it is anything else, they are disappointed and even humiliated. I'll bet you know these feelings. Whatever the grade, students probably will ignore any written feedback from the instructor, even though this is the most valuable information. If they have earned an A, what is the point of reading it? They cannot do any better. If it is a weaker grade, they have to fight feelings of disgust and defensiveness to listen to and learn from the criticism.

Lost in all these intense feelings is any appreciation for what they have learned. Grades are intended to measure learning. But they overshadow what you have gained on a deeper, intellectual level. Because

Is Success the Same as Getting Good Grades?

SUE BROWN, Ph.D.

RESIDENT DEAN OF FRESHMEN, HARVARD COLLEGE

HARVARD UNIVERSITY

Good grades are certainly one indicator of success, but in my experience, they are not the only measure. Motivational speaker Tony Robbins says that "success without fulfillment is failure." While Mr. Robbins is not ordinarily quoted in the halls of Harvard, I find this adage to be true for some of my students. By all external gauges, they are already successful: they are at Harvard studying to become doctors, bankers, and lawyers, and they are doing well in their classes. But they are not happy. They are not thriving.

Why? In the quest for good grades, some students do nothing but schoolwork. They enjoy their classes to some degree, but neglect all the other things in life that can bring fulfillment, like relationships, hobbies, and sleep. They are feeding part of themselves, but not all. They take no time for reflection. They burn out. Other students are getting good grades in classes they have no passion for because someone expects them to follow a certain career path, and they haven't given much thought to whether *they* want to.

So, how does one find fulfillment in college? *Do what you love, do it well, and the rest will follow.*

the feelings of validation and rejection can overwhelm a more balanced view of success, and because others judge our worth by grades, it's easy to forget what is lasting: knowledge, wisdom, and understanding. In fact, your grades do not measure what *you* want or value. They crudely measure what *your instructor* wants you to learn. You forget that you are there to learn, not to please the instructor, so your studies are driven by external pressure not internal curiosity. So rather than appreciate the lasting lessons you will carry beyond college, you have a set of assessments testifying to your ability to know what others want from you.

Measuring success this way changes the way you make decisions.

Most students make choices based on whether they get good grades in a subject rather than on a desire to learn anything in particular. They might choose one college over another on the basis of what they think will help them achieve the best record. They choose some courses just to get good grades. This hurts the mission of education at its core.

And it means that you are doomed to disappointment because you cannot always be the best. It is physically impossible for everyone to stand alone at the top of the mountain. There are only a limited number of seats at any top college, and of course, there is only one person at the top of every class within that college. Students generally accept this notion, as some people will win and some will lose. "That's life," they say. Or, at least, it is a good preparation for life. But it has a terrible effect on your view of college. It suggests that college is filled with losers. There are going to be a lot more losers than winners in a situation like this. College life starts looking more like a championship tournament with 63 losers and only one winner. Is this how you want to measure success?

Obsessing about grades will encourage you to forget what you have learned as soon as the final grade is recorded. Honestly, what is the point of remembering Aristotelian ethics once your "Classics in Philosophy" course is on your transcript? No one is ever going to test you on this again, after all. That is why those who graduated from college long ago have nightmares about facing an exam again. They cannot remember anything after the real final ended. Some of that is natural and inevitable. But more of it stems from the short-term reward system of letter grades. That system encourages us to focus on what is important to the professor, to learn what is most likely to appear on the exam, and to master just enough to earn the best grade possible. Now we have completely forgotten the reason to become educated.

Think about why you are in college, and you will realize that grading is ridiculously shallow. The deeper mission of a college education is to absorb and understand the material to change the person you are, to be *infused* with what are you are learning. If learning and infusion are better and more enduring goals, you will be less concerned about the approval of the instructor and more focused on owning your education.

A final reason to keep your grades in perspective is to avoid thinking of your college experience as just a step to some later achievement. College life loses its value as a precious period of personal and intellectual development when it becomes so utilitarian. This is most painfully on display among pre-meds. When we call them "pre-meds," we acknowledge that they attend college primarily to get into medical school. Students who are pre-medical are not actually living in the moment. They do not appreciate where they are or what the place can do for them. They are simply looking for the ticket to get on the train.

Not surprisingly, professors have mixed feelings about pre-meds. While we respect their ambition, their work ethic, and their desire to serve others, we also feel a bit abused by them. We would like to teach them something, but they would like to get a ticket punched. This is particularly painful for those who teach them required pre-med courses such as physics. Physics may be the most important of all sciences, and yet most students take physics only as a requirement for medical school. They have very little if any interest in the subject matter itself. But physicists love physics. They respect the field. They have made it their life's work. And yet here is this group of students in lecture, listening eagerly, not because they care about physics, but because they want an A. That is very disheartening.

Of course, I do not deny that grades are useful and important. They offer a shorthand for feedback, quickly telling you what an instructor thinks. They are used to determine academic standing, scholarships, admissions to graduate and professional schools, and job searches. I am not telling you to ignore your grades. I am suggesting that you keep them in perspective. Obsessing over grades, being crushed when they are low and thrilled when they are high, focusing only on pleasing an instructor, and measuring your education's worth by your GPA, is a tragic mistake.

Successful or Learned?

So allow me to offer an alternative to the definition of success based on achievement and good grades. Consider the idea that a highly successful college student is a *learned person*. Rather than gaining satisfaction from a high GPA, learned people feel contented by the richness of their understanding and the breadth of their curiosity.

Claiming an Education

LEAH BLATT GLASSER, Ph.D.

DEAN OF FIRST-YEAR STUDIES and LECTURER IN ENGLISH

MOUNT HOLYOKE COLLEGE

After many years of teaching, advising, and serving as an academic dean at Mount Holyoke College, I still find myself turning to Adrienne Rich's convocation speech at Douglass College back in 1977 to answer students who ask me how they can be most successful in college. Rich's address was delivered to college women, and her speech is especially important for women to absorb, yet it applies to all college students: "You cannot afford to think of being here to receive an education; you will do much better to think of being here to claim one. One of the dictionary definitions of the verb 'to claim' is: to take as the rightful owner; to assert in the face of possible contradiction. 'To receive' is to come into possession of: to act as receptacle or container for; to accept as authoritative or true. The difference is that between acting and being acted-upon."

In my work with first-year students, one of the most important things I want them to learn about the transition from high school to college is the necessity of making this shift from "receiving" to "claiming." The shift involves moving from passive note-taking to active engagement and participation, from the quick click on Google to interacting with college reference librarians, from quietly taking notes on lectures to seeking conversations with faculty members during office hours or at the local cafe, from expecting to "be advised" by one authoritative advisor to seeking dialogue with a web of advisors who will suggest an array of options.

Claiming an education involves rethinking what education means and "unlearning" two common high school habits: "receiving" advice as a series of directives rather than suggestions, and treating grades as wages that validate self-worth (in which moving from a B+ to an A is like a pay raise). Given the pressure to gain economic stability upon graduation, these are difficult habits to get beyond. Students often begin college with the illusion that a particular set of grades or a certain major will lead to happiness, and financial success. Yet those who cling to this belief inevitably find that their grades and spirits suffer in equal doses. To "claim their education," students must begin with an open mind to the possibilities and pathways that are neither prescribed nor shaped by others; they must also shift from a focus on grades to a focus on learning.

Two examples come to mind that capture the kind of "unlearning" that must happen. Prize-winning playwright Suzan-Lori Parks, who graduated from Mount Holyoke College in 1985, began college with the echo of advice she had received in high school. She thus started college as a chemistry major, but as she explained years later to Mount Holyoke's theatre majors, "I was dying in the lab." In her commencement address in 2001, Parks quoted her "very stern English teacher" in high school who advised her against studying English. Indeed, I remember her description of this high school edict when she came to my office to discuss her first paper for my writing seminar, and then the way her voice filled with energy and excitement as soon as she began to speak about literature and language. In college Parks learned the importance of listening to her own voice, what she would later refer to in her speech as "inner ear training." She allowed herself to take pleasure in what she loved most and began to claim her education by pursuing aspirations of her own making, recognizing her talents on her own terms.

My next example is a current student who began college with the well-cultivated belief that the pathway to good grades was to take notes and memorize dutifully. But despite spending many hours studying silently in her room, she was on academic probation at the end of her first semester. Our weekly meetings began by discussing her grades, but I quickly shifted to questions about what she was learning and encouraged her to meet with her teachers. She returned to describe lively conversations on the texts, her papers, and her ideas. She decided not to drop "Critical Social Thought" at mid-semester, despite the poor grades she had received, because of her fascination with the material and her developing ability to accept criticism as feedback rather than judgment. She began to "claim" by shifting her focus from grades to content and thus actively participating in shaping her education. Making the decision to push through a course for which she had the potential for a lower grade had a secondary result of better grades overall. Further, she had formed a partnership with a dean, her advisor, and her teachers and had learned a critical lesson for succeeding. Seeking help was an opportunity for active learning, a sign of strength rather than a source of weakness and shame. She even learned that it was okay to have failed in her first semester, and that such failure was pivotal to her realization of how to succeed.

I welcome each new incoming class with the words of Adrienne Rich. Claim your education, I repeat. It is an essential repetition that goes to the heart of what every good college should be teaching its students.

They approach their college experience by asking themselves: What do educated people know? How do they feel? What is their demeanor, their approach to life? Learned people set goals based on what it means to be learned, and they enjoy the rewards of that pursuit, including good grades. As a freshman, or a soon-to-be freshman, you should think about these questions, as their answers can set goals that you alone will measure, independent of the grades you receive.

What does it mean to be learned? Most colleges already have answered this for you, by developing their distribution and core requirements. These requirements force you to take courses from a combination of disciplines—making you well-rounded, at least on paper. Some colleges have you take specific "core" courses. Columbia University, for instance, tells to you take "Major Cultures" and "Contemporary Civilization." You can argue with them over what is a "major" culture, but you cannot argue about taking the course.

Some other universities have taken the opposite tack, believing that the definition of an education should be left to the student. Brown University undergraduates have complete control over their curricular choices; there are no distribution or core requirements at all. Johns Hopkins University offers a slightly different approach by requiring relatively simple and easily completed distribution requirements with no core curriculum.

So, it matters how your college defines what it means to be "learned" because it will shape your course selections profoundly, but I suggest that you craft your own definition. How you do this will help you make choices about your intellectual life. This should be an ongoing exercise, adapted to new conditions and to different stages. A freshman can and should disagree with a senior on this question because they have different needs and levels of maturity. But whatever the phase of your college career, you should step back, be thoughtful and purposive, and own your education. I try to encourage freshmen to take a moment from the thrill of a new college life and from the institution's curriculum, emphasizing requirements, to consider what it is that they want to *learn* while they are in college. It is a simple question, and one to which surprisingly few have given any thought.

I once met a young woman who was determined to double major in psychology and biology. On the face of it, these two fields have a great deal to do with each other. But as a practical matter, their curricula and their requirements do not overlap very much. She was determined, nevertheless, and had mapped out for me every course she would need, semester by semester, from her freshman year until graduation.

I told her that she had proven that such a double major was doable. "But have you," I asked, "proven that it is wise?" She looked at me strangely. She was a determined woman, and I was offering an inconvenient thought. I said, "Think about the opportunity cost of what you're doing. By setting out all these requirements in front of you, you've given up a lot of academic and intellectual freedom. You have failed to give yourself the chance to think about what you want to know and what you think should be learned."

I said to her, "Don't you think it's important for a modern person to know something about Africa? Our educational system is woefully ill-equipped to teach us anything about Africa. So when you get a chance to take a class from an Africanist, you should jump at that chance. As we move into this century the issues, problems, and opportunities of Africa are no doubt going to be important. And on what basis will you understand them? How will you be able to read the newspaper?" The same could be said of any number of places, like India and China, but I did not want to belabor the point.

I let her go on her way, and she promised to give it more thought. But I could also have told her that the marginal utility of having an impressive dual degree would be far outweighed by the loss of a wider understanding of the human experience—not just its politics. Every learned person, I could argue, and she might agree, should know something about Renaissance art. To know nothing about Leonardo or Michelangelo or Raphael is to overlook how the modern aesthetic landscape was changed by their pens, brushes, and mallets forever. How about the poetry of Emily Dickinson or the writings of Gabriel García Márquez? Should we not know something about the ancient world—not just the stuff covered in your sixth grade history class, but on a deeper level of poetry and philosophy, art and architecture?

I challenge you to think this way. Consider your own ignorance, and make a plan to fix it. What do you want to know? What are your curiosities? What do you think you ought to understand? Think beyond college requirements. They are just maps to take you to an educated place. But you can draw that map yourself. And that map should be wide and exploratory, to cover the territories you did not know existed when you started. That is the power of a liberal education. Not only does it help you understand the world you know; it exposes you to the world you don't. It prepares you to be a learned person for life, somebody who has sophistication and an appetite for many things—an appreciation for the subtle, the beautiful, the unexpected. This does not require true expertise; undergraduates mistakenly expect that earning a degree in biology, for example, will make them a biologist. If we can back off of that expectation, then the joys of a wider, exploratory education that feeds lifelong curiosity will become more obvious. To go to college for the credentials is to grossly underestimate its value. To go to college expecting expertise is misguided. Far better, and more lasting, is to set your sights on becoming a sophisticated, curious, and learned person.

♣ *Put It in Perspective*

Colleges, especially competitive ones, attract people who define success by their good grades: that's how they get in, after all. But grading can obscure higher values of education: exploration, experimentation, and learning grounded in curiosity. This is a serious matter. Grading distorts the goal of becoming a learned person rather than simply a person with a high GPA. If you focus only on good grades, you will fail to appreciate or absorb all that a particular course has to offer. Why

The Liberal Arts and Other Endangered Species

DAVID N. DEVRIES, Ph.D.

ASSOCIATE DEAN FOR UNDERGRADUATE EDUCATION

CORNELL UNIVERSITY

In the jittery, anxious world of Twitter, texting, tumbling markets, and widespread uncertainty, the liberal arts have come to occupy a place in the public consciousness rather like poetry. The vast majority of human beings alive on the planet now, as well as the vast majority of human beings who have ever lived, have never had a need for the liberal arts, nor for poetry. Even among the age group to whom highly selective colleges and universities cater, the liberal arts matter little. The stressed-out, over-achieving teenagers clambering to enter elite institutions constitutes a tiny fraction of teenagers in the United States. What we offer in these institutions is like poetry: a difficult endeavor taken up by a very few people *willing* to suspend their usual hurry and distraction for what, on the surface, seems to many others not worth the effort.

Not everyone agrees that the liberal arts have value in today's society. Nearly 35 years ago, Caroline Bird wrote an essay "College Is a Waste of Time and Money." The essay became widely anthologized and was a staple among college composition courses in the late 1970s and through the 1980s. Much of Bird's argument rested on money: a college education was not enough of a guarantee of lifetime earnings potential to justify the expense. And besides, many college students in the early 1970s were disaffected, "sad," and bored. They weren't getting much out of college. Flash forward into the new millennium and Bird's article continues to find echoes: "Bottom line: College, particularly an expensive private college, is a high-risk investment, which, for many, won't pay," personal-finance columnist Scott Burns wrote on MSN.com in October 2007.

The mercantile attitude toward higher education is reflected in *Forbes Magazine*'s defense of its annual rankings of U.S. colleges and universities. Universities and colleges "are selling a product that, to the typical consumer, is the second largest expenditure made in a lifetime, after the purchase of a home. Just as *Consumer Reports* and J. D. Powers and Associates help people wanting to buy cars, so ranking organizations like *U.S. News & World Report*, the Princeton Review, and *Forbes* provide consumers with assistance in choosing a college" (www.forbes.com/2009/08/02/best-colleges-methodology -opinions-ccap.html).

Money comes and money goes. Banks rise and fall. The marketplace is no place upon which to build a foundation. The liberal arts, however, are not commodities to be consumed. *They are states of mind to be acquired.* The marketplace, despite the granite, steel, and glass facades behind which the great barons of commerce conduct their business, is full of uncertainty. A sound liberal arts education helps students cope with uncertainty. Immersing your mind in the intricacies of physics, history, literature—or any of the other disciplines on a liberal arts campus—encourages flexibility, receptivity, and the chance to investigate, explore, and ultimately choose based upon an educated decision-making process. You will learn to think through spending time with the liberal arts. You will learn to forge a position based on more that whim or sentiment. You will learn to wield the difficult strength of intellectual passion.

listen to something if it is not on the test? This may simplify academic life, but it cheats the mission of a liberal college education. So I reject the notion that success should be measured by grades.

Instead, I suggest that you think about what it means to be learned, to obtain an education that is motivated by curiosity rather than by the achievement of good grades. A lot of doors will open for any student who gets through a top college. But if you set aside the obsession with credentialing and the need to earn grades, then you have created space to consider what should be learned. If you put your grades in perspective and elevate the goal of learning, you will be motivated to find answers to difficult questions. What are the underpinnings of our system of values? How do dictators achieve and retain power? What literary traditions come from Africa or South America? What is the appeal of a Brahms symphony? How did the Japanese recover from World War II, and what lessons can we draw from that?

When students draw energy from their curiosity, not only do they learn much more and love their academic experience, but they *also* earn good grades. In fact, they are the ones who are the superstars. Grades are simply a by-product of their passion for learning. It is not the other way around. Great students are powered by curiosity, enjoying the pleasures of discovery and appreciating that hard work deepens that discovery. And *then* they earn the grades that others can admire. If you approach your education with enthusiastic, committed curiosity, you will do the hard work you need to get good grades. And when you are done, walking in your commencement, you will carry with you a rich intellectual legacy that is far more enduring than a good-looking transcript. You will be *learned*.

Build an Adult Relationship with Your Parents

In one remarkable—but not unusual—week, I had visits to Johns Hopkins University from two sets of parents. One father flew to Baltimore from Singapore to argue, on his daughter's behalf, over an academic policy. What distinguished this visit was not the distance traveled, but that the policy was so simple and unshakeable. His daughter was more than a semester's credits short of graduation, and yet he claimed that the university had suggested she could graduate early. We had not. He was wrong and flew a long way home empty-handed.

In the second case that week, a student's parents had flown from Oahu, Hawaii—for the second time in two weeks! The mother had visited alone the week before. Now both parents were on my calendar, joined by their son. They came because their son had been struggling academically and was on probation. As I sat with this couple, questions ran through my mind. Why had they come so far for such a short appointment? What did they think they were going to accomplish by sitting with me? What kind of relationship did they have with their son that they thought this was a good idea? The son certainly was not comfortable with this and sat through most of the appointment staring off into space. What could I tell them to get them to leave this young man alone? And, of course, *should* they leave him alone? What role should they play in his college experience—his intellectual development and his personal life—that would help the student succeed and mature to adulthood?

An Open Letter to New College Students about Parents

KATHRYN STUART, D.M.A.
DEAN OF STUDIES and
VICE PRESIDENT FOR STRATEGIC INITIATIVES
OBERLIN COLLEGE

Dear new college students,

You've graduated from high school and have been accepted to the school of your choice. You've finished helping your parents pack your belongings and are ready to start the trip to your college. Already, your parents are giving you advice—and lots of it—about what to do and not to do (and *how* to do whatever it may be), as though they have not had nearly 18 years to help you make good choices and "do the right thing." You may be feeling testy, nervous, anxious, sad about leaving your family and friends, but generally eager to start college. And you *really* don't get the way your parents are acting.

Your parents are liberally ladling out this advice because they suddenly realize there may be a few really important things they haven't told you, and they also may be having a hard time remembering their own experiences leaving home. And, most importantly, you are their child, they love you, and they desperately want you to succeed—happily and in good health—at college and beyond.

The arrival on campus brings orientation sessions. During one, some dean suggests that students and their parents should talk, before parents leave campus, about how students will communicate with their parents—both the good and the not-so-good news, the accolades from professors as well as the occasional bad news about midterm and final grades (not all of which may be what you were accustomed to earning in high school). The dean says that the role your parents play during your college career may be critically important to your success and happiness in college, whether or not you can imagine this right now. You will also choose a number of advisors and mentors from the faculty and professional staff members you meet on campus who will provide you with a range of support that will enhance your education.

Like Oberlin College, most colleges and universities state their educational goals for students. At Oberlin these include

- to graduate students who have learned to think with intellectual rigor, creativity, and independence;
- to offer a superb liberal arts education;
- to open the world to its students and develop in them the skills and knowledge they will need to engage with and navigate in highly diverse communities and in a global society;
- to nurture students' social consciousness and environmental awareness;
- to provide outstanding preparation for success at the highest level of graduate and professional education and in careers.*

These statements help us understand and appreciate the value of a college education. A student who accomplishes these goals will also learn about the importance and pleasure of giving back—to family, friends, and community.

From the moments of transition that nearly all first-year students experience to commencement, a student profits from the support of family. It is up to you, new student, to "take the high road" with your parents by establishing and maintaining open lines of communication. Ask your parents to communicate with *you,* saving their calls to college officials for times of emergency. Realize that if you establish this plan for regular, honest communication as a new student, your parents may be more ready than you'd expect to accept and respect your growing independence. If you can communicate as an adult with your parents, chances are good that you will be comfortable developing important student-mentor relationships with your professors. And your growing maturity and independence will help you to enjoy success in learning how to learn, to become an engaged participant in your community, and to thrive in your college career.

Wishing you and your parents an exceptional college experience,

Kathryn Stuart
Dean of Studies, Oberlin College

* Excerpted from *A Strategic Plan for Oberlin College,* March 5, 2005.

As I outline the second habit of highly successful students, I will try to dig into your most important relationship, the one you have with your parents.[1] This relationship is central to your success as a student, just as it is in all aspects of life. Figuring out how to make this work is a tough job. Your parents love you. They are worried about you. They want you to "succeed," though you might disagree on what that means (especially after reading about Habit #1!). Many of us who work for colleges think that your parents are too interfering and hovering, which is why we call them "helicopter parents," though that term might be more clever than real.[2] We know they mean a lot to you and that you have been making decisions together for a long time. I will make the gentle suggestion that you work on a new way to relate to your parents, one more appropriate to your new life in college. And so Habit #2 on the Dean's List is *Build an Adult Relationship with Your Parents*.

In Constant Contact

It might surprise you to know that not long ago, parental indifference or independence was the rule for college students, probably including your parents, if they went to college. Weeks might go by before most parents would call their children in college. They might never exchange letters. College students rarely talked to their parents about the courses they were taking. They didn't tell their parents how well they were doing in those courses. Students wouldn't ask for advice and rarely got it. Parents never received a transcript, nor did they ask for one. No one had mobile phones or e-mail (we didn't have computers), so students and parents generally lived in separate worlds.

It is possible that those of us who went to college in this era (and that includes your parents) could have avoided the many mistakes we made by listening to our own parents. But the choices were ours to admire or condemn. We were becoming adults. We had to cope with the uncertainty of an open environment, make choices, and live with them. And when those choices turned out to be poor choices, adults had to adjust and change direction.

But now you might not be surprised if your parents flew across the world to have a 20-minute conversation with a dean about your grades. Those same people would have been astonished and embarrassed had *their* parents, your grandparents, done the same. Today's students think nothing of texting, e-mailing, instant-messaging, or tweeting their mothers or fathers, or both, every day, usually several times.[3] I have been in the elevator many times with a bunch of students, and at least one of them is talking to his or her mother on a cell phone. Your parents may have written to your grandparents from college, but they could not imagine a technology that would track them down in an elevator. Students now routinely make most of their choices, from courses to majors to summer internships, in conjunction with their parents.[4] Some do not make a move without consulting them. And they seem comfortable with that, for the most part. Those same people—your parents—would probably have reacted to their own parents' involvement with horror and resentment.

The irony is stunning.

Nevertheless, today's college parents ignore that irony and step boldly into every decision. When I talk to parents about course selection, for example, they always use the word *we*—the first-person plural: "We have been looking at the course catalog this term, and we were thinking that it might be best to take the organic chemistry lab this term instead of next term. That's important, since Roberta will be a doctor. What do you think?"

I would like to say, "Why are you talking to me? Why did you make this phone call? Why are you making these choices about courses? Why are you referring to the decision-making body as *we*?" In the summer before freshman year, I get many phone calls from fathers and mothers before having met their son or daughter. The parents simply have stepped into the breach and decided to ask me what would be the best courses for their student to take in the fall. "We've been looking at the pre-med requirements, and we think we should take calculus this term. What do you think if we took physics?" I usually react to this by gently suggesting that they put the student on the phone rather than making the call themselves. But what I am really thinking is, "Who do you think is going to take this course? Are you coming down from Hoboken or flying in from Chicago every Monday, Wednesday, and Friday?"

Beyond course selection, parents want to know how classes are going. A mid-term exam in microeconomics is coming up on Tuesday.

Separation Anxiety

SUZANNE DUKE, Ed.D.

RESIDENT DEAN OF FRESHMEN

HARVARD UNIVERSITY

I came to my position straight from graduate school, armed with a doctorate in human development and psychology, a deep interest in the developmental processes of young adulthood, and a subtle sense of trepidation about how much I needed to learn about the practice of higher education. As I spent my first few months immersing myself in the new language and culture of "deaning," I came to the realization that my work with parents was, in fact, a lesson in human development.

During the first year, both students and parents undertake a process of separation. Students encounter newfound freedoms. They move from the highly scheduled high school environment to one of making their own decisions about which courses to take, how to structure their time, and what kind of social life they want to have. These freedoms require separation from parents—from parents' expectations, well-intended interventions, and in some cases, parental control. Parents undergo a similar and equally challenging process. For nearly 18 years, many parents have been actively involved in their children's lives. They know how their children spend their time academically and socially. Parents are physically present to celebrate their children's successes and to support their children in times of distress. When their children leave for college, parents must find a healthy balance between supporting their children while giving them room to develop the skills necessary to become strong, independent adults.

The process of separation is hard for both parents and children. However, deans and other members of the college community can help both students and their parents negotiate the challenges of separation in a way that makes both groups feel supported and understood.

"Are you ready for it?" they'll ask. The next week they'll call again: "How did the exam go? What grade did you get? Were you at the median, above, or below? What does that mean for your final grade?"

If you think this is the way your parents ought to behave, step back for a moment. You should not doubt their love or concern, but you can question their methods. Do they really need to ask those questions? Do you have to answer them? Is there another way to talk about college? What are pros and cons of making your parents active partners in your education?

Finding Your Own Way

There are moments when parental concern is both effective and touching. For example, students can struggle with a lot of health problems, particularly with emotional health. Coping with these challenges requires a lot of support, understanding, and help from parents, family, and friends. If a student is battling depression, it is critical that the parents know about this, educate themselves on the situation if they are not familiar with it already, and do what they can to support the student's effort to overcome that challenge.[5] That may mean understanding that their son or daughter needs a leave of absence to take care of his or her health. It may mean appreciating that the student's grades last term were the consequence of these struggles, not reflective of some broader problem that cannot be overcome.

Parents offer students a reality check that is needed just as much as emotional support. Do you know what you are doing? Are you thinking about life after college? Are you focused on your studies or on video games? Are you meeting interesting people or just hanging out with your roommates? Are you staying healthy, with enough sleep and exercise? Are you thinking through your options or just following what everyone else is choosing? Have you found a way to have fun without ending the evening in a drunken stupor? Have you remembered to apply for a summer job? Your parents will still look after you, even if you are on a distant campus. And they should.[6]

But there are too many cases in which parental concern crosses into interference that is not healthy, engaging, or supportive. This makes it very difficult for you to make decisions or to learn how to make the

A Time of Transition

RAIMA EVAN, Ph.D.

ASSISTANT DEAN

BRYN MAWR COLLEGE

Your parents were no doubt involved in your college application process: accompanying you as you visited different schools, talking with you about their finances, and helping you decide which college or university to attend. During the summer after your high school graduation, they probably talked with you about what courses you might want to take during your first semester. That fateful day arrived in August, and they took you to college, lugged your belongings into your dorm room, and attended an orientation ceremony with you. Then, strangely—even though you might have fantasized about it for weeks—they left. You're suddenly without them. Now what?

Some students react to the start of their first year of college by luxuriating in their freedom from their parents. They do everything they want to do when they want to do it. They go to bed at all hours. They do things their parents definitely would not have given them permission to do in high school. And when their parents call them, they don't return their phone calls—to the point that deans receive worried phone calls from parents, asking them to check on the status of their son or daughter because he or she hasn't responded to a phone message for days. Other students react to the start of their college experience by calling, texting, e-mailing, or skyping their parents several times a day. Neither approach is going to be healthy in the long run.

College is not just an intellectual journey; it's an emotional one too. You're going to meet new people with backgrounds different from your own, and you're going to discover things about yourself in the process. But you're also going to discover things about yourself in relation to the people who have been involved in your life from the beginning: your parents.

It's understandable and natural that in the first days and even weeks of the freshman year, you may want to call your parents often for advice, information, or just plain comfort. But as the year unfolds, things are bound to shift. You may have different needs of your parents now that college life feels more familiar, and you have other sources of advice and comfort around you. Maybe you don't need to call your parents as often. Maybe you begin to recognize how different some of your values are from theirs. Maybe you share a lot of the same values, but you just want to decide something for yourself before you call them to discuss what courses you plan to take next semester or whether you want to study abroad during your junior year.

It can be dislocating when your relationship with your parents suddenly feels different. It's often much easier to start a new relationship with a friend, roommate, or mentor than it is to recognize that your relationship with your parents is changing. But just because the relationship is changing doesn't mean it isn't still a central part of your life and theirs. The transition to this new way of interacting will take some time for everyone to adjust to. Transitions, by definition, can be bumpy, even rocky. In my role as dean, I've talked with students who tell me that their parents call them or text them several times a day—often to the point that it becomes burdensome. They feel responsible for being the emotional support for their parents or siblings; they feel guilty about developing their own lives at college; they may even feel pressured to return home on weekends.

I have urged these students to try to set limits for their parents by establishing mutually agreed-upon times to call one another. I've also urged them to turn off their cell phones when they're studying for a test, writing a paper, or—of course—attending their classes. Finally, I encourage them to take advantage of our counseling center. A counselor can help students better understand what's going on at home and help them develop strategies for coping with family concerns. With time, the great majority of parents will respect and nurture their daughter's or son's growing sense of independence. They'll be there when you need them, and they'll give you the space you need when you want to be in charge of your decision-making.

But perhaps the difficulty you're having in the first weeks of college is not that your parents are calling you several times a day. Perhaps you're the one who's making the phone calls. If homesickness is making it hard for you to enjoy your college experience, this,

continued

too, deserves attention. It may feel very difficult to reach out for help when you're feeling homesick, but remember that you're not alone at college, even though it may sometimes feel that way. Talk with your parents when you miss them, but talk with someone at your college too, whether it's a friend, roommate, advisor, or counselor. It's important to develop a network of support at college, just as you had when you were in high school.

It's widely recognized that going to college is an important coming-of-age experience. But what people often don't realize is that growing up is a process that takes place throughout one's lifetime. It isn't something that happens in one fell swoop over the course of your freshman year or even over the course of your entire college career. So be gentle with yourself and try to take it one step at a time. Your parents are growing too, so if you're having some trouble getting adjusted to all the changes in your life, keep in mind that they're going through a lot of changes too. With patience and understanding on both sides, you can be sources of support for one another during your freshman year and beyond.

decisions that allow you to own your education and your life beyond. Unhappy pre-meds often share the sad story of taking more science courses with dread. They are not—or are no longer—inspired by the idea of becoming a doctor. But in highly competitive and expensive schools like Johns Hopkins, parents of many pre-meds have the explicit understanding with their children that they are going to college to prepare for medical school. There is no room for rethinking this goal or for building other interests. It is not difficult to imagine the pressure on these students. If they want to continue enjoying life at that college, they had better take a prescribed set of courses, major in biology or neuroscience, earn good grades, and go through the medical school application process successfully. That is the inviolable contract between parent and student.

And yet, some of the time, these plans do not go as expected. A pre-med might have sailed through high school, earning A's in every subject and gaining entrance into some of the country's top colleges. But when he goes to college, he discovers that the amount of work that he did in high school pales in comparison with the amount he must now do. And he finds that work is both highly independent and too demanding. He begins to think that physics and organic chemistry are beyond his reach or, at least, that he does not find them interesting. All of this is a terrible surprise for someone who had been planning to be a doctor since he was a child.

Now, he is stuck. His parents have clear expectations for him, but those expectations do not fit his reality. Yet he talks to his parents every day, tempting him to lie or to avoid the central problem in his life. He has to tell them things are fine when he knows that they are not. The relationship begins to fray.

I see this dilemma with painful frequency. One of my advisees faced this problem for several semesters. After her second term, she went on academic probation for struggling in her science classes. She insisted to me that we not copy her parents on her academic probation letter.* And she lied to her parents for over a year about her situation. But one day, her father opened a piece of mail that was not addressed to him and discovered that, in fact, his daughter was failing her science classes. The resulting conflict was a terrible thing.

What was startling to the student (and a pleasant surprise to me) was that, after they had calmed down, her parents understood that their daughter did need to change direction. They slowly began to appreciate that majoring in biology was probably beyond her reach, but that she could continue to take some pre-med courses to keep her options open. In the long run, the confrontation between parents and daughter was healthy. They were able to begin a dialogue about the meaning and direction of her education in a way that allowed their daughter to take ownership of her education and her future.

While this story ended happily, there are plenty that do not. Many other students tell me that if they do not major in biology and go on to medical school, their parents will not pay for a Johns Hopkins educa-

---

* Normally, universities send parents a letter, alerting them that their child is doing poorly, but it is within the student's rights to ask to keep this information private. The university's relationship is not with the parent but directly with the student. This is both appropriate and legal. Federal statutes preclude universities from sharing information with parents without the student's permission.

Untethering the University Student

MAURA GREGORY, M.A.

EMILY A. ZENICK, M.A.

ASSISTANT DEANS, SCHOOL OF FOREIGN SERVICE

GEORGETOWN UNIVERSITY

Parents of the students we know have directed their children's education since birth. From consistent communication, beginning in nursery school, to tracking their students' progress in elementary school via Blackboard, parents are accustomed to being in the loop. They are very involved in students' decision-making, even after students arrive at college. Yet the concept of the hovering parent seems foreign to us university administrators only one generation removed from our advisees.

In our time, attending college was a rite of independence from parental control. It was an opportunity to prove ourselves by living on our own and making our own decisions. We were allowed to make mistakes—our parents expected it! The best part of being able to make mistakes while away from home was that mom and dad would, for the most part, have no way to know you were in trouble. Phoning home on Sundays for weekly check-in was the extent of our interaction with families. God forbid things got so out of hand that mom and dad were actually contacted by university officials. The last thing anyone wanted was for parents to get involved; such intervention was akin to having mom protect you from the school bully during recess—*not cool.*

Not only that: everyone revered the decisions of administrators and faculty. Mom and Dad backed them 100 percent, knowing that their answer to any problem was an answer, not an invitation to negotiate a better outcome.

Our expectations of universities were also different. College was a stepping-stone (albeit an important one) to finding a job (one that paid us enough to live on) and starting a new era of independence in life. Today, tuition is paid in the hopes that graduates will be handed a much sought-after *future.* Consumerism of education has led to an increased expectation that the university will take on the role of parent in following the student's every move.

Whatever the causes for changes in expectations, there are successful strategies to "untether" students from their parents to achieve a healthy balance during this transitional phase in life. To begin, parents need to move from the role of directors to informed advisors. University officials try to help students make good decisions, but they cannot be the decision-makers. The Family Educational Right to Privacy Act (or FERPA, also known as the Buckley Amendment) prevents university officials from sharing what is considered privileged information with anyone other than the student, despite who is paying the bill. Students who give mom and dad log-in access to their academic records need to understand their role in communicating with their parents instead of hoping the university advisor will play mediator when we are unable to do so by law.

Parents need to allow their students to resolve conflicts at college on their own. Overly involved parents render students powerless in everything from course selection to resolving roommate conflicts. We are not advocating a total detachment from a student's education, only a recalibration that sets up the dynamic of the student as director and the parents as mentor.

tion. If I suggest majoring in a social science, for example, to minimize the imprint of the sciences on their curriculum, the student will say to me: "I might as well transfer right now. I'll go to my local community college and pay for it myself because my parents want me to be a doctor. And they will accept nothing less than the plan I started with." It is tragically ironic that because student and parents are so intertwined, when things go wrong, many students see no choice but to lie. As the reality of your life drifts from the version held by your parents, you might be stuck with a similar dilemma: live a lie or tell one.

Another risk of an excessively tight family circle is that it can delay the maturing needed to live successfully beyond college walls.[7] An adult, independent life calls for the ability to cope with great uncertainty. Life in college can lull you into thinking your routine is normal, permanent, and ongoing. But of course, on the day after graduation, life changes, and it will never be the same again. The framework of daily classes, clear goals, and adult support no longer exists. It is neither fair nor prudent to shield you from this inevitable reality by being so interfering in your daily life. You need to learn how to make decisions and own them if you want to be a responsible and effective adult.

Parents who are too involved in a student's daily life, consulting with her as she makes decisions about courses, majors and minors, and even club activities, are crippling her, delaying her ability to grow and to become independent. Such parents mean well. They see a long record of how their advocacy and guidance has helped their child enjoy great experiences and academic success. But when the values and priorities of parent and child conflict, excessive involvement makes healthy separation very difficult and painful, and even a practical impossibility. And yet we know that separating from our parents is critical—by definition—to becoming independent adults.[8] So the stories of hovering "helicopter parents" may be exaggerated,[9] but they make us gasp because we know that students need to fly alone.

What these stories fail to tell, though, is how many students help in keeping those helicopters aloft. You may have become used to having your parent drive you everywhere, manage everything for you, take you to lessons, sign you up for classes, be sure you go to summer camp, help you with college applications, and on and on. It's hard to turn off that faucet of help.

Many students like the feeling that their parents are their friends. They say they have an open relationship in which they can talk freely about their lives. And on some level, this is a healthy thing; open communication and a loving, friendly relationship is obviously something to be treasured. The problem is that when the relationship is too tight, both parent and child are delaying the inevitable. They are making it more difficult for a student to manage his or her own intellectual development, choose a professional life, and achieve personal maturity.

Building a New Relationship

In this era of parental intervention and involvement, let me offer some thoughts on and approaches for finding a new relationship between you and your parents. I hope that these suggestions will help you build a healthier, but independent, relationship rather than disrupting it and doing it harm.

First, try to imagine a different kind of relationship with your parents. It is hard enough to manage this relationship without thinking that it could be different. Your relationship will evolve anyway, so you might as well be proactive in taking it where you want it to go. This may seem a more pressing challenge or need for students who have obviously suffocating relationships with their parents. But it should be a priority for every student. What would it be like to treat each other as adults who respect each other's decisions? If that is not imaginable, then can you imagine a more trusting relationship that respects independence? What would it be like to make decisions separately? What would life be like? Could the parent let the child make mistakes, suffering the short-term fallout for the benefit of maturity and modesty?

A second approach is for you to become less needy of your parents. Of course, students will always need their parents' love and support. I am not suggesting that you never listen to your parents again. But be aware that you are deepening this interdependence by continually asking for their advice and approval. When you ask for such support all the time, you begin to think you need it, and your parents become convinced you do too. This neediness creates an opportunity for a parent to think that you are not capable of making decisions on your own or with anyone else. You are signaling that you are not ready to grow up.

How do you fight this neediness? Look to other people when you are indecisive: your faculty or academic advisor, roommates, residential assistant, people in class, new friends, other trusted adults, religious leaders, your Girl Scouts den mother—anybody but your parents. How about an uncle, a cousin, a grandfather, a brother or a sister?

More obviously, you can decide that you want to make these decisions yourself. It is okay to make mistakes because *it is more important to grow up than to be right.* You should take some prudent risks to show yourself that you do not need others' advice as much as you think you do. Perhaps your parents can be first among equals when you need help, but you can learn to rely on your own judgment first, with the input of many others as well.

A third approach for creating healthy distance is to be more proactive in finding out what your opportunities are. For example, if you have decided that being a doctor may not be right for you (most of us are not doctors, after all!), you will need to fill that void. You need to figure out your alternatives. If you and your parents have been expecting that you would grow up to be a physician and now you have nothing—no plans, no ideas, and no way to create any of these—your parents will have a legitimate worry. They are going to think that you now have no direction, and they will be right. They might conclude it would be better for you to be an unhappy doctor than a wandering soul with no job. That conclusion is absurd, of course, though understandable. From your parents' vantage point, you can seem to be in the midst of doubts and confusion, where you were once so directed and self-assured. In the absence of any reassuring work or thinking on your part, the irrational can and will take hold. And it will take even more work to undo those feelings than if you had done the work immediately and independently.

The same will be true of a student whose parents expect that she will have a specific major. At Johns Hopkins, for example, biomedical engineering is a very popular major. Much of its popularity, I believe, comes from the word *medical*. But this major is not for everyone, even if medicine is a lock for their future. It is an extremely rigorous program, and the issues and puzzles of the field may not be of real interest to a given student. A pre-med might simply not be able to pass key requirements, so he had better have a new plan.

That poses a special challenge, demanding an alternative. You will need imagination, work, and exploration to find that alternative. You have to overcome any delusion that something better will just come along. You have to stop the momentum to nowhere. You need to face the possible (but usually imagined) embarrassment of admitting a poor initial decision and anticipate the likelihood that your parents will object. You imagine their arguments: "We are sending you to the most expensive college on the planet to what end? What's the point of your education? Where are you going? What are you doing with our money?" Your anxiety, in anticipating theirs, is going through the roof. You would rather stick with a failing major than face this argument.

Consider two ideas before you do. First, you may be wrong. Your parents may be more understanding than you think. Maybe you have been assuming they would object, and they won't. But if they do, you can face this challenge with greater confidence if you take charge. Do the research online, have the conversations, get help from Advising, sit in on other classes, and peruse books from other disciplines in the college bookstore. You can be deliberate about your search and share with others exactly how you are doing that search. Your parents will find it very reassuring if you offer them a specific *plan to build a new plan*. You can show them that you have given the problem active thought and tell them you are investigating alternatives consciously and responsibly. You can share with them that you have taken steps in finding a new major and considering other careers by using Academic Advising, investigating internship choices, and going for counseling at the Career Center—a rarely used but invaluable resource. Letting go of a dream, like becoming a doctor or majoring in biology, will be difficult for you and your proud parents, but they will respect the aggressive work you are doing to find a new path.

A fourth approach to building separate lives is one your parents may not appreciate: you can simply say no to them. One of the most awkward, but important, moments in your education comes when you realize that *you* own your intellectual development—but your parents do not see it that way. Parents rightly have confidence in their vision, built on longer experience, deep understanding of their child's development, and perhaps their own professional lives. So their views have great merit, but those views may simply not square with that of the student. You may have to say to your parents: "This is my life, and I have to make my choices and live with them. I respect your advice; I hear what you are saying. I know that you are worried about me. But I've thought about it. I've listened to many people, done the research, considered my options, and this is what I'm going to do. It is not what you had in mind. But I'm just going to have to say no."

This could be a terrible moment. It may be impossible to implement or even imagine. Most people want to avoid moments like this, hoping that the person with the different opinion comes to this conclusion naturally without confrontation. But sometimes clear, respectful confrontation is necessary, though the real script might be better than the one above. You may learn that, in order to step away, your parents may need a little bit of a shove. And parents will have to accept and respect the courage it took for you to say no.

A fifth and final approach: do not say anything to each other. This generation of parent-student relationships is built on an expectation of regular, even constant, communication and consulting.[10] When this contact is preferred by both sides and supported by new technologies, regular communication is understandable. But neither side has to communicate all the time, nor do they need to do so as regularly as they may like. A brief conversation every few days, or (heaven forbid!) once a week, to say that everyone is all right would be a healthy break from too much detailed reporting and consultation. It might even make the conversation more meaningful and reflective. There is no particular reason to make more than that phone call; there is no need to check in every day or every afternoon. You can simply choose not to reach out to the other. Distance is not such a terrible thing. We all need space, and this new life where parent and child are physically separated by ivy-covered walls is not a simple extension of life back at home. Parents need to hear the message indirectly, as well as directly, that their child is working on forming her own life, feeling her own way, creating her own sense of priorities, and tailoring her values to her current situation.

If you use these strategies in part or in sum, you will find that you are creating some sensible and healthy distance between you. Students are taking a risk to make some choices, but they can explain those choices and then live with the consequences. Parents need to have some faith that those consequences will be positive. With a child who earned his way into a top college, isn't that faith justified? Hasn't your son or daughter proven to be responsible already?

I acknowledge that some of the consequences of independence will be negative and serious. Students can and do make very poor choices, enmeshing themselves in unhealthy romantic relationships, abusing drugs or alcohol, or ignoring their studies. I will talk about some of these and their impact on academics in Habits #9 and #10. But most students are responsible and healthy, and they deserve the benefit of the doubt and the room to grow. They need the chance to use parental advice in a careful manner that shows that they will weigh that advice against that of others and against their own judgment.

In Loco Parentis

MATTHEW LAZEN, Ph.D.
DIRECTOR OF STUDIES, BUTLER COLLEGE
PRINCETON UNIVERSITY

Parents: can't live with them, can't live without them. College is a time when you learn to live independently, making decisions for yourself, and this independence is perhaps the foremost of the many skills you learn *outside* the classroom in college.

In most cases, the students at top colleges have been primed for successes by highly engaged parents. Yet, at a certain level, this intense engagement can become pernicious. Every college administrator has faced parents demanding some special dispensation or even attending academic advising sessions with their child. We also see the effects of parental involvement indirectly, such as when students choose certain educational paths because of parental pressure, not because of personal passion. Now that college costs are so high, most parents expect return on their investment, and this leads some of them to intervene excessively, forgetting that one of the main purposes of college is to teach students to think independently and expansively.

There are many compelling reasons for students to wean themselves from their parents' protectiveness. For one, they will be the ones to live with their decisions about majors or careers. Many different majors can lead to the career of your choice, and a decent salary is only one component of happiness: liking what you do and enjoying a life outside of work are nice, too. Moreover, thinking and acting autonomously is one of the most valuable skills anyone will develop in life, one that will be cherished by future employers. College is an ideal time to learn independence. Students can spread their wings, knowing that caring faculty and staff are always available for support when needed.

As much as it is vital for students to cultivate their independence in college, parents can and should be valuable partners. Parents will be a source of wisdom and inspiration for students for all their lives. Deans and faculty can, in turn, help balance out parental influence, giving students the security and the license to explore and even

continued

risk failure. It is important that campus contacts do not become surrogate parents, however. For a long time, universities have been considered to act *in loco parentis*—in the place of parents—but it is the student who needs to assume the place of parents. In the end, students must learn to seek, decide, and act for themselves. With the autonomy and support it offers, college is an ideal environment to learn this valuable life lesson.

You can acknowledge that you lack your parents' perspective and experience but recognize that your judgment cannot become refined and mature without the chance to make mistakes and learn from them. You will not grow into a strong person without the chance to be tested and strengthened. Isn't that an important family priority for the college years?

✣ Put It in Perspective

The students who populate good colleges excel by setting ambitious goals and then meeting them with aggression, determination, and brains. If they change or broaden those goals, they will succeed in meeting them. Habit #1 suggested the importance of moving away from academic goals that are too limited—getting into a famous college and getting a high GPA—to a wider vision of being *learned*. For adopting Habit #2, you and your parents should set a more conscious goal to create healthy distance and independence between you.

The stories of "helicopter parents" who hover are often exaggerated—usually by people of earlier generations who experienced much greater distance. Many of today's close relationships are healthy and are supported by ever-refining communication technologies. Friendly, encouraging, and useful relationships have obvious value. All these relationships are underpinned by love and genuine concern. But other relationships are destructive, creating unrealistic expectations that trap students in academic programs in which they struggle. In the long run, parent-student relations that are too close can suffocate the student and delay the development of the healthy skills of independent thinking and accountability.

I've offered a number of ways to create some separation—imagining a new relationship, becoming less needy, proactively investigating the future, saying no, and not saying anything—but such strategies will not work without some perspective and a longer view. It can be very hard for a college freshman—or a senior for that matter—to do this. This discussion can accelerate the development of seeing the long-range benefits of healthy independence in young people. But parents, who do have the skills and wisdom to see the necessity of independent decisions and adult responsibility, will make it easier, or not so hard, by just backing off a little.

Work the System by *Understanding* the System

F ounded in 1876 by the donation of a wealthy Baltimore business-man and train magnate (whose first name truly was Johns—not John), Johns Hopkins University is now well into its second century of guiding research, taking care of patients, and educating students. The architecture on Hopkins' Homewood campus in North Baltimore is in the Georgian style, meaning that there are a lot of brick buildings with cupolas and white trim. There are brick paths everywhere.

Even though Hopkins students are surrounded by the structures of a large and complex institution built a long time ago, with plenty of history, they seem to think that the university was created the day before they moved into their dormitories. From their point of view, maybe that makes sense. College students tend to be self-absorbed and even a little selfish. That is appropriate; it is a time for them to focus on their own development—intellectual, emotional, and otherwise. So it is no surprise that before they arrive, students give little or no thought to their college as an institution or its history.[1]

But it can also be a time when students can look around to understand, at the very least, how the university's workings can affect their lives. As a new student, you should ask, "Who are the people on this campus, what do they do, how are they organized, what do they care about, and how do I fit in?" These questions are not likely to occur to you—until you get in trouble! At that moment, it is too late to figure out that the people of a college or university do matter. In fact, *before* you arrive, you can and should learn who populates a university. That knowledge will ensure a richer, more fruitful experience because you'll be able to appreciate the culture and work within it. That is why Habit #3 on the Dean's List is *Work the System by Understanding the System.*

Who Are the Faculty?

Faculty members are the most important people on campus, but they are also the most misunderstood. To most students, the faculty are *teachers*, people responsible for their education. In many cases, students have only a glimpse at these people, mostly as they lecture. Luckier students, who are more deliberate about the experience, make every effort to meet faculty in a smaller venue, such as a seminar. But even the most enterprising student will not see a faculty member more than three or four hours a week—and usually much less than that.

Indeed, you might elevate a professor to "mentor" even though you have met with her only five to eight times, with less than four hours of contact. So there is some mystery about the faculty. Who are they? What are they doing? What are they doing when they're not with you? Does it matter? Does it have an effect on you? This knowledge will be critical in making the most of your faculty relationships—itself a key to success.

Despite these mysteries, students still look up to faculty as role models. Many of the most successful and intellectually engaged students, in fact, want to become professors themselves. They look at these intellectual giants as mentors and role models and think, "What a life that would be!" They find the idea of teaching and doing research very exciting, though they are not sure what either activity involves. One of the main reasons students want to go to graduate school or want to teach at the secondary or primary level is that, aside from their parents, teachers and professors are the most omnipresent of all adults in their lives. They simply have no other professions on which to model.

But before you start dreaming of being a professor or getting to know faculty members, it is a good idea to know who they are and what they do. College professors started their academic careers much the way that you are. They went to a good school with a caring faculty and did exceptionally well. They learned how to thrive in an academic environment, which gave them a sense of purpose and meaning among the books and laboratories.

But it is a long haul from an engaged undergraduate to a full professor. Naturally, the academy expects a high level of training. With almost no exceptions, professors have Ph.D.'s—doctor of philosophy degrees earned in graduate school. The term "doctor of philosophy" dates back to the Middle Ages when most academic study was philosophic in nature, normally the philosophy of religion.[2] The tradition has not changed in title, although you can earn a Ph.D. in many different disciplines.

A doctoral program is rigorous; that much is obvious. What is less known is that if you are a graduate student, you are being trained primarily, if not exclusively, to conduct research. The classes you take prepare you for that enterprise, introducing you to the scholarly literature in particular subfields of your new discipline and teaching you how to use and analyze that literature. These studies, as well as work outside the class, are designed to help you master a wide range of research: the classic research that is the foundation of your discipline, the research that is being published today, and those works in progress that are presented at conferences.

Graduate students take seminars primarily and work closely with faculty members and mentors. The number of graduate students in a department varies by the number of faculty that can support them. Training a graduate student is very labor-intensive, so most departments will limit their numbers, but those numbers also depend on the funding available to the program. In the sciences funding may come from research dollars secured through grants. More commonly, funding is determined by how many courses the faculty must teach, as this affects the number of teaching assistants (TAs) that professors need.

Undergraduates like you belong to the whole college or school, but graduate students belong to a department such as English or biology. These departments handle admission to their graduate programs themselves, rather than through a larger admissions office like the kind that admitted you. Departments also handle the structure of graduate education and manage financial support. I started off with 25

MICHELE RASMUSSEN, Ph.D.
ASSOCIATE DEAN and DIRECTOR, ACADEMIC ADVISING CENTER
DUKE UNIVERSITY

Many of us who work at universities and colleges are pleasantly surprised to be at a graduation ceremony or other campus event and hear the words, "Mom, Dad, I'd like you to meet my mentor." We might not look over our shoulder or do a double take, but the effect is still the same. I'm your mentor? *Really*? How did that happen?

And therein lies the mystery of mentoring. Unlike advisors, who are assigned administratively and have a well-defined set of roles and responsibilities with respect to student learning, mentors typically step into this role for students without really being aware of it. Good advising can lead to strong mentoring relationships, but a good advisor does not necessarily have to be a mentor to his or her students. Similarly, mentoring may have little to do with helping students select courses and find the ideal major, two of the functions we often associate with academic advisors.

If asked, most college students would say that they would like to have a mentor, but I'll bet if you asked them how they would go about getting one, they would have no idea. So, how do you find your mentor?

We could start by listing some surefire ways *not* to find one:

▶ Miss professors' office hours. Initiate contact only if you need to contest a grade or ask what you missed when you were absent from class (because you had to leave early for spring break in Daytona Beach).
▶ Eat meals and take coffee breaks only with peers (or by yourself, if your friends aren't available).
▶ Choose napping over those otherwise interesting-sounding seminars and lectures.
▶ Trust no one over 25.

Mentors are not going to be members of your peer group. As a young adult, you haven't yet accrued the life experiences—which include the less-than-great ones, by the way—to be a mentor to your

continued

lab partner. A mentor could be a professor, a residential dean, or your graduate-student teaching assistant. Your mentor might be the career counselor who helped you find a summer internship or the assistant coach of your fencing team. Your mentor could be anyone on your college campus who takes an active interest in your life, to whom you go for advice or just for conversation. Your mentor can introduce you to people on campus (and beyond) who can help you realize your goals, and your mentor can offer consolation when things don't quite work out as planned.

Having one (or more) mentors in college is rewarding because you have invested in adult relationships that are qualitatively different from—but similarly beneficial to—the ones you have with friends and parents. Expand the network of people who can support you: this skill will serve you well in all future endeavors. So, let the mentor searching begin!

other graduate students in political science at the University of Wisconsin–Madison. That is a large size for any graduate program. But that was intentional; the department wanted us to compete with each other for funding after the first year. It worked, apparently. Only eight of us eventually earned our doctoral degrees; that is fewer than one in three. And it gave us a preview of the tough winnowing process that awaited us in our careers as professors.

Aside from this kind of intense competition, graduate students must survive many personal challenges to complete a doctoral program and then reach a professorship. Not everyone is well funded through graduate school, so some students may have to take out loans. This is probably not a good idea, as faculty are not well paid. So financial pressures can force people to drop out. Another pressure is time. It takes many years to complete a graduate program, and many students do not have the motivation or self-discipline to sustain it. A third factor is family. A lot of graduate students get married and may start a family. Unfortunately, this means that a lot of women graduate students drop out of the program to raise children. It is very difficult for parents to have the self-motivation, the discipline, and the quiet needed to be a serious student on a graduate level. I have great respect for those that do, but many young mothers simply do not have the support to succeed. That makes the finding that the majority of Ph.D.'s awarded in 2009 went to women all the more remarkable.[3]

There are at least two more academic hurdles students must clear in graduate school. The first is a series of exams designed to test their mastery and the use of the literature that they have been studying. These are often called comprehensive exams or "comps," written exams that last four or five hours each. If a graduate student survives these comps—and there are usually three of them, but programs vary in requirements—then she has become something called "ABD," or "all-but-dissertation." And of course the second hurdle is researching and writing a lengthy paper called a dissertation.

Being an ABD is the no-man's-land of academia. Graduate students at this level may have a regular teaching gig needed to pay the bills, or they may be teaching assistants, research assistants, and the like. Some lucky few get research grants, but most people have to do something for cash, which will distract them from completing the program. Teaching assistantships are the most common, so if a TA is not as responsive or helpful as he or she could be, it is because the TA has a lot of other work to do to keep moving forward toward a doctorate. And now you begin to see the tension between teaching undergrads and getting a TA's "work" done. Teaching is a necessary burden, but often an obstacle to the job of completing a research project or dissertation.

A dissertation is a graduate student's effort at contributing to the field with new data and new thinking. In many humanities and social science disciplines, this is like writing a book. In the sciences, it often means a series of related articles, some of which could be published independently in scientific journals. Scientists rarely write large monographs or books on a particular subject. They usually stick to writing shorter articles that are published in peer-reviewed journals. Even with the preparation of a strong program and the support of a great faculty, completing a dissertation is Herculean. It demands enormous focus, skill, and time at levels a grad student has never before experienced.

Again and again, both in graduate school and beyond, there is this emphasis on publishing and research. It is fundamental to university life, yet it is a feature that escapes the view of most undergraduates.

Research not only preoccupies graduate students and professors, but it also consumes any real time that could be devoted to training them in how to teach. No graduate school that I know of spends more than a few hours, or at most a few days, training graduate students how to teach and focus on their roles as teaching assistants.[4] Johns Hopkins offers a day of training sessions to boost the effectiveness of TAs. But this is not a deliberate effort to train them as future professors who would have to stand in front of students or lead seminars. A university usually provides this training indirectly, giving students a variety of teaching assistantships and the opportunity to teach a course of their own. Hopkins does this regularly in summer programs and in Intersession, a three-week period in January between the two main terms. But all these teaching experiences amount to learning on the job; there is no specific effort directed at showing graduate students how to teach. This may be a very unfortunate feature of academia, but it is certainly a common experience for graduate students and junior faculty.

What's in It for You?

Now take a minute to consider the implications of this system on you as an undergraduate.

Junior faculty—meaning those who have Ph.D.'s but who are still trying to earn tenure (or a permanent position)—have come out of graduate programs knowing relatively little about how to do the teaching job they have been asked to do for undergrads. They do not exactly know how to teach; they are finding their way as they go. So if you have graduate students or young professors as instructors, there will be a tradeoff. Those instructors will be energetic, creative, enthusiastic, and passionate about their subject. But they may show that passion by overdoing it, assigning too much reading and writing, or simply trying to cover too much ground in too short a time. Their lectures may be disorganized or overly organized. They may not know how to prompt a discussion or how to structure that conversation in a way that has them speaking less and the student speaking more.

You can be sure that junior faculty members know what they are talking about, however. Having come out of graduate school in the last five years, they will have been at research's cutting edge and will be on

➤➤ A Community of Students and Scholars ◄◄

BRIAN T. GIBSON, Ph.D.

ASSISTANT DEAN OF UNDERGRADUATES and

DIRECTOR OF ACADEMIC ADVISING

RICE UNIVERSITY

In searching for the right university or college, students and parents consider an array of variables including reputation, size, academic offerings, social culture, amenities, and location. However, opportunity for faculty-student engagement—getting to know professors on a more personal basis—is often underemphasized. Even if decisions are made with exactly this in mind, full understanding and realization of the benefits is elusive. Mentoring and advising in college consist of much more than suggesting courses and checking graduation requirements. Developing relationships with those providing the mentorship and advice is critical. Unfortunately, a lot of college graduates, including some current faculty members, have never had this type of interaction with a mentor, so it can be difficult to envision. Developing an ideal academic community on campus or within an undergraduate residence takes careful planning, consideration, and facilitation.

At Rice University, the residential college system is specifically designed to afford opportunities for faculty members to become integrally involved. Some serve as Masters, tenured faculty members who live on campus in the residential colleges. Masters oversee all aspects of life in the residential college, but they are uniquely qualified to develop their academic community by engaging faculty associates (some of whom live in residence as resident associates, like me). Faculty associates are professors who associate with and frequent their respective residential college for meals. They also engage in numerous events and programs throughout the year. Regardless of university structure, or strategy for facilitating faculty interaction, the benefits are unequivocal to both students and faculty members.

Students benefit from consistent interaction with faculty members, especially in a casual setting without artificial barriers and awkwardness. No matter the discipline, sharing ideas and engaging

continued

in thoughtful discourse is instrumental to learning and broadening perspectives. Students can gain a fuller understanding of a faculty member's profession, whether related to research, teaching, or service goals. Students might find an opportunity to get involved in a research project, especially with the ever-increasing focus on interdisciplinary research. Just as often, they simply gain knowledge about an area to which they have never been exposed. It is all part of developing an intellectual community where immersion results in learning by default.

But it would be a mistake to think that the faculty offer only discipline-specific perspectives. Faculty members are people, too, with their own interests, hobbies, and passions that influenced their decisions to pursue their academic careers. Most are more than willing to share their personal experiences of how they got to where they are today, and many students are shocked to hear that most did not follow a planned route. I know many of my students are surprised to hear about the academic success and struggles that I experienced along the way. Especially when students are struggling personally, faculty members with years of experience can often refer students to lesser-known resources on campus. Even listening to the frustrations a professor might have with students who shirk responsibilities in the classroom or in the advising process can really provide perspective and open lines of communication.

The bottom line is that the better a student knows the faculty, the greater the potential benefit. To illustrate my point, imagine the ease of obtaining a personal letter of recommendation from a faculty member who really *knows* you. It can make the critical difference.

These relationships benefit the faculty, too, both professionally and personally. Students keep life exciting for us by consistently challenging us and helping us see the world through new perspectives. Whether conversations revolve around current events, travel, music, books, sports, relationships, or hobbies, understanding undergraduate student culture, interests, and concerns plays a pivotal role in our ability to do our jobs.

Engaging with college students significantly enriches the lives of faculty. The personal satisfaction gained from helping students consider, create, and complete plans to reach their goals is difficult to describe. It's not unusual to hear my associates comment on thank-you notes from students and how much they mean to them. A few of us even keep folders of correspondence to reflect on occasionally.

In short, most of us enter higher education to further knowledge and to make a difference in students' lives. We cannot do either effectively without serious engagement.

top of the literature as is no one else in the field, even full professors. They have spent years mastering it, and they are ready to share it. The problem is that they may not know *how* to share it.

More fundamentally, you must remember that your instructors are researchers first. In nearly all colleges, the reward system is very clear: you can earn a tenured, permanent position on the faculty by publishing solid research. The more the better. As young professors add more and more articles or books to their curriculum vitae, they become more likely to win tenure. This can be a singular preoccupation of young faculty who want to be promoted from an assistant professor to an associate professor. This title change may seem very unimportant to you, but to professors it represents a critical moment in their careers. In order to get positions to do as they like academically or just to keep their jobs at all, they must first prove to their senior colleagues that they are worthy of staying on the faculty for a long time. That proof comes primarily, often exclusively, from the quality and quantity of scholarship they have produced. This is a demanding system, but it has produced a higher education system that may be unrivaled in the world.

This situation is ironic for the best students. The institutions that are the most focused on traditional scholarship, generally at the expense of teaching, are the ones that attract the best students in the country, if not the world. Those students tend to gravitate toward the larger universities with bigger reputations. And yet those reputations were built on the backs of academic publishing, not on great teaching.

The proof? Talk to the graduates of these schools. A small liberal arts college like Oberlin or Bryn Mawr graduates people who love their professors and were taught exceptionally well by them. If you were to ask the same question of a Harvard University graduate, she might be hard pressed to name any professors she knows well. It is unlikely that she had a strong or personal relationship with them. Harvard professors are focused on their research, and their assistant professors are preoccupied with earning tenure—which they often do not get and must leave for another job. That is one reason why Harvard professor Richard Light tells students in his *Making the Most of College* that getting to know the faculty may be difficult but is worth the effort.[5]

Complicating this challenge is that "research" means different things to different disciplines. In the sciences, most research takes place in a laboratory, staffed by graduate students who are working on their own research in the context of the research of a mentor-professor. This research, generally supported by grants from foundations or the government, generates a lot of revenue for the university. Such revenue can pay for a lot of "overhead," the administrative costs of running the place. Managing that laboratory is in itself a full-time job. There are graduate students to oversee, materials to purchase, grants to secure, and of course experiments to manage and analyze. Gathering data is a very labor-intensive experience. Making sense of it, writing it up, and finding an audience through conferences or journal submissions requires an enormous amount of time and a lot of intellectual energy.

Faculty members in other disciplines conduct other kinds of research. This research might be quantitative, looking at data sets such as the polling results that might be interesting to a political scientist. Archival work done by a historian requires travel and a great deal of time, sifting through years of documentation. Archaeologists must work in the field, often in brutal conditions, to manage their digs. There is no department that escapes the pressing need for publishing, although the kind of publishing that takes place varies a great deal. Philosophy professors tend to focus on one or two books that take many years to write. An English professor might do the same. But other disciplines such as sociology or anthropology focus on publishing a series of journal articles.

In summary, as you look at the university and the most important people within it, the faculty, you must understand that their training, their careers, and their daily lives are dominated by research and its

Connecting with Faculty

COLE M. CRITTENDEN, Ph.D.
ASSOCIATE DEAN OF UNDERGRADUATE STUDENTS
WHITMAN COLLEGE
PRINCETON UNIVERSITY

Top students apply to top universities because they want to learn from the best scholars in the world. Whatever else a school may offer in terms of extracurricular activities, the academic reputation of its faculty ultimately determines the school's prestige. World-renowned faculty is a major selling point of top schools, but many students who choose a school for its academic reputation may find themselves in their senior year of college without having made a meaningful connection with a professor.

How can this be? Top schools offer excellent faculty-to-student ratios and small class sizes, and many of these schools have organizational divisions such as residential colleges or faculty advising programs that aim to help students connect with faculty. But simply bringing faculty and students together in the same place—even in smaller numbers and more intimate settings—will not by itself guarantee meaningful connections. Faculty at top schools are busy with teaching, research, publishing, the tenure process, and committee work, not to mention their own personal lives. Moreover, programs designed to increase faculty-student interaction may give students more one-on-one time with faculty, but these various programs in no way reduce the many demands on a busy professor's time and attention; on the contrary, such programs probably add to those demands, meaning that faculty-student interactions may be more frequent but less conducive to creating the relaxed atmosphere where social connections based on common interests—academic and otherwise—thrive.

Students themselves must work to forge close mentoring relationships with their professors. There are three things students can do to build strong relationships with faculty:

❶ actively seek out classes where they will be more likely to get to know a professor personally;

continued

❷ initiate academic conversations outside of the classroom;

❸ initiate nonacademic conversations outside of the classroom.

Most top schools now regularly offer small seminars, often as early as the freshman year, to offset the larger lecture courses. These seminars are an ideal way to get to know a professor. By making a conscious choice to start early in these smaller settings, students will come to know more faculty. Students should not be discouraged by an application process; introductory-level seminars generally do not call for any prerequisite beyond curiosity. Small classes may seem intimidating precisely because they are small, but no one is expected to have brilliant insights and comments all the time. Sometimes the best way students can show they have done their preparation for class or can participate in a discussion or project is to ask good questions.

Regardless of class size, students should continue the academic conversation outside of class. Many professors take advantage of Web-based programs to give their classes an interactive component beyond the classroom or laboratory. But all professors are available individually, normally by office hour appointments, and often by e-mail. Faculty hold office hours because they expect visits from students, yet many students fail to take advantage of this one-on-one opportunity. Students who are doing well in class may think that they need to be struggling in order to gain something from office hours. And students who are struggling may feel embarrassed to admit their struggle, believing that it may harm their grade. All students should try to build a relationship with their professors, regardless of how well they are doing.

E-mail is a good way to reach faculty, but students should remember that faculty are not peers. The tone of e-mails to a professor should be professional and respectful, regardless of how friendly the professor seems. Keep in mind that a response may not be immediate; faculty do not generally live on campus or keep student hours.

Initiating nonacademic conversations with professors outside of the classroom may prove a bit more daunting. Rest assured, however, that faculty teach because they want to get to know students, and this is particularly true at top schools, where faculty generally expect their students to have active, interesting personal lives.

Inviting faculty to an extracurricular event is a great way to build relationships. Even if a professor cannot attend, the invitation will probably be remembered.

Most schools have active residential communities and dining halls, so inviting a professor to a meal is another appropriate way to initiate contact outside of the classroom. Some schools offer organized programs that allow students to do this, but students should feel free to extend their own invitations. If the idea of a one-on-one meeting seems intimidating, students might try inviting faculty to a group meal. Good conversation is often easier and livelier in small groups. However students choose to organize it, a meal is a good way for students to learn more about their professors, and for faculty to learn more about their students.

Some lucky students may find that close relationships with faculty come easily because faculty themselves make it a priority. But no student should feel that he or she can be a passive recipient of a close mentoring relationship. Most faculty want good relationships with their students, but they may need help from their students to make good advising and mentoring possible. The tangible and intangible rewards of such relationships are numerous, including strong letters of recommendation, contacts in fields in which students may be interested, enduring friendships, and improved teaching and learning. When students put forth the effort, their professors are very inclined to reciprocate, benefitting both student and teacher alike.

publication. To put it bluntly, teaching undergraduates is not the most important of the activities at a university. This revelation can come as a real shock to undergraduates like you. You are now moving from instruction by high school teachers, who were paid exclusively to teach you and who were under no expectation to publish, to an environment in which the reverse is true.

"How is this possible?" you might ask. "How can I be unimportant? It is my education; isn't this a college? Aren't they supposed to teach me? Aren't there alumni who came here and have been happy with the instruction? I'm paying a lot of money for this education—over $40,000 a year. How can I not be important?"

Let me be clear: undergraduates are important, just not as important as you might think or want. College students absorb a lot of time and energy from even the most productive of faculty. Many faculty members are devoted to their undergraduates and teach them with great enthusiasm. They love their students' energy, their enthusiasm, and their spirit of learning. In contrast to their graduate students, who must be very professional in their approach, undergraduates bring a freshness to the discipline. There are also many faculty members who take a great deal of pleasure in advising students, talking to them about their lives, their studies, and where they are going. These faculty tend to be the most gregarious and outgoing of the community. But just remember that you are not the sole focus of the faculty, even in colleges that educate only undergraduates. Faculty members are not successful or hired because they are gregarious or outgoing. They are hired because they are effective scholars, scholars who get things on paper and send them out into the world.

What can you do about this? You can begin by appreciating the strain on faculty to do things other than talk to you or lead your classes. When a faculty member seems distracted when you go to her office, it is because she *is* distracted. She may be under unreasonable pressure to produce something. She may be behind schedule to do that. Her personal life or other responsibilities may be slowing her down from the principal task at hand, which is to produce research. And you complicate this problem by arriving on her doorstep.

In most cases, faculty are sympathetic. They want to talk to you, but they also feel pulled in another direction. They know that they may not get full credit from a demanding research university for helping undergraduates. And while advising students or instructing them is certainly in their job description (if they have one), the university and their colleagues will be less concerned about the energy that they have shared with their students than with the publishing record that they can show.

To make this difficult situation more challenging for faculty, they have many other things to do. Faculty members serve, on a rotating basis, in administrative positions, including department chair and director of undergraduate or graduate studies. Professors also have to sit on a variety of committees. The department might have a committee, for example, to recruit and keep other faculty. There might be many college-wide or university-wide committees on which faculty are asked to sit, such as Study Abroad, Student Research, and Curriculum, along with many search committees to interview job candidates. These committees and other work around the community are broadly defined as "service." And that rounds out the three areas in which a faculty member is evaluated: research, teaching, and then service.

Again, you can see that your education is only a small fragment of the work life of a faculty member. While student learning and well-being are the direct responsibility of high school teachers, those considerations are only part of a wider range of responsibilities that a college professor has. In a system with so many demands, research most prominent among them, good teaching happens mostly because of goodwill and enthusiasm, not necessity. Certainly, professors are obligated to teach one to four undergraduate courses a semester. But they are under no particular obligation to do that very well. So if you are expecting to get uniformly excellent attention from talented "teachers," I am sorry to report you will be disappointed.

But do not despair. If you recalibrate your expectations, and look to find professors on their own ground, you will be rewarded over and over. Finding exceptional professors that excel in teaching and who care deeply about undergraduates will take effort. A lot of students rely on word of mouth to find out the best professors. That sometimes works, except that one professor may seem "interesting" to one student and not to another simply because students differ in subject matter interests or learning styles. Nevertheless, it is a good idea for you to ask around and to use whatever resources the university has for publishing online or paper student evaluations of instructors. And by remembering that faculty are not entertainers but scholars, you can enter into their wider world of ideas, discovery, experimentation, and understanding. Don't look for them just to teach, but engage them in that wider world. That might mean visiting them during office hours with specific questions in mind or to push an idea. It might require that you look for research opportunities in their labs or on their archaeological digs. And it would help if you asked them what they are researching and how it is going.

Such efforts are worthwhile. Faculty are by far the most important

people on any campus—more important than the president, the provost, the deans, the staff—anybody. These are the people that give an
academic institution its backbone, and their attention will give your
education the richness it deserves. It will just take more effort and empathetic understanding of the challenges they face to make that relationship successful.

More Players
The President
....

While the faculty are the most important people on campus, there
are other key players. The most misleadingly important person on campus is the president. He or she does lead the institution, and no doubt
his or her personality and priorities affect the culture profoundly. But
understand that most of a college president's job extends outside the
walls of the campus. So his or her direct impact on your life is limited.
Instead, college presidents work closely with alumni. They coordinate
with local, state, and national officials. They may represent the college
or university on larger boards and associations such as the NCAA.

But by far the most critical job of a college president is to raise
money. You may think that you and your family pay a lot of money for
a college education—and you do! The cost of a college education continues to rise all the time.[6] For many, financing this seems impossible.
At Johns Hopkins tuition, room, and board totaled well over $44,000 in
2008-2009 and is likely to keep going up indefinitely. But what might
come as a surprise to you is that this represents only a fraction of the
money needed to keep the institution alive.

I have already told you about one of the major sources of funding,
grant money won by various faculty members, often in the sciences or
engineering. A variety of institutions also rely on revenue from other
tuition payers, such as students who go to summer programs and
those who attend various forms of continuing education at night.

Whatever these sources provide, fundraising and endowment resources are critical for the college to survive. Supported by the development office and the alumni relations office, presidents raise money
in a variety of ways. They manage annual funds, which are campaigns
that ask every alumnus, alumna, and friend of the college to donate

Advice or Advising?

MARGARET BRUZELIUS, Ph.D.
DEAN OF THE SENIOR CLASS and
LECTURER IN COMPARATIVE LITERATURE
SMITH COLLEGE

If there's one thing a college student gets a lot of, it's advice. Parents and grandparents, aunts and uncles, guidance counselors and teachers, friends—practically everyone has advice to share: study hard, do pre-med, don't do pre-med, take a small class, take lecture classes, satisfy all your requirements, explore new fields, have fun, join a team, participate in extracurricular activities, keep your nose to the grindstone, etc., etc. When you get to college, you will probably have an "official" advisor, a staff member or professor with whom you will meet to discuss your academic plans and who will help guide you as you register for class. But there are many other people on campus ready and willing to give you advice. Professors, deans, teaching assistants, librarians, roommates, dorm mates, hall mates, and fellow students who are only too happy to recount their experiences and offer suggestions.

Yet with all the advising that goes on, both official and unofficial, every year students complain that they got no advice, or bad advice, or that someone told them something that turns out to be completely untrue. So how do you get good advice? How do you know which advice is good?

Asking Is Important!

Asking for advice is an excellent habit to get into, but remember that just because you've asked for advice doesn't mean that you have to take it or that the advice you get is worth taking. You are under no obligation to follow the suggestions that you've asked for—you're just asking. In general, professors and deans will not have their "feelings hurt" if you ignore their advice, so you should cross that off your list of things to worry about. For bigger decisions, asking more than one person is a good way to get a cross section of points of view. If you receive versions of the same advice, you know that it's worth considering. That still doesn't mean you have to *follow* the pattern, but at least you know what the standard answer is.

continued

Ask an Expert

You cannot get good advice if you ask the wrong person. The same professor who is a wonderful advisor about larger intellectual and academic issues can be either quite foggy or simply misinformed on details of procedure. If you are seeking information about specifics about college mechanics—registration, planning to graduate early, questions about study abroad, and so on—ask the professional on your campus: a dean, the registrar, the director of study abroad. Ask the pre-professional advisor for pre-professional advice. Your college has someone whose job it is to answer questions about careers in veterinary medicine, business, nursing, and public health. Don't assume that knowledge in one field equals knowledge in all fields.

Think Critically

Professors can be wonderful advisors, but their advice, like that of everyone else, comes from personal experience. If you admire a professor, it's easy to think that her advice is definitive, but remember to ask yourself some questions first. Do you want to follow her career path? Do you want to be a professor? Do you even want to go to graduate school? Really? If graduate school is not an immediate interest to you, you might want to take that course on the history of rock and roll rather than the advanced seminar in sociology that will get you into a grad school that you aren't even sure that you want to go to.

All advice—even when given by knowledgeable and good-hearted people—is *only* advice and is *always* limited by the experience of the person who gives it.

Take It with a Grain of Salt

If grown-ups can give unhelpful advice, recommendations of fellow students can be even more misleading. It is astonishing how often students take advice from each other without giving it the tiniest bit of thought. Just because John Q. down the hall didn't like the professor who taught history doesn't mean that you will not.

Even people you really like and admire can have vastly different experiences in classes because of things you know nothing about and that have no relation to your experience. That doesn't mean you should never talk to anyone about courses or, worse, never listen to anyone, but it does mean that you almost never have the whole picture. Learn to receive negative—as well as positive—judgments with a critical ear.

The grain of salt—your critical judgment—is the most important part of advice giving and taking. Advice is free, and people hand it out daily, often without giving it a great deal of thought. As a student, you need to be aware that the famous professor whose lectures you love can still give you lousy advice. Or he may give you great advice which you still feel unable to follow. Evaluating advice is a process: the more you work at it, the better you will get at asking questions that elicit good answers.

Going from high school to college means moving from a model of learning that emphasizes preparatory material to one that emphasizes your strengths as a thinker and a learner. You will be asking more difficult questions of the material you are learning, questions that may have no definitive answer or that have answers that may take years to develop. The same goes for the questions you are asking about your studies: the answers you get will be more complex, and there may not be one right answer.

money each year. That donation can be as small as $10 or $20 or more than several hundred dollars a year. These programs try to maximize participation to create a broad sense of commitment and belonging to the financial responsibilities of a college. After you graduate, you will almost certainly be approached by your alma mater regularly for the rest of your life. If you are a parent who went to college, you already know this.

The principal job of the president, however, focuses on working larger donors. These are people, generally alumni, who, after some time and development, become very interested in particular campus projects. It should not be a surprise to you that many of the buildings on a college campus are named for major donors. On occasion, a sentimental college will name a structure after an important administrator, a president, or a beloved faculty member. But, for the most part, a university will name buildings after people who have given a lot of money to build that very facility, often tens of millions of dollars. And when you have that kind of money to give, you want to work directly with the president of the college. And that is why the president spends a great deal of time traveling, meeting people, and developing relationships, with the ongoing expectation that he or she will ask those people for money.

The president as fund-raiser is a strange concept to most undergraduates. At Johns Hopkins, students think the president is the most important administrator on the campus. He is certainly the most recognizable and most famous, partly because he leads important ceremonies such as convocation and commencement for the university. Many college presidents are dynamic personalities, excellent public speakers, successful scholars, or people known from other accomplishments such as public service or the leadership of a foundation.

So it makes sense that you'd think the president is in charge. This is probably why, when parents are particularly upset, they might send an e-mail or a letter directly to the president. Yet nearly every one of these messages is forwarded by a secretary or other staff member to the proper person; the president of a university or a college simply does not have the time to work out the particular problems of a given student. He or she might be sympathetic, but when it comes to the particular problems, a president is powerless. He or she has to rely on other people to solve these problems. It makes more sense for you as a student (or as a parent) to learn who does what and talk to that person. When you try to solve a problem by going over someone's head, it makes them look bad.

So it is important and useful to understand what the president does, to realize that what he or she does is very different from what you imagine, and to appreciate that you need to learn who else is in charge in order to solve your problems.

Other Administrators

On most college campuses, the second most important individual is the provost, sometimes called the vice president for academic affairs or just the dean of the faculty. This individual is responsible for the direction and leadership of the entire academic enterprise: research labs, libraries, the development and recruitment of faculty, and the relationship between the various academic departments and the curriculum generally. In larger universities, the heads or deans of various schools report to the provost. If you are going to a university that has a medical school, law school, or graduate school, the deans of those schools answer to the provost. In smaller colleges, the provost will deal with a lot of day-to-day academic administration. This might include a variety of policies related to academic life, deadlines, grading, progress toward graduation, and the like. At a larger university, those issues are relegated to the deans of the respective schools and their support staff. But it is important to know that the provost is the number two person because academics are more important than anything else.

There are usually a variety of other vice presidents at a university, such as one for development, and another for finance and administration. But for your purposes as a student, the next level of leadership is occupied by deans. Deans are the people who have the most hands-on experience with the management of the institution. They are the people who supervise all of the various administrative and academic divisions at a university. There are generally three types of deans. The highest of these is a school or college dean, who is the principal leader of the School of Arts and Sciences, the College of Engineering, and so on. Academic deans are in the next group. They usually report to the school's dean. These are people who deal with academic advising, curricular development, faculty relations, and managing academic programs like study abroad, summer programs, and so on. These people are the most responsible for your day-to-day experience in the classroom and with faculty. Finally, at the same level as academic deans, there are deans in student life. Student life officers focus on the residences, athletics, counseling, career services, multicultural affairs, dining services, Greek (fraternity or sorority) life, and all other pieces of a student's experience that are outside of the academic.

Other offices and services—such as financial aid, the bursar, admissions, and the registrar—fall under the academic or student life deans. The registrar's office is a smaller office worth noting here because of its importance to the academic experience. Registrars manage enrollment, making sure that classrooms are filled with students taking a class from a particular professor. They register students for their specific courses, then gather their grades and maintain transcripts.

This should give you a sense that there is a large army of lower-level administrators who handle all of the day-to-day functions of the university from registration to bill paying to plant operations, managing the recreational facilities and programs, and on and on and on. If a college administration is doing its job, most of these people, including the deans, are fairly invisible. This is one of the reasons that most students have never heard of these people. But it is important to know that these people can help every day, and when you get in trouble.

♣ Put It in Perspective

I have outlined the principal players in a university so that you understand their functions, limitations, and pressures. It is easy for you as a college student to be focused on your life, as defined by friends, activities, and classes. But that life takes place within an institution with concerns larger than yours and with a horizon stretching long before you arrived and reaching far beyond your time in college.

The most obvious and important example of these larger concerns and longer horizon are the faculty. This group of women and men represent a long tradition of discovery and scholarship, have been trained through rigorous programs, and are successful at navigating a demanding culture and profession. They are not teachers. They are scholars, committed to pushing the bounds of their disciplines. Undergraduates are invited into their world, but this invitation is not always to a place where undergraduates are the center of attention. Professors have rich and complicated lives outside of an undergraduate's view, packed with research agendas, conference schedules, and other responsibilities, from managing the department to training graduate students and sitting on countless committees. Universities and colleges have a wider responsibility than educating young people. They preserve, protect, and create knowledge.

Knowing the demands on faculty, you can better take advantage of the academic environment. You can blend into it, use it, absorb its values, and appreciate its pressures. So now you do not have to take it personally when a professor promised to meet you but didn't show up because she is on a dig in Syria or presenting a career-making paper

Making the Most of Academic Advising

MICHELE RASMUSSEN, Ph.D.

ASSOCIATE DEAN and DIRECTOR, ACADEMIC ADVISING CENTER

DUKE UNIVERSITY

While perhaps not quite as maligned as dining or parking, academic advising is one of those features of undergraduate life that students say are in the most need of improvement. The reasons for students' dissatisfaction with their advising experiences are as diverse as the students themselves, and perhaps this is part of the problem.

Most freshmen start college without ever having had an individualized advising relationship. To complicate matters, colleges don't always do the greatest job articulating the purpose of academic advising in ways that make sense to an 18-year-old. Advising should be a process of engagement, give and take, listening, and feedback. But often students want a transactional relationship, where they are told what courses they should take. Some students may expect their advisor to be a collegiate guru, someone who will watch over them omnisciently, impart knowledge, and show them the path to enlightenment (or at least medical school). Others would prefer not to have to deal with an advisor at all, since they know what courses they want to take and don't need some random old person getting in the way.

For the majority of students who fall somewhere in between these two extremes, academic advising is often like a AAA membership: you're told you need it, but you really don't give it a second thought until something breaks down. (And then it better be *right* there!)

Although you may be perfectly content with an advising experience that consists of information being produced on demand, you could be missing out on something really important by limiting the extent of your advising relationship to biannual meetings to go over course schedules. Whether advisors are faculty, deans, or student affairs personnel, they have two things in common: they know how college works and they know college students (after all, they used to be students). When you meet and communicate with them regularly and tell them what you hope to get out of college, why you chose your school over someplace else, what you're worried about, and

continued

what you're interested in taking (say, an acting class, even though math will be your major), you are not wasting your time or theirs. Rather, with each meeting and e-mail you are giving your advisor the details she needs in order to know you as an individual, details she will remember when a course, program, or opportunity seems tailor-made for you.

At most colleges there will only be a handful of professors and staff who will know students for all four years of their undergraduate career. The advisor is likely to be one of them. So don't cheat yourself out of an advocate by discounting your advising relationship to the bare minimum.

Remember, you got into college in the first place because you are smart, self-motivated, and good at figuring things out. If the sole purpose of academic advising was to ensure that students have access to a repository of graduation requirements, college regulations, and deadlines, we'd have assigned you a copy of the Undergraduate Bulletin instead of a human being. Luckily for you, we didn't . . . so make the most of it!

at a distant conference. You were just the victim of a distracted and pressured researcher torn in many directions, though still trying (in this case, failing) to do the right thing for you. As you gain more perspective, you will find that institutional and professional understanding like this will make you an effective coworker, colleague, and friend in your life after college. By understanding the players in the game, you will be able to get what you need while being a part of the enterprise of learning and discovery.

Approach the Curriculum Like a Great Feast

One of the best features of some Jewish weddings is something called the Viennese table. This is a long table or a series of tables with the most extraordinary array of desserts. All kinds of delights await—cakes, pies, pastries, chocolate mousse—everything you could imagine. When a friend of mine got married years ago in Miami, he and his wife offered a Viennese table with great flare. The waiters lit various flambés, so the table appeared to be on fire. The band introduced it with a flourish. What followed, of course, was the wonderfully difficult choice of which of these confections to try. You had only a certain amount of room on your plate, and having had dinner, you had only a certain amount of room to put it.

The other problem was the temptation to try only the things that seemed familiar, like the cheesecake or the German chocolate cake. But because there were so many new and different things to try, it took a long time to survey the table and figure out your best strategy. Would you try to come back for more or would you load up your plate this time? Would you take tiny slices of a variety of things or big slices of just a few things? Given how unusual it was to have so many choices, it seemed almost stupid to focus on one or two options. So most people, as the line grew longer and longer, decided to take as thin a slice as possible of as many different kinds of things as they could fit on their small plate.

By now, you have figured out the obvious academic analogy that I am building. The college curriculum is very much like a Viennese table. It is wide and complicated. It offers many, many different choices—some of them very familiar, some of them completely strange, using terms and names that you have never seen before. The choices from both the Viennese table and the college curriculum could all be delicious. But some of them simply seem more appealing than others.

Subject matter that seems familiar, such as political science or economics, may look more appealing than the offerings of a lesser known discipline, such as sociology or anthropology. Coursework in biology, likewise, is something students are already familiar with. If you are good at a familiar subject, that would make it even more appealing. In contrast, a subject like cognitive science might seem a little mysterious and a little daunting. I can make only a certain number of choices; I can't put all of this on my plate. Cognitive science seems like a bit of a risk. I'll go with biology.

When students sign up for classes, particularly if they are freshmen who have not yet gotten to campus, they will feel the same time pressure that I did in a Viennese table line. They have a limited amount of time to gather any information, and that information is incomplete. After all, at the Viennese table, you cannot put your fork into a variety of choices before you put them on your plate and take them to the table. The same would seem to be true for a college curriculum. If everyone is registering at the same moment online, from wherever they are around the country or around the world, the time pressure is quite intense. So students make choices precipitously and without fully considering their options or alternatives.

But what may matter most, as you approach either a banquet table or a curriculum, is your attitude before you get there. And that attitude may depend on how much panache you need to get excited. At the Jewish wedding, the build-up to the Viennese table is intense, as everybody celebrates both the generosity of these offerings and their variety. It is part of the show and the wish for a future of abundance. And it is something for which the host family has every reason to be proud.

Colleges feel the same way about their course offerings, but they are much less inclined to present it with equal flourish. We make little effort to do so, probably because it seems a bit unseemly to create an atmosphere of excited anticipation about the variety of choices. Part of our reservation comes from the fact that we are so familiar with your choices. We work with sociologists, for example, so we know the content of their courses. We are familiar with the faculty and their areas of specialty. The variety of course offerings does not seem like a big deal to us. But if you are coming to a strange subject for the very first time, you probably need more than a little encouragement to feel excited about that subject and its equally unusual peers. Yet academics are not particularly good showmen—unlike the caterers at Jewish weddings!

Instead of flaming desserts and a 20-piece band, I offer Habit #4 from the Dean's List, *Approach the Curriculum Like a Great Feast*. We'll look at the reasoning behind the university's offering this amazing fare and the tactics you can use to explore it. Knowing that this effort will fall short of stacks of custards and chocolate fountains, I also will give you a few tools to navigate and make sense of this staid environment and help you shape an attitude of academic celebration, anticipation, and desire to put a wide variety of choices back on your plate to sample and savor. If you are deliberate and self-conscious in exploring and make it a habit of your college experience, you may be surprised to find delicacies you never thought existed and for which you have great talent.

The stakes are high because there is an important link between exploration and success.

Sampling Your Way to Success

Academic exploration, both in its attitude and its outcome, is critical to being a highly successful college student. A successful student has nurtured an open, liberal education, an education that is ongoing, exciting, and filled with curiosity.[1] Such an approach will last far beyond graduation, outlasting the short-term gains of good grades or even the prestige of a degree. Better to build an appetite, therefore, than to fully satisfy it. You cannot separate exploration from a successful education.

Sometimes it only takes an unintentional elective, taken just for fun, to unleash a cascade to a rich experience. You might stumble onto anthropology, for example, and discover that the exploration of gender roles, ideas about sexuality, or religious tenets is so exciting that you cannot wait to open those books, go to those classes, and do research. You will find that the power within you comes out and is evident everywhere. Good grades will fall as easily as rain on a spring afternoon when that commitment comes from inside you. You find you are willing to do the extra work, to talk to professors in an excited, interactive way, and to think deeply about what you are learning.[2]

It is vitally important, then, to be deliberate and open-minded in finding the niche, the academic home, within which you will prosper. This is a personal exercise, one special to you alone. And your college wants you to find that home, too. Colleges want to support this kind of exploration. Some of them will do this in a way that pushes you to explore, through distribution or core requirements of various kinds. But most colleges are happy to see students look around on their own, and to do this in a way that is tailored to the individual and independent of others.

Finding a path does not have to be accidental, but your path will belong to you if you are creative about building it. For example, a college may have a strong and popular program, like Johns Hopkins' neuroscience major. Anyone choosing that would follow a large crowd, and that choice might be a good one for you. But a student could add his own twist, adding a French minor or a second major in classics. This can make his choices uniquely his own, creating balance and contrast to other students. This is the kind of surprising choice that always draws attention from employers, graduate schools, scholarship committees, and other people who look at your record. They look at this kind of contrast and imaginative exploratory curriculum with a bit of envy.

Indeed, many college graduates look back with some regret and wistfulness, wishing they had been a bit more imaginative in their choices. They regret having stumbled onto certain subjects, such as the history of art, so late in their undergraduate career that they could not take more of those kinds of courses. When you take an exploratory approach, when you embrace this habit from the Dean's List, you will look back on your college choices and record of success with great satisfaction, not wistfulness and never with regret.

Watch That Metaphor!

MARGARET BRUZELIUS, Ph.D.
DEAN OF THE SENIOR CLASS and
LECTURER IN COMPARATIVE LITERATURE
SMITH COLLEGE

One of the things I notice in conversations with students is how the metaphor of warfare pervades their speech. They describe themselves as winning and losing in the battle zone delimited by daily college life. If you find yourself in a position where your classes are not going well, if you are having trouble in your living situation, or if you are simply unable to imagine what's coming next, beware the language of battle! Such language by definition creates winners and losers.

Students in trouble often describe themselves either as a beleaguered citadel on the point of surrender or as a combatant outmaneuvered by a crafty, ruthless opponent. The foe is rarely clearly denominated, but is, rather, an amalgam of college, classes, professors, never-ending demands, and fellow students who seem better prepared, richer, and better-looking. Everything appears to oppose and impede their progress.

The language of warfare is embedded in the language of intellectual argument. As Lakoff and Johnson point out in *Metaphors We Live By*, metaphorical constructs have a systematic quality that structures our thinking: we *demolish* or *win* arguments, or use *strategies* to *defend* our ideas lest we get *shot down*. Such language is also engrained in sports culture, which, despite gestures to the losers, exists to enshrine and financially reward winners. It is found as well in the language of commercial competition, where the acquisition of luxury objects is enshrined in the pages of every newspaper and magazine in the country.

Rather than viewing the college experience as a battle, you can choose to think of your education in other ways—as a dance, for example. Dancing is a skill that can be learned and that all can enjoy. You don't have to dance like Justin Timberlake to be a great partner and to have a good time.

Another way to think about college is as a form of agriculture.

continued

Every year you go back to the same field and sow new seed, but in ground that has been prepared by previous years' cultivation. Every year there's a crop, but every year is different. Every year builds on the hard work of the previous years.

Comparing your college career to dancing or agriculture may seem a little silly. But we all use metaphors when dealing with life's challenges. You can choose the language of battle to describe the college experience, but you are then committed to the language of win or lose, do or die. Choosing another metaphor—one that does not create false dichotomies—just might help you through!

Ask the Right Questions

The process of making those good choices begins with asking the right questions. So ask yourself the following five questions when you look at your college's curriculum of majors, minors, and courses:

❶ What do I know and what do I want to learn?
❷ What is required?
❸ What skills do I want (and need)?
❹ Where is the surprise?
❺ How do I make room for academic opportunities like study abroad?

What Is Worth Knowing?

The first question—what do I know and what do I want to learn?—is the most important one of all. Remember, of course, that a college experience is profoundly educational. This may seem obvious, but asking what to learn is often the last question asked by students. They usually are more preoccupied with fulfilling requirements and expectations. That's understandable. Figuring out what to learn is a big challenge, requiring perspective that few freshmen possess. But if you focus on requirements, taking courses to "get them out of the way," you are giving up a lot of intellectual freedom to follow your own curiosities. You're creating obligation when education is a gift. So let me suggest you put requirements down a peg and think about better questions regarding your education.

You can begin by taking some stock of what you learned in high school. How rigorously did your teachers cover their subjects? How deeply did they push you to reflect, analyze, and criticize? How much ground did they cover? Compare the course offerings at your school with the course catalogue or even a semester's schedule at your college. That will help you think about what you know and what you don't. You see a course on African colonial history, for example, and ask yourself if you know anything about that. Probably not. How about Roman Republican government? Or subatomic physics? Do you want to learn these things?

Another approach is to consider knowledge that everyone should share. For example, one could argue that everyone should know something about daily life in China, the history of South Asia, theories of international conflict, or revolutionary thought in Latin America. You might believe it is important to understand the fundamentals of Western civilization, as shaped by the Greeks and Romans. Everyone should probably find out what Cicero had to say.

If a college has an open curriculum, one with fewer core requirements, students have the freedom—along with the responsibility—to decide what they want to learn. They can decide whether it is important to focus their attention on Latin America or on neuroscience. But as young people with little exposure to the world, they can have trouble appreciating the wide range of choices available. They need to be self-aware enough that their definition of what should be learned is incomplete, just as their definition of what is "interesting" is limited by their knowledge. In other words, when one is ignorant, it is hard to know what one is ignorant about.

Since you may not know what you don't know, you might need some help. Here is one place where your parents can be helpful. As experienced adults, parents should have a wider sense of their own ignorance and so an appreciation of how a liberal education can fill those holes. Parents with this kind of self-awareness can encourage you to take intellectual risks, like they did when offering you new food, a trip to a local museum, a new book, or any new challenge. Parents

Exploring the Curriculum

MARCY KRAUS, Ph.D.

DEAN OF FRESHMEN

UNIVERSITY OF ROCHESTER

We know what we are, but know not what we may be.

Hamlet, act 4, scene 5

It's freshman orientation and you are excited to *finally* be at college. You discuss with your advisor your first semester course schedule. As a student who has dutifully followed the advice of your teachers and parents for many years, you may be disappointed that the answer to your question "What should I take?" is "What do you *want* to take?"

Until the beginning of the twentieth century, being an educated person meant following a tightly organized sequence of courses. Choices were limited, and the concept of the elective course simply did not exist. Contrast this scenario with what is available to today's college student—a choice of hundreds of interesting classes with titles like "The Beatles, the British Invasion, and Psychedelia"; "Topics in Literature and Human Rights"; and "Vision and Art: Physics, Physiology, Perception, and Practice." What happened to Calculus I and Calculus II? While it can be exciting to have choices, freedom can create confusion and sometimes anxiety. What courses will look best on my transcript when I apply to graduate school? Which classes will help me find that all-important summer internship? Is it the course that will challenge me or the course that will prove to be the easy A?

College is a critical time to explore and develop skills and interests that are important not only for your major and your first job, but for the successes you hope to achieve throughout your life. To make the most of college, choose courses and subjects you are passionate about. You will be most successful in classes that coincide with your academic strengths and match your intellectual interests. Rarely will new students have had an opportunity to test all of their potential interests before beginning college. In the first year, find a balance between those courses that are recommended and those that sound interesting.

Ask yourself what courses you can see yourself interested in, even when studying at two o'clock in the morning. Consider courses that coincide with your proven strengths while balancing those with classes that will help you further develop important skills. By choosing only courses that will assure a high GPA or are required for your major, you will lose out on opportunities for exploring new interests and career possibilities.

Small, discussion-oriented classes are good ways to get to know a professor well. Look for courses that will challenge you, since they will stretch and push you to refine your intellectual abilities. Students often look back on those courses as high points of their college careers.

One of the myths of college is that a liberal arts major is not as wise a career choice as a more technical or pre-professional path. Don't use this reasoning—or anxiety—to select a major on the basis of job or income prospects. Your major alone will not determine what your job will be. By actively choosing courses that interest you, researching your career choices, and fully and enthusiastically engaging in all aspects of college life, you will find your way.

Your educational choices belong to you, so engage *actively* as you and your advisor discuss your interests and goals. If you are honest with yourself, you will be happy and successful in college.

can follow that logic into the college curriculum and support you as you explore.

But if your parents do not see education in this way and you are lost, your college can help. Academic advisors love to help students find an academic home that matches their skills and interests. This may take a lot of conversations, and a lot of failed experiments and even struggles, but the journey is well worth the effort. Finding out what you don't know and setting down the path to learn is a noble and worthy quest.

Another way that your college can help you decide on what to learn is through its requirements for majors, minors, and graduation. So it is sensible to ask, "What is required?"

As I've suggested, if you ask *only* this question, you are giving away too much freedom. But you must balance freedom in course choices against the realities of requirements, most importantly for your major. The best way to do that is to appreciate that you can choose a major for your own personal reasons. I suggest in Habit #5, *Understand That Majors and Careers Are Not the Same Thing*, that you avoid making that choice because you think it is the only one to get you where you want to go. When students choose a major for better reasons, such as the desire to learn more about a subject and gain the skills associated with that discipline, then *"requirements" is just another word for courses that they would take anyway*. "Requirement" and "choice" become exact synonyms.

Try to look at this process of evaluating a major backwards. If you do not like the requirements for a major, then you probably will not like the major. It is like suggesting that you might like jambalaya when you do not like rice or shrimp or peppers or hot sauce or any of the other ingredients. You cannot like the end product if you do not like what goes into it. I acknowledge that some things may have to be endured, but those should be minimal. Think about the path, not just the destination.

If you find the path through the requirements appealing on the whole, to better understand the field, you can explore the rationale for these requirements. For example, the sociology department at Johns Hopkins requires a series of skills courses in statistics and research methodology to help students build the analytic skills they need in that discipline. But sometimes the reasoning behind requirements may not be so obvious. You can always ask. Any professor in a given department will be able to tell you why certain courses are requirements, and if not the particulars, then at least the spirit of them. Why is it necessary, you could ask, for a history major to know something about the history of many continents? Why not focus on just one?

It is also worth noting that required courses need not be taken all at once or right away. Think of these as something that should be spread out over time. The requirements of the pre-med curriculum cause the most problems in this regard. Students interested in medical school are on a tear to get through the requirements. That means their first two or even three years are jammed with things they think they must do, so their whole attitude towards their education becomes pressured and compressed. Yet those requirements—a year each of math, English, biology, and physics (the last two with labs), and two years of chemistry (also with labs)—can be spread out over time, and thus made more manageable. They do not have to be completed quickly to "get them out of the way." To get help with pacing yourself in taking courses, seek out an academic or pre-med advisor on campus, who knows how the pieces can be moved around in ways that suit your interests and preferred pace.

Shop for Skills

Building specific skills is another way to make choices in a large academic curriculum. Some of the most important skills include a foreign language (very common in the social sciences and humanities); statistical skills for programs like psychology and sociology; and calculus, a fundamental skill for the understanding of physics and all engineering fields. Laboratory skills are critical to all natural sciences. Other skills might include computer skills, accounting and other business skills, and some forms of leadership training.

You can look at your course selections as a way to shop for skills, filling a shopping cart rich with possibilities. Each course offers a new add-on, and the entire experience becomes a way to shape what you can do. For example, let's say that you are drawn to philosophy. You find the puzzles challenging, the courses exciting, the ideas inspiring, and the faculty welcoming. You're thinking, though, "What can I do with a degree in philosophy?" If you find yourself asking a similar question, try to recall my advice to think of your coursework as a way to gather skills. Indeed, philosophy majors learn a variety of important skills, often without knowing it: the ability to build and to analyze

Freedom to Choose

JOHN P. LOGE, JR.
DEAN OF TIMOTHY DWIGHT COLLEGE
YALE UNIVERSITY

One fall during orientation, a first-year student came to see me, clearly upset about something. She became teary and said, in as composed a way as she could manage at the time, "Is it true I can take whatever courses I want?" Upon hearing that the answer was yes, she seemed stunned. When I asked whether she would like me to help her choose courses that might be of interest, she enthusiastically responded, "Yes, please!"

Many college freshmen feel anxiety about selecting courses because it may be the first time they have ever decided which classes to take. In choosing first-year courses, following the criteria below can help, as can thinking about how courses may complement one another on a schedule. Students should select courses

- in majors they may be considering or plan to complete,
- in disciplines not represented in their high school curriculum,
- taught by the great teachers as they hear and learn about them,
- that complement each other (to explore connections),
- that do not complement each other (to discover connections),
- for practical reasons (requirements for postgraduate plans),
- that follow a personal interest.

It can be easy to discount personal interests when choosing courses, but sometimes it is appropriate to follow a passion or to satisfy a curiosity. Remember: you're free to choose!

complex arguments, to write well, to argue in public, and to absorb great amounts of complex information and make sense of it. These abilities are all vital in most professions.

But there are a variety of skills that philosophy majors do not get as a result of their studies. They will not learn how to lead a group, to apply the theoretical to real, or to manage personal conflict. That is where electives, a second major, or a minor comes to the rescue. A handful of business courses might do the trick, adding some practical and applicable skills. They could take a computer course or learn a foreign language. If you see a single choice, like what to take or what to major in, as one piece in a wider skill-set building strategy, you are more likely to make bolder, more imaginative choices that work together. You will get a richer *and* more professionally useful education.

Take a Chance—Be Surprised

Taking a rational approach to the curriculum—asking what to learn, what is required, and what are worthwhile skills—does not always help you catch some lightning, coursework that really excites you, courses that not only answer your questions but give you new ones. You may be missing something great, because no strategy can capture serendipity and luck. We often limit ourselves to what we find "interesting," a judgment that requires us to know something about the "interesting" thing. But how do you know if you'll like something you don't know?

I can only suggest that you do all you can to be open to serendipity. That could mean dropping in on a lecture you passed while walking down a hall; asking a friend for the most surprising and inspiring choice he had made; clicking randomly on a department Web site or its course listings; looking for the strangest course title in the catalog; really using any "shopping" period at the beginning of the term to look around, rather than taking your early choices as final. Take a course you might think irrelevant or off the wall. If you are consciously open to surprise, you will always be intellectually fresh and alive. Things that are unfamiliar are often far more stimulating than things that are more familiar. By building in surprise, you will stumble onto people and ideas that you never knew existed, and yet they are wonderful and enjoyable.

Your college might have programs that help you be surprised. Johns Hopkins has an "Intersession" of three weeks in January designed to promote serendipity. This winter session offers more than 100 one- and two-credit courses taken pass/fail, so it lacks the pressure or commitment of the traditional terms. Some recent Intersession courses were "War and Victory in Ancient Rome," "Medicine and Membrane Proteins," "I Want to Be Humphrey Bogart," and "Introduction to Ba-

➤➤ How Should Your Major Change You? ◄◄

ANYA BERNSTEIN, Ph.D.

DIRECTOR OF UNDERGRADUATE STUDIES and SENIOR LECTURER

COMMITTEE ON DEGREES IN SOCIAL STUDIES

HARVARD UNIVERSITY

At an information session on the major that I direct at Harvard, a first-year freshman asked a remarkably prescient question for an 18-year-old: "How do you hope your students will change as a result of their experience in this program?" My response had very little to do with the content of the curriculum: "I don't care whether your values and beliefs *change*, but I hope that you will be forced to critically examine them, and hold them up to the challenge of empirical evidence."

College is the first and possibly the best time for students to think critically about what they believe and why. College students are nearing adulthood, and most are away from home for the first time. They have the maturity and self-awareness to reflect insightfully on important questions, and the time to do so, before they start jobs, get married, have children, and pay mortgages. A major allows students to delve into a discipline or subject, but more importantly, it gives them a lens through which they can think about big issues: Are humans basically good, bad, or blank slates? Are there fundamental truths, and if so, what are they? Is morality universal? Why do people keep making the same mistakes through history?

The in-depth work required in any major provides students the analytical, research, and presentation skills needed not only for college, but for life. While different majors afford different skills (a humanities student will learn to analyze texts, while a scientist will learn how to generate and test hypotheses), all majors give students practice in making arguments orally and in writing, and in analyzing the arguments of others. These skills are essential to any professional career.

In the end, it doesn't matter what a student majors in, as long as that major opens her mind and teaches skills. That is how your major should change you.

sic Electronics." If your college has programs like this, whether it's a January term, guest lectures, or teas at the dean's house, take advantage of them. You may be surprised.

Study Abroad

Studying abroad is one of the best curricular examples of blending the planned and the serendipitous. On the one hand, it can take a lot of time to prepare for going abroad to study. You will want to learn the language, which usually takes years. This is truly worth the work and commitment because meeting new cultures on their own terms is both the most respectful and empowering experience you can have in college. But language is only the beginning. If possible, adding course work related to that particular country or region would be very useful, too. Going to South America for the first time might be a bit daunting, and probably not as fulfilling, if you don't know something about Latin American culture, history, literature, and art.

Most European universities offer a level of instruction that requires expertise and skills to meet success. Oxford University, perhaps the most famous of all study-abroad destinations, does most of its teaching through one-on-one "tutorials." There, students meet "dons," or teachers, in their offices to discuss readings and to read papers aloud. This is an exciting learning experience, as you can really own what you are studying, but it also demands confidence and skills to handle the pressures.

Study abroad offers the greatest challenge to science and engineering students. Students in most of these fields have chosen a fairly regimented and prescribed set of courses that must be done in sequence. Because everything is already laid out for them, it can be very difficult for them to step away for a semester or two. It is certainly possible to continue advancing their studies while overseas. There are many fine science departments and universities all over the world, and most American universities are building closer ties with them.

But for better or worse, American science faculty are skeptical about sending their students to study biology in France or genetics in India. Faculty argue that the vocabulary of science is so particular

GEORGE LEVESQUE, Ph.D.
ASSISTANT DEAN FOR ACADEMIC AFFAIRS
YALE COLLEGE, YALE UNIVERSITY

In college, you get to decide what courses to take and when to take them. This newfound freedom to study what you want can be at once exhilarating and overwhelming. You will have literally hundreds of courses and dozens of majors to choose from, but you can only take four or five courses at a time. How do you decide?

To begin, make sure you are thoroughly familiar with the undergraduate requirements at your institution. These requirements are designed to ensure that students develop general tools of learning and communicating while acquiring the research skills of a particular field of study. Many students fall into the temptation of viewing these requirements as an obstacle course, and the goal becomes finding ways to jump the hurdles as quickly or as easily as possible. Resist this tendency. However bothersome required courses may seem, they reflect a purposeful educational philosophy and can provide a useful blueprint for you to develop your own goals. Fulfilling these requirements should not be the goal of your education, but they supply a good starting point and some structure for your choices.

Whatever the number and rigidity of the requirements at your college, you are likely to have much freedom in deciding how to fulfill them, and it will be up to you to build a coherent plan of study that corresponds to your particular interests and abilities. To help you identify some particular courses that you might want to take in your first year, consider the following:

▶ Which courses did you particularly enjoy in high school? Why? Was it the subject matter, the style of learning, the nature of the assignments? Look for similar college courses in which you can build on these interests.

▶ What kinds of books do you read in your free time? Are there subjects that continually fascinate you but that you have not been able to study formally? See if your college offers courses in those areas.

▶ Think about your favorite extracurricular activities. What inspires you to devote time to them? Look for courses that would allow you to develop a broader perspective on these interests and strengthen related skills. As a corollary, look for extracurricular activities that might complement your coursework, either because they are similar to or very different from your academic interests.

▶ Before deciding on a major, think about those subjects you might be interested in pursuing, and take courses to explore those interests. Be aware that any major has prerequisites that should be completed before junior year.

▶ If you plan to major in science or apply to medical school, consult the special advisors who can help you reach those goals. Most colleges have a special pre-medical advising office which can offer advice and answer questions. Keep in mind that many courses in the sciences must be taken sequentially. Prospective science majors and pre-med students should start their math and science sequence in freshman year.

▶ Choose courses for which you are prepared. The relevant academic departments can offer information and guidance about placement, but if you are ever unsure, ask questions. Keep in mind that at many colleges, students are permitted to change their course selection during an early "drop/add" period; don't be bashful about talking to the instructor if you think you are not in the right class.

▶ If you attend a large university, be sure to take at least one small class each term that will offer you the chance to participate in discussions.

It would be impossible (and unwise) to map out at the beginning of your studies a firm schedule of courses for the next eight terms. Still, some thoughtful reflection and careful planning will help you explore the curriculum intelligently.

The increased independence that accompanies the transition from high school to college does not mean that you should make these decisions alone. Seek advice from a variety of sources. Many colleges match first-year students with faculty members or professional staff to serve as advisors, and some colleges also have

continued

advising centers where you can go to find answers to a variety of questions. Take advantage of these advisors, not only to acquire information but also to talk about your short- and long-term goals. These advisors can also help you to think about how extracurricular activities and summer opportunities can complement your coursework. Remember: you are going to college to gain an education, not just a degree. With thoughtful reflection, careful planning, and good advice, you will accomplish both with great satisfaction and success.

that even the most fluent student would spend a lot of time simply orienting themselves to the things they already knew in an American setting. Whether these biases are fair or not is not appropriate to argue here. But it does mean that a chemistry student, for instance, will find it difficult to go abroad during the year. And so, if that student feels it is important to go abroad, she will need to move some science requirements out of that term and negotiate with her major advisor to approve courses taken elsewhere. That will take time and planning.

The same challenge faces students who have serious commitments to activities and especially to sports. Training, practice, and game schedules may make it impossible to be away at any time during junior year. For student athletes who have worked all their lives to hone physical skills and mental toughness, junior year might be the peak of their playing careers, a time when other students turn to them for leadership.

There are a number of solutions to these obstacles to studying abroad. Think of your requirements, whether for a major or for medical school, as dominoes to be moved around the board. Most pre-med students take physics their junior year, often the time to study abroad. Remember that physics (and its lab) is offered over two semesters, and those semesters can be separated; you can, for instance, take Physics I in the fall, then have a semester abroad, and take Physics II either in the summer or in the next fall. (All of this depends on how often your college offers physics, of course, and whether it will allow you to take summer courses there or elsewhere. But most places are flexible.) Or you can move the course to senior year. Or you might have AP credits for physics, so you don't have to take it at all.

Understand that all things are possible if you ask for help and plan carefully. If studying abroad, even for a January term or in the summer, is a priority, *then do it.* No sport should ask of you a 12-month commitment, and even if it does, you can run and lift weights anywhere, not just at home. Find flexibility in your curriculum and get help from an academic or study abroad advisor. It is well worth the effort.

✤ *Put It in Perspective*

Going to college is a fleeting opportunity and an honor. A college education gives you the credentials and tools to succeed professionally, certainly. But always remember what the experience can do for you intellectually, spiritually, and emotionally. College is an amazing time of life, a time that will never come again. Unless you are very enterprising and energetic, you are not going to take another course on the history of the Ottoman Empire, or Japanese calligraphy, or the poetry of William Shakespeare. It just won't happen. Professional pressures, family obligations, and the lack of time will make it difficult to be as selfish intellectually as you can be right now. This is an ethereal moment that will vanish as quickly as it arrived, and it is crying out for you to grow in every way.

Consider this: you have only 40 courses, often fewer, that you can take during your college career. *Just 40.* (And that's at the high end; you can graduate from some colleges with 36 or even 32 courses!) And after each term, another four or five courses go by, never to be seen again. Doesn't it make sense to work really hard to find a group of courses that is balanced, diverse, surprising, interesting, and challenging? Should you really fill that group with courses you are taking just to "get them out of the way"? Why not make choices that inspire you to get up for class, ready to learn and engage and debate and read and think?

When I first became a dean at Johns Hopkins, I met one of the school's most famous alumnus, Michael R. Bloomberg, the founder of the Bloomberg media empire and, at this writing, mayor of New York City. I told him I was excited to become the new dean for advising and was ready to try something new. He looked me straight in the eye and said, "Don't screw it up." I laughed, but I also knew that he was very serious. The job was important, and the opportunity was precious. And that is what I am saying to you about your exploration of the rich feast, the Viennese table of college courses.

Think it through and don't screw it up.

Understand That Majors and Careers Are Not the Same Thing

When you go to college, you expect to learn something, of course. But most students are not really sure what that means. Learn what? And why? For Habit #4, I talked about seeing your choices as a great feast. But you may want to ask why you are eating at all. Really, *what's the point*?

Answering this question has become a lot more pressing recently, as the cost of a college education spirals without end. Everyone knows that college graduates do better than others economically, earning more and having access to important professions like the law and medicine. But I don't think many people have figured out *why* they do better. People go to college assuming that good things will happen for them professionally. They'd rather not consider that there might not be a good connection between a course of study—a major—and a career. To the contrary. Most college students I know, and their families, *invent* the connection to better justify the expense and effort of going to college at all. Political science majors become lawyers. Biology majors become doctors.

I am sorry to report it is not so simple. And that is why Habit #5 on the Dean's List is *Understand that Majors and Careers Are Not the Same Thing*. You'll find that this is a very helpful thought. It allows you to explore intellectually and find an academic "home," or major, without worrying about what professional implications that choice of study might have. You can blossom in that field, be it art history or neuroscience, knowing that the skills, confidence, and sophistication that comes of any good college education can help you in any professional pursuit.

But it might take this entire chapter to convince you of this. I'll begin that effort by trying to explain why our university system sends such conflicting signals about its purpose. Those signals are at the heart of the confusion. Am I training for something or getting a liberal education (whatever that means)? I think that the root of this confusion is our ambivalence about expertise.

The Ambivalence of Expertise

Americans are ambivalent about expertise. On the one hand, we respect that experts in science and medicine, for example, have brought us the marvels of technology and modern healthcare. We appreciate the depth of knowledge and the extraordinary skill necessary to make such contributions. On the other hand, we worry that premature commitment to a profession or academic discipline is elitist and exclusive. Pushing a student into an advanced track means that another path is excluded, an outcome that feels wrong to self-styled egalitarian society.

American higher education reflects this ambivalence. It begins with the premise that 18-year-olds are not ready for graduate or professional studies, although they are considered so in countries like France and Britain. Instead, Americans want a wider, well-rounded educational experience. That attitude may originate in the beginnings of American colleges, many of which were founded to educate ministers for service to God.

Whatever the reason and the roots, American education has created a contradictory intersection between breadth and depth. You can see breadth in two ways. Most obviously, U.S. universities support an extraordinary range of academic disciplines. Even small colleges offer dozens of programs, led by a wide array of faculty, often in departments with fewer than five members.

Second, American colleges have developed requirements that both reflect this diversity and enforce it. Students may or may not want to take classes in a wide range of fields, but they often have little choice.

They must take a diverse set of courses, sometimes very specific courses. These core and distribution requirements might reflect a long academic tradition of studying the Western canon of literature or history. Or they might come from today's concerns for scientific and technological literacy. Together, the structure and history of higher education puts a premium on breadth, a belief that a well-educated person knows a lot about many things.

Mapped against this value is the opinion, held by many scholars, that having a wide set of interests marks a person as not "serious." They think that for academics to be legitimate, it must require a high degree of depth and hard-earned expertise to make it all worthwhile. This attitude probably stems from their own training and traditions, where scholars have mastered a common vocabulary and methodology. Given that professors gain credibility and professional security from digging deeply into their fields, it is no wonder that they expect undergraduates to do the same. At some research universities some faculty members consider their undergraduates to be "junior graduate students." This school of thinking demands that a large number of upper-level courses should dominate the intellectual life of an undergraduate.

This view will become familiar to you right away in freshman year. Suppose you are interested in studying biology, perhaps with an eye toward marine sciences. Your college is likely to assign you to a faculty advisor in biology. If he is typical of many research biologists, he will be excited to meet a new student interested in the field. He might tell you to pack in the lower-level sciences—general biology, biochemistry, cell biology, physics, and lots of chemistry—to get to the upper level courses quickly, even to reach graduate courses. Understand his enthusiasm, given his own professional choices, but know that his advice might not work when you have to take distribution and writing courses, and that you might be unsure about biology to begin with. You might not really understand all that biology involves, even if it seemed interesting in high school. So, right there, you are experiencing the culture clash between the expertise this faculty member wants you to have, and both the college's and your own ambivalence about trying to become expert.

A Major Decision

GEORGE LEVESQUE, Ph.D.
ASSISTANT DEAN FOR ACADEMIC AFFAIRS
YALE COLLEGE, YALE UNIVERSITY

If you are unsure about what you intend to major in, you're in good company. Most students arrive at college with several possible majors in mind. Did you know that many students graduate with a major they had never even contemplated when they first arrived? The good news is that there is usually no need to choose a particular major at the outset of your college education. Indeed, it is often best to let the decision grow out of your academic experiences.

Your career options after college have little to do with your choice of a particular major, almost any college career advisor will tell you. With a few specific exceptions (like engineering and medicine), most employers and graduate schools are primarily concerned with an applicant's transferable skills. They want to see evidence of discipline and creativity, analytical and interpersonal skills, the ability to communicate, and the willingness to learn. Many of these skills are inferred from the successful completion of a college degree and from an applicant's extracurricular and employment experiences. This is not to say that the courses a student takes are irrelevant or inapplicable outside the classroom, but employers and graduate schools want to know you are trainable to do the work they want you to do. Put another way, the *facts* you learn in your education (such as the causes and consequences of the French Revolution) matter less than the *skills* you gain in the process of learning them (whether it be considering evidence, evaluating competing interpretations, or postulating and testing an argument).

Although you need not be overly anxious about the choice of a particular major, the choice is not unimportant. If the goal of pursuing a major is to develop further the skills of research, analysis, and articulation, then you should pick a major that inspires you to develop these skills. For many students, a variety of subject areas could serve this purpose equally well, so your final decision may depend on the particular course offerings, available faculty, and requirements of the major at your school. Use your first two years to explore different departments, and see if the topics and modes of inquiry interest you. In most departments, an introductory lecture course can be a good way to learn about the field, but keep in mind that lecture courses are not always the best way to assess your interest in the subject matter, and faculty teaching styles can vary widely, so beware of drawing too many conclusions from one course.

At most colleges, majors are sponsored by academic departments, and they reflect different approaches to studying the world. Disciplines associated with the arts and humanities, for example, interpret the range of human thought, expression, and activity in the past and present. The social sciences investigate the behavior of groups and individuals. Disciplines in the biological and physical sciences examine natural phenomena from the microscopic to the cosmic. The lines between these disciplines can be blurry, and many colleges sponsor interdisciplinary majors that bring a variety of perspectives to topics of study, but a consciousness of these broad categories may help to inform your exploration.

Take comfort in knowing that few colleges require you to declare a major during your first few semesters in college. However, in order to keep your options open, you may need to make some decisions as early as freshman year. Students considering a major in the natural sciences or foreign languages will need to follow a sequence of courses throughout all four years of college. Introductory courses are prerequisites for intermediate courses, and so on. It may not be impossible to complete a major in these fields without beginning in freshman year, but it will very difficult without summer study. The selection of a particular major does not determine your future, but with thoughtful reflection and careful exploration, you can identify a major that will serve your future interests well. Keep in mind the big picture and the kinds of skills and habits you want to cultivate. You cannot possibly exhaust the curriculum at your college in four years, but you can further develop the tools of learning and apply them to whatever endeavors you pursue after college.

Majors ≠ Careers

In a pressured environment with steep tuition bills to pay, it is not surprising that you and your family might set aside these mixed signals and conclude that a major leads to a specific career. But let's consider the evidence that there is no link between majors and careers.[1] The most obvious evidence that this link is false can be found among a college's alumni. Alumni relations offices track their graduates to find donors and to know which of them has greater resources. So they know, as accurately as anyone can, what career choices their alumni have made. At Johns Hopkins, and probably at all top colleges, these offices can see that alumni go on to do hundreds, if not thousands, of different things. All of their careers differ from one another, even if they have joined the same profession, such as journalism or the law. Their journeys vary from one another enormously, and they end up in very different places, literally and figuratively.

There are two ways of looking at these "data": you can go forwards or you can go backwards. If you go forwards, you take the list of majors and find out what happened to those people. For example, English majors from Johns Hopkins diverge into dozens of career paths: lawyer, doctor, teacher, bureaucrat, public servant, management consultant, and so on. This holds true across the curriculum with any group of majors, including those that appear to be a little bit more "practical," such as economics or psychology. Like many top colleges, Hopkins does not offer undergraduate degrees in marketing or business, but it is likely that even students with those majors at other colleges go on to do many different things as well.

Another revealing exercise is to look at career development backwards. Take a given profession, say urban planner, and then look back to see which major those people had. This proves the point again. Lawyers who went to Hopkins majored in a wide variety of subjects: history, earth and planetary sciences, philosophy, Latin American studies, and mechanical engineering. It is true that in some professions there are some majors more commonly found than others. Political science majors are more likely than any other student group to choose the law. Biology majors tend to go on to medical school at a higher rate than do undergraduates in any other major. But from my view of these records, these kinds of choices are not well connected, and there is too much variation to show clear paths from major to career.

In fact, graduate and especially professional schools often look for those who have studied in a variety of disciplines. A medical school would be very interested in a student who had majored in art history, provided that the student has done well in the science classes that were the pre-medical requirements, such as physics and calculus. Medical school committees construct a class, so they need diversity of opinion and background, in addition to obvious variety in race, gender, and ethnicity. The same is true for law schools, which do not want only political science majors in their classes.[2] They have a special interest in creating different perspectives on life because that affects the richness and quality of debate. That means that a distinctly novel candidate, such as an electrical engineer, has an excellent chance of admission. Such a student would enrich the school and would also be very attractive to a law firm, particularly one interested in, say, intellectual property, patents, and corporate litigation. So it helps to be both distinctive and to offer valuable complementing, not redundant, skills and expertise to any given school or firm.

Why the Disconnect?

Let's dig deeper into this puzzle. Why is there a disconnect between majors and careers? I have suggested one possible explanation, the ambivalence in American higher education toward expertise. Because Americans are not committed to in-depth training at the undergraduate level, it makes sense that this stage of education should remain highly flexible and therefore not predictive. For example, a political science major usually takes between 12 and 15 courses in that discipline. Departments vary, but they generally want you to take a wide variety of courses even within that discipline: "Political Theory," "International Relations," "American Politics," and "Comparative Politics." So even if you were to write a focused senior thesis, which might deepen your understanding of one area, you're still taking a fairly random group of courses. The same would be true for most departments, particularly in the humanities and social sciences.

This randomness is compounded by the expertise of the faculty.

The Meaning of Majors

M. CECILIA GAPOSCHKIN, Ph.D.
ASSISTANT DEAN OF FACULTY FOR PRE-MAJOR ADVISING
and ASSISTANT PROFESSOR OF HISTORY
DARTMOUTH COLLEGE

As assistant dean of faculty for pre-major advising at Dartmouth College, I have spoken with students (and their parents) and listened to them struggle with the decision of what to major in, and also whether to take on multiple majors (or minors). In these discussions I invariably find myself asking students why the college even asks them to choose a major. Some students are at a loss for a coherent answer. Others reply that a particular major is necessary for their chosen career goals.

I then make the following points:

▶ The importance of your major isn't in the knowledge you've gained but, rather, in your ability to gain and manipulate that knowledge.
▶ A double major isn't inherently better than a single major.
▶ Students (and their parents) radically overestimate the link between majors and career options.
▶ Employers value how you think, not what you know.

Let's unpack these points. Colleges and universities ask you to choose a major because an academic focus allows for increasing your sophistication of thought, writing, and research skills within a discipline. The goals are critical thinking, intelligent assessment of evidence, synthesis, and the creative application of knowledge. In one sense, learning to excel within a discipline—any discipline— makes you smarter. Graduating with a history major doesn't make you a historian; a biology major doesn't make you a biologist. It means that you have developed these high-level, valuable skills within the context of the discipline of history.

Likewise, having more than one major is fine, but it doesn't mean you are getting twice as much out of your education, or that you are graduating with twice the qualifications. It just means that you followed two parallel paths to the same goal.

You may need to master certain content to reach your goals. Medical schools ask you to be competent in a body of knowledge that you can acquire in college. Some employers may have a particular need for someone who speaks Spanish. If you want to become a computer scientist, it makes sense to take computing courses. But in all cases, graduate school, medical school, and employers (and so forth) are interested in your ability to acquire knowledge, to manipulate that knowledge, and to draw conclusions from that knowledge—not necessarily in whether you have knowledge to begin with. This has never been so true as today, when knowledge ("content") is freely available (think Internet) and when, moreover, it is changing so rapidly.

How does any of this relate to your future professional life and goals? Most highly educated people will change professions repeatedly over the course of their careers—by one estimate, perhaps as many as 10 or more times. The knowledge that one must have in any profession is also changing rapidly. What is valued, thus, is not the "stuff" you know, but the ways in which you can adapt to new challenges, assimilate new information in a productive fashion, absorb new information, and adapt to new parameters. These are precisely the skills that liberal education fosters, in part by asking you to develop high competency in a single discipline (a major), and in part by asking you to work at a high level in different types of classes and different disciplines (general education requirements). This is why colleges ask you to take a variety of courses in a variety of areas. Breadth is as critical to liberal education as depth. In this respect, a double major might actually inhibit you from taking the broad array of courses that fosters broad perspective.

We urge you to "find your passion" and "major in what you love" because we know that passion and sincere engagement encourage the intellectual self-discovery that *is* critical to success and happiness. You are far more likely to do better academic work if you are dealing with content and ideas that are inherently exciting to you. In other words, studying something you love will more effectively hone the intellectual and cognitive skills that *are* of great value to graduate programs and future employers. More important, self-knowledge will maximize your ability to make professional choices that will result in your own happiness.

Most academic departments make an effort to hire a range of professors whose interests collectively represent most, or at least much, of the discipline. Since academics try hard to avoid stepping on each other's toes, they will not push for the creation of a seamless curriculum where courses complement each other. There are exceptions to this, particularly in the sciences and engineering. There, success in upper-level courses depends on expertise gained in the lower levels. But for the most part, if students take courses from many members of a department, they will be taking a scattered, incoherent set of courses.

Now take this incoherence and look out over many universities. Since the coursework offered by each department varies by who is teaching, by what they teach, and by what they are interested in, then you can see that there is no *one* meaning to a degree in political science. This is true simply because each program is unique. No one is bothered by this. I am not. And employers anticipate this incoherence by training employees to fill in the gaps in their knowledge. (Engineering programs are an important exception to this observation. Engineering programs undergo rigorous accreditation, requiring them to be uniform—within reason—for a given program, like electrical engineering. Still, not every electrical engineering department looks exactly the same, so there will be some variation despite all efforts.)

Another reason that majors and careers are not linked is that they evolved as separate cultures with different rewards, leadership, and missions. Academic disciplines like English or history developed from a wide variety of intellectual histories and traditions that date back many centuries. They were not created for vocational training. British and French universities, for example, met the needs of the upper class by offering a "formal" education, while guilds evolved to train craftsman through apprenticeships. The kind of hands-on education offered by the guilds had nothing to with reading literature or the Bible. In fact, literacy was limited generally to the clergy and the nobility. "Practicality" and the application of knowledge was not central to the development of universities. To the contrary, in fact. So there is no historic reason to expect a link between academic majors and work.

This historic separation is perpetuated by the resistance of most elite colleges to develop anything that is obviously practical or skill-building. That is just not how they define their mission. Learning the skills for doing a job, from management to accounting, lacks the intellectual depth that academics respect. Even if academics had the inclination to focus on skills, they could ask a good question: which skills? The modern economy is too complex and changing for a group of faculty to anticipate and then teach specific skills. Technological innovations from the laptop to the Internet underscore the transient nature of economic demand. So, to the extent that the academy teaches skills at all, it teaches skills that are flexible and in constant demand: how to write cogently, how to speak with clarity, how to gather and synthesize information, how to argue rationally, how to consult sources, how to speak a foreign language, and so on.

Economic development also has fragmented the job market, further disconnecting majors from careers. If there was ever a short list of careers open to college graduates—minister, priest, teacher, bureaucrat, lawyer, doctor—that list now numbers in the thousands. There are hundreds, perhaps thousands, of industries with countless career tracks within them. The combinations are staggering. If there are thousands of careers, with many more born every day, then how could a list of 25 or even 50 majors predict their choice? Rather simply, they cannot. Careers develop and evolve from many factors beyond academic credentials: personality, family connections and traditions, preferred geography, desire to follow a loved one, values and mission, and simple luck. The power of chance is always underestimated. But luck may be the only way to explain how we meet people that help us find a job. You may just be lucky that some jobs fit you. How did a job open at a time you are ready? How did you see that posting at all? Maybe just dumb luck. So, how a job, or series of jobs, coalesces into something that could be called a coherent "career" might be a matter of cognitive flexibility and chance as anything else.

And as you get further away from your undergraduate experience, the less and less importance you will put on your major to determine anything. If your parents went to college, ask them. They already know this, as their lives have drifted from their undergraduate studies to many new areas, carried by the often unpredictable tides of life. Your own parents probably can prove the point that majors do not link well, and usually not at all, to careers and life choices. In that sense, majors do not matter at all to begin with.

The Mystery of the Missing Major
Choosing Your Major from the Inside Out

JOSEPH HOLTGREIVE, Ed.M.

ASSISTANT DEAN and DIRECTOR OF THE

MCCORMICK OFFICE OF PERSONAL DEVELOPMENT

MCCORMICK SCHOOL OF ENGINEERING AND APPLIED SCIENCE

NORTHWESTERN UNIVERSITY

Choosing a curriculum, or major, is one of the first decisions you will be asked to make as you begin your college career. This choice may cause you anxiety, given that it feels like the decision that will have the biggest impact on the rest of your life.

But where to begin? Many students begin by focusing on external issues such as future job markets. I often hear students and parents ask questions like "What majors will be in the highest demand four years from now?" and "Which majors earn the most money?" Nothing is wrong with these questions unless they are driving your choice of a major. I believe your choice needs to be student-centered.

A student-centered decision begins with the question "Who am I?" rather than "What will someone pay me to do?" Putting yourself at the center of your choice requires you to look inward as you begin the curriculum selection process. Ideally, you should choose a curriculum that both ignites your passion and accentuates your strengths.

Imagine you are a detective who has been hired to unravel the mystery of who you are. Keep in mind that the mystery of who you are has been 17 or 18 years in the making, not just the last 4. You are not simply trying to answer the question "Who am I today?" but rather "Who have I been and how does this impact who I will become?"

Officially on the case, your first job is to compile a list of key witnesses to your life, including characters from all chapters of your story. At the top of your list should be the first people on the scene, your parents and siblings. They offer insight into your history which predates your own memory. Next, include other important people from different parts of your life: special teachers, extended family, and friends may see things about you that your family don't see.

They can provide unique perspectives on your strengths, interests, and weaknesses. Because it can be extremely difficult to have an outside perspective on yourself, it's vital to acquire this through other key characters in your story.

Clues can come from unlikely places. Some things that were true about you as a young child remain true about you today. Identifying these truths may help you recognize their continued role in your life. Aspects of your intellectual curiosity, your "fascination DNA," have also remained persistent. Your job is to uncover these truths, as well as the new curiosities you have developed, in order to answer the question, "What kinds of problems do I like to solve?"

Each detective has his or her own approach to finding the truth. For example, a potential engineering student may find she is most interested in hands-on experiments to explore and test various theories. Or perhaps she enjoys solving problems through the development of computational programs. Other potential engineers may be more intrigued by analytical problem solving using mathematical models to predict behavior. Investigating your preferred style of problem solving can help you constructively narrow the field of options when it comes time to choose a major.

Good detectives reveal the truth by following leads and asking the right questions. As you prepare to interview your witnesses, organize your questions in a way that is meaningful to you. Focus on personal characteristics and not the application of these characteristics to a profession. During this stage of your investigation you are painting a self-portrait, not reaching a conclusion. You may consider asking:

- What kinds of problems did I enjoy solving as a young child?
- What types of things could I spend hours doing when I was younger?
- What are some things I do well?
- Tell me a story that illustrates how I am unique.
- List things with which I have consistently struggled.

As you listen to the testimony of your witnesses, keep in mind that you are looking for emerging clues and patterns across this spectrum of perspectives.

continued

Through this process you will begin to identify your strengths and the types of problems that interest you. Record your interviews so you can revisit these conversations as you come to various crossroads throughout your college career. These will serve as rich reminders of your past as you reflect on what direction to take for your future. Each time you listen, you will hear something new about yourself or discover new meaning in your witnesses' words.

Once you have completed your initial investigation, you should have a better picture of your overall strengths, interests, and weaknesses, as well as a fuller understanding of the types of problems you like to solve. You can then begin the process of matching these insights with potential majors and careers. Hearing others' perspectives on your life can be eye-opening and fun, but ultimately, you need to take ownership over your choice of a major.

Remember that no two paths are the same and that the journey is far more meaningful than the destination. Keep yourself at the center of your choice of a curriculum, and you are certain to have a successful and rewarding career.

Choose Wisely

You might be stunned or at least surprised by the idea that majors don't matter. You might think: "Great, just great. *Now* how am I supposed to pick a major? Doesn't this choice matter at all?" These can be scary questions, particularly if you thought the reason to go to college was to get a degree with a major. Such questions may be disturbing if, even as a freshman, you already think of yourself as an "econ major" or an "international studies major" or a "chem major." Isn't that one of the first things freshmen tell people about themselves? Wasn't this the main reason they chose this university or that college? Wasn't that how the college pitched the academic experience?

When facing these unsettling questions, try to consider these ideas. If it does not matter what you choose as a major, then

▶ Be yourself: create your own personal identity and academic mission.

▶ Don't just live with your choice—love it: you're free to choose any major you like. It doesn't have to be practical.

▶ Know the true value of your education: no matter what you major in, your decision will have its own payoff.

▶ Don't be so hard on yourself: keep your college education in perspective.

Let's take these one at a time.

Be Yourself

"So, what's your major?" That is so common a question in college as to be trite, even self-mocking. Students enjoy answering that question anyway because the answer provides an immediate identity, a shorthand that allows a new acquaintance to understand your interests, priorities, and even ambitions. People will continue to ask you this question, but in a new form, when you are in the work force: "So, what do you do?" The need to categorize like this must be fundamental, perhaps a modern way to discover a person's standing. Or it might be more practical. If you answer this question, then I have a starting point for our conversation, a generalization I can tap into.

"Math major? Wow, you must be smart (or a geek)." "Biology major? I bet you're pre-med." "Majoring in economics? I hope you'll hire me some day." "Philosophy? (Insert laughter here.) You're planning to have no job?" These generalizations and predictions are nonsense, of course. They are gross oversimplifications. But when a student thinks that her major defines her, then she is setting this trap for herself.

A healthier alternative is for you to describe more richly what you are studying within a discipline, what you find especially interesting, and how you are planning to further explore those things. Perhaps you are intrigued by the cellular functions of spinal neurons, or the essays of Sartre, or the phenomenon of black holes, or the reasons for partisan bickering in Washington. Try to avoid saying, "I'm a biophysics major." It might be quicker, but it's not as accurate.

If a friend of yours loves a particular course or finds inspiration from a special professor, then encourage him to share that about himself. Or maybe there are other aspects of his college life that mean more to him—music he is writing, a political cause he has embraced, a play he is producing, or a team he is leading to its best record in a decade. Isn't that a better, richer way to say who he is than "I'm an English major"? He is either defensive at that moment—"Yeah, yeah, I know you can't get a job studying literature"—or sending a simplistic or even misleading signal about who he is.

Don't Just Live with Your Choice—Love It

Many discussions about majors center on whether they are "practical" or not. I don't think any of them can be defined that way, especially in more traditional colleges. Nevertheless, the division between "practical" and "impractical" lingers. Humanities programs such as art history, history, English, classics, and creative writing may have extraordinary faculty, but these disciplines seem a bit self-indulgent, anachronistic, and intellectual. In other words, they are impractical. This prejudice may explain the general decline in humanities studies. Other programs, like economics, political science, and international studies, seem to be more obviously applicable to certain careers. Choosing the "impractical" disciplines is stupid, the "practical" ones savvy, particularly in light of rising tuition costs.

But I think this is a matter of branding, not reality. Economics seems to have something to do with money, business, or finance, when really it is the study of self-interested behavior. Political scientists rarely know anything about public policy or the law, focusing more commonly on the processes of decision-making. Both are "social sciences" for a reason. They work to make a science of the study of social phenomenon. International studies has the marketing advantage of having "international" in its name, making it sound important or at least timely in a world dominated by a global economy and military conflict. Yet much of the field is either theoretical (e.g., why do nations fight?) or simply a combination of other traditional social science and humanities disciplines. If the study of history is impractical, why is it a critical part of any international studies curriculum? In fact, all of these majors will serve the same set of general purposes by deepening your understanding of the world, enriching your life with beauty and complexity, and giving you widely applicable analytic and communication skills.

What matters most, without a doubt, is that *you must love what you study*. If this is not your main reason for choosing a course of study, or if your other reasons have priority—it's "practical"; it's defensible to your friends, parents, and family; it's better known or more popular— you are doomed to mediocrity. You will not have the same internal motivation or fire to do the extra work needed for excellence. You will find yourself doing things you *must*, filling your academic life with resentment, rather than pursuing what you most *want* to know. And that resentment will not just poison your intellectual life. It will make the achievement you may want, measured by grades or any other scale, more difficult to reach.

Certainly, some students can overcome that challenge, excelling in an area without loving it. They have the self-discipline, the work ethic, the study skills, and the pressure of family and their own expectations to "gut it out." I admire those students. There are many more of them than I would like, and I have to watch them sorrowfully. But is this why they worked so hard to get into college? To be trapped? Did they want their education to be liberating or imprisoning?

Know the True Value of Your Education

Let's suppose for a moment that you buy what I've just argued. "OK," you say, "I'll major in archaeology. But my parents are going to kill me. They're going to think I've wasted their tuition money!" It's true. Parents dominate decisions on majors. That is an inescapable fact in today's academic environment, as discussed more fully in Habit #2, *Build an Adult Relationship with Your Parents*. That is understandable. If your parents are shouldering all or most of the growing tuition costs, they want to have a sense that this investment of $200,000 or more is going to pay off. Given the high financial stakes, they want to be assured, if not guaranteed, that there is going to be a good job, a lucrative career, and financial security on the other end of this experience. So, they would say, if you go to the University of Chicago and you major in psychology, there had better be a clear payoff. You will be able to go on to be a psychologist, and psychologists make a good amount of money. So everything will work out just fine.

But this reasoning is a convenient delusion. Chicago graduates with majors in psychology go on to all kinds of careers, I am sure. Some no doubt become therapists, though this is not an easy profession in which to achieve financial success: there is much more to such success than academic choice. But most psychology graduates do not become therapists, as a consequence of the very factors I mentioned above, not the least of which is serendipity.

A more important point is that the preoccupation with the false link between majors and careers distracts students from the real value of a college education. As I argued in Habit #1, *Focus on Learning, Not on Grades*, the real payoff is to become a learned person, one who has begun a life of rich exploration and self-conscious education. Such a person gains motivation from curiosity and enjoys the success that comes to people who love what they do. I believe it is more important to focus on process because it is in the mastery of life's smaller triumphs—learning a difficult concept, overcoming a misconception, finding a way to better communicate—that one builds the foundation for professional success and financial security. Isn't this the kind of payoff any parent wants?

Don't Be So Hard on Yourself

A final advantage you can enjoy by separating decisions about majors from career planning is that you don't have to get it right. If your major doesn't matter to your career (or doesn't matter much), then you don't have to worry about setting your career in motion right now by picking the perfect major, before you even know what you're doing professionally. Maybe the choice of majors really isn't all that important after all.

What? How couldn't it be important? Isn't college important?

Of course it is important. But the mission of earning a college degree might not be what you think. It does not determine your fate. You are not destined by the choices you make in college because there are many more you will make in life, some much more important: whether you marry and whom, if and when to have children, how you will choose to raise them, how you will infuse your work and personal life with strong values and integrity, and whether you take care of your health. You will make choices throughout your life, many of them much more serious than whether to major in biology or history.

While picking the "right" major does not guarantee academic success, it is very important. You need to make many other choices just as effectively, from how you study to what courses you choose within your major and without. (And that's why Habit #6 is *Don't Just Work Hard—Work Smart*.) You must enjoy the mission and content of your discipline if you are to succeed.

So this choice of a major—and its professional implications—needs to be put in a wider perspective within the college experience, within your family's dynamic and decision-making, and in your life. By doing that, the pressure will diminish. You can be confident that good, but not perfect, choices are good enough.

A Story

A story will help pull these four thoughts together. An advisee of mine (I will call her Alice) went to Johns Hopkins intent on majoring in biology and then going to medical school—a plan that is all too common. She had done reasonably well in the sciences in high school. When she got to college, she signed up for the basic slate of pre-med courses: chemistry, calculus, and biology. She also signed up for a couple of anthropology courses, mostly out of curiosity.

As the first semester progressed, Alice began to admit that she was not really interested in the science courses. Every time she had to crack the books, get down to business, and study every day, she became more and more resentful of the fact that she had to take these classes. They were neither interesting nor stimulating. They were no fun. Not surprisingly, she did not do well in these science courses. At the same time, she was prospering and loving her experiences in anthropology. Eventually, Alice figured out that she needed to spend much more of her time studying that discipline. And as a result, she earned better grades and was much happier.

But the story did not end there because such decisions are never easy or simple. Alice still felt the pressure from her parents and from within herself to major in biology. Her parents would have agreed with her fear, if she had ever talked to them about it, that choosing anthropology would be professional suicide. They never said to her, as some parents have to other students, that unless she majored in biology and then went to medical school, she could not attend Hopkins at all. But Alice's anxiety ran deep, reflecting a deep tendency in student culture to be practical.

This thinking is understandable, particularly for first-generation college students and for students from families with lesser means. It is difficult to have faith that a humanities major will make for a good life. And if you define college in the narrow terms of gaining credentials by achieving high grades within a limited list of majors, and not in the larger frame of learning, then concepts like "exploration" seem self-indulgent.

So Alice continued to waffle back and forth between biology and anthropology. And she continued to struggle academically until she finally resolved to minimize the pre-med courses she had to take and finish the anthropology major. She eventually had the talk with her parents, who grudgingly supported her decision and bowed to the reality of her grades.

But how will the story end? Does Alice go to medical school, or does she choose another path? A year after graduating, Alice decided that she did want to apply to medical school. She was fortunate that her grades from her anthropology major helped her cumulative GPA, despite a poor performance in the sciences. She worked hard to prepare for the MCATs, and her application was strongly written and enthusiastically supported by recommenders—including me. And she did get accepted, if only to a few schools. She is happy, and her parents relieved. But none of them knew it would happen this way—and all of them should have embraced what made Alice special from the beginning.

❖ *Put It in Perspective*

Picking a major, on the face of it, appears to be the most important decision you can make as a college student. If we believe that myth, then the choice of major has an endless cascading effect on what we do, where we go, and how successful and happy we will be. Aside from making this decision far too pressured, this belief is a crutch, invented to give comfort to those who wonder whether going to college is worth all the work, trouble, and money. They need reassurance of a clear "payoff," and that payoff, they hope, is a secure future with a good job.

Students from great colleges do enjoy successful careers, but not because they chose the "right" majors. Instead, they have succeeded by absorbing a more meaningful set of values and priorities, in which they put a premium on learning, understanding, and empathy. Most of them absorb these values, and the other rich benefits of a liberal education, without conscious effort. It just happens, thanks in part to the challenging and diverse environment they enjoy for four years. But for many of them, those years would have been a little less stressful and anxious had they known that their course of study would have so little impact on their professional direction, that majors and careers are not the same thing.

If that thought *had* occurred to them, they would have been free to pursue intellectual curiosities. They might have enjoyed their success as learners even more because the motivation had come from within them, not from without. They would have noticed that any major they could have chosen would have given them a richer understanding of the world and many of the intellectual tools to deepen that education after graduating. And they might have taken a few more moments to celebrate the marvelous ambivalence of American higher education.

So I hope you can learn from their mistakes and, instead, pick your path with hope and an excited love of learning.

Don't Just Work Hard—Work *Smart*

Let's start with a fictional story about a student I'll call Rajiv. When Rajiv was a freshman at Harvard, he took a course on microeconomics. He really had no idea why he took this course, though it did seem vaguely practical, and it certainly was sophisticated and mature to talk about economics, a famous discipline about which he knew nothing. The other novel feature of the experience, for him, was that the course was taught as a big lecture. He had never been in a lecture course, let alone a lecture hall, in high school. It seemed very cool and collegiate to be with 300 or 400 other students, furiously taking notes and looking up at a brilliant professor. She was a young economist, pregnant and married to the man who taught the macroeconomics course that followed in the spring.

Everything was new about it—not just the subject matter, the professor, and the setting, but the real challenge of figuring out how to master this course and do well. Rajiv frankly had no idea what to do, despite his considerable academic success in high school. Naturally, he started with buying the textbook. When you go to public high school, as he did, you do not buy any textbooks; the school gives them to you, with the threat of death if you damage them. But here he was, buying his first textbook, which was very cool—and expensive.

"I had better read this thing," Rajiv thought. Everyone seemed to do their reading and work in the library. He guessed that is what you do in college. Some of his friends studied in their dorm rooms, but there was a mass migration to the Harvard libraries every afternoon and evening, especially the main library, the Widener. So Rajiv followed them. He could have gone to the main reading room, where most students work on large tables. But he chose to explore the *stacks*. Stacks are where all of the books are kept on shelves, floor after floor after floor. He made his way up to the fourth floor to look for what is called a *carrel*, a sort of a cage or working space.

Not really sure why he had made this choice, Rajiv settled down to crack open his brand new economics textbook. He brought with him a blue highlighter. This also was new. The idea of marking a textbook seemed vaguely illegal to someone who had been to public schools, which might have explained why he chose the most remote part of the library to do it. But with highlighter in hand, Rajiv began to read the assigned chapters. This economics textbook focused a lot of attention on economic policy, its development and reasoning. It explained debates about minimum wage, for example, as a way to illustrate key concepts. He read carefully and began to highlight furiously. It all seemed very important, and he was enjoying his newfound freedom to deface the book without fearing arrest.

As time went on that gloomy afternoon in the stacks, Rajiv began to realize that he was *highlighting most of the book*. He had converted a textbook with white paper pages into a textbook with blue pages. On any given page, there were only a few sentences that he did not highlight.

At the time, he did not worry about this, just noting how strange it was. But once he took an exam, Rajiv realized that the professor had no interest in public policy debates. Nor was she going to test his unstructured absorption of gross amounts of highlighted material. In fact, she wanted him to solve problems, to apply conceptual skills to a new situation. While the textbook may have been part of an awakening interest in public policy, the lessons within it were not readily applied to exams.

Those exams, and the optional assignments that Rajiv should have done, were all based on conceptual graphs showing, for example, the intersections of supply and demand. The exam asked for a solution to a problem: What is the stable cost situation? Where does this particular product reach price equilibrium? Where is demand? How can you know that this product was given out for free? The professor asked nothing about monetary policy (and, of course she would not—that is *macro*economics).

Rajiv probably could have figured this out in advance if he had actually gone to "section." He did not know what that was because high school did not have sections. As it turned out, a section is a separate meeting of a class, generally run by a graduate student, at least at a research university like Harvard. It is in section that teaching assistants, or TAs (they call them TFs—teaching fellows—at Harvard), help you make sense of the lecture and then actually do the kinds of work that you would do in an exam.

But he had no idea; the section was optional. He figured anything that was optional was not important. As it turns out, *everything* in college that is optional is important: the additional readings, the added assignments, the study sessions, the review sessions, the sections. If students take advantage of all those resources, they are more likely to understand the material and what is going on. But to Rajiv's way of thinking, that was just more work, and since there was already a lot of work, why add to that?

It took a lot of time, time he did not really have, for Rajiv to understand these lessons. He stopped turning his textbooks blue, but he really needed someone to tell him that studying is a strategic, focused exercise. Successful students think about how to study. They do not just "study," diving into material, thoughtlessly trying to memorize it all. They absorb material selectively, building a framework of understanding that can be useful in new situations. And that is why Habit #6 from the Dean's List is *Don't Just Work Hard—Work Smart*. By developing this habit, you will enjoy a richer learning experience, and you'll spare the lives of a few extra highlighters.

Making Smart Choices

If you want to get everything you can out of a college academic experience, you need to become highly self-conscious about how you are studying and using your time. Let us say, for example, that you are taking a course in medieval history. You are assigned a mountain of reading from books you buy and others on closed reserved (meaning that you cannot check out them out) in the library. According to the syllabus, you have to read this in a certain order by a certain time and prepare for a series of exams.

Now what?

You have some choices. Your first is that you can read it all—every book, every line, every word. Isn't that what a "good" student does? No point in rebelling here in a system that seems to reward compliance. So your choice appears to be obedience or failure. The professor says, "Read all this material," and that is what you will do. And you will do it on the timeline the professor demands. "That will take a lot of time and discipline," you say to yourself, "but I am up to the challenge." Failure is not an option, says the good student, so obedience it will be. Unfortunately, while this headlong approach may appear diligent and respectful, it does not call for engagement with the material, nor for understanding it.

Second, you could choose to read as little as possible, figuring the lectures ought to be enough. After all, you reason, why would the professor talk about some things and not others? The professor knows what is important, and what is important to him or her is what will be on the exam. You can do the readings later when midterms or finals arrive. "Cramming" is pretty common in college. After all, nobody is paying attention to what you are doing—or not doing. Your parents are not there. They are not around to look after you. No one will ask you, "Have you done your homework tonight?" No one will treat you like a child.

But there is a third way that is neither unquestioned obedience nor irresponsible cramming, a better way that demands ownership of your intellectual journey. This calls for strategic thinking and self-discipline, carefully and deliberately making decisions about what is important and when it must be done. The strategic student—rather than opening up her brain, attempting to pour everything in, and hoping for successful regurgitation—manages the information by choosing how to approach learning.[1] And by learning I do not mean memorizing. Memorizing does not help anyone make sense of anything. You are not really thinking. You are just shoving information into an imperfect memory bank.[2]

The strategic student approaches the readings and even the lec-

Three Keys to Success

CARL P. THUM, Ph.D.
DIRECTOR, ACADEMIC SKILLS CENTER
DARTMOUTH COLLEGE

Doing well at any competitive college or university requires three things: (1) setting personal goals, (2) developing learning strategies, and (3) planning. Students who come to colleges like Dartmouth are intelligent and, to one degree or another, motivated to do well. Successful students share these characteristics:

1. Personal Goals

Students' goals in high school are pretty clear: they want to do well, be organized, and get involved so they can be admitted to a good college or university. Yet many of those same students don't have clear goals as first-year college students. Students should view goal-setting as an important and ongoing process. It's a good idea to record all goals for college in general, for the term, and for the week, and review them on a daily basis.

To do well at a competitive college, students must work hard. Even the brightest and most self-directed students tell me that they have to work hard to do well.

2. Learning Strategies

There are many studies on how and why new college students lack effective reading, note-taking, and time management skills—the techniques that college work demands, especially if students want to do well.

No one's to blame; it's simply the difference between high school and college learning. But college students must learn these skills in order to succeed in college. Most of these techniques are pretty basic, involve common sense, and are easily learned. They can be found in books on study skills, on the Web, and in academic support centers that almost every college and university has.

3. Planning

Most students who do well at Dartmouth use some sort of schedule. A good schedule is both specific and general. It's specific in that it notes the structured activities of classes, labs, work, study times, athletics or exercise, and meetings; it may also include meals and personal time. An effective schedule is more than a to-do list: it's your life for that day and that week.

As a part of scheduling, I encourage students to make a four-year plan for their time at college. It should include courses they want to take as well as other things to they want to accomplish: study abroad, internships, and extracurricular activities. A term schedule that lists the weeks of the term and the quizzes, midterms, papers, presentations, and final exams gives students a bird's-eye view of when the major academic events are. Successful time management relies heavily on a concrete and specific set of personal goals. Time management is the vehicle by which one's goals are accomplished.

tures—which I will discuss shortly—more carefully and deliberately. That student asks questions *while studying*: Why am I reading this? What am I supposed to get out of this? What kinds of questions will this answer? Will I be able to solve a problem based on what I'm doing and practicing? How do these readings and concepts connect to one another? How do they connect with those discussed in lecture?

Let us go back to the example of the medieval history course, but with the strategic student in mind. On an exam or in a paper, she will be asked to "connect the dots," a useful if clichéd expression. But there are a lot of dots in a history course. The blizzard of dates, locations, treaties, names, and concepts explains why some students do not like the discipline. In this case, she might be asked about the Hundred Years' War. An exam question might be "What impact did that conflict have on European development?" It is not enough to know the basic facts of the war; she must make some distinctions among the many possible answers to that question. It is not enough to give a laundry list of political or economic impacts listed in the textbook or mentioned by the professor, which may be something the obedient student could do and the crammer wishes he could. Instead, she has to create a hierarchy of impacts, to see how they affect each other. In other words, she needs to make thoughtful decisions about which things were more important than others.

The strategic student does not just try to memorize the facts—when the Hundred Years' War started, its duration (it was longer than 100 years), and who was involved—because that is a very difficult exercise without a framework in which to put those facts. She takes note of illustrative facts, just enough to see how the bigger picture fits together. And she does that by engaging the material, by asking what it all means, and by getting help from instructors and others when that mean is unclear. She understands the difference between passive *absorption* and the selective effort at *understanding*.

Getting Lectured

A lecture is an odd way to learn. It is a technique dating back to the Middle Ages, when religious scholars and legal experts would stand before their students and lecture for hours. Perhaps these lecturers assumed that the students had nothing worthwhile to say. The cleric or lawyer or scholar was far better educated, by definition, than their students or pupils. So it made sense that they would speak and others would listen.

Despite its anachronistic and hierarchical history, lecturing has many merits. It is an efficient way for a scholar to tell a student what is important, as time limits demand a focus on the necessary. A lecturer can provide clear frameworks and theories to make sense of the excessive volume of information. It is deeply ironic, then, that scholars use a passive teaching technique to tell students how to be more interactive, strategic, and thoughtful. But if done right (and that "if" is important, as not all lecturers are equally talented or effective), a lecture can be a crucial tool to the strategic student.

Just as ironically, many students see a lecture as a passive, redundant opportunity to absorb information, rather than a chance to make sense of that information. Sit in on almost any college lecture, and you will see this happening. The lecturer stands before dozens, even hundreds of students, using computer technologies or just a blackboard to make his or her points. The students furiously take notes. Most of the time, their heads are bowed down to their notebooks as they try to write down everything they are hearing. Students would acknowledge that it is impossible to transcribe every word (although if they could, they would), so they settle for summarizing nearly every sentence that is spoken. In fact, when the lecturer provides notes, perhaps online in advance, then they do not need to take notes at all. The transcription is done, they reason.

Note-taking, then, becomes another way to say "transcribing," reducing the student to the role of court reporter. It is odd that hundreds of other students are doing the same thing in a monumental act of clerical redundancy. When they can, they will make an audio recording of the lecture or get the podcast, so that the capture of the lecture is complete. And the hierarchy is secure: I speak, you listen.

You could argue that a lecture is a terrible way to learn, which may explain why many students are inattentive, sleeping, texting, e-mailing, or just absent. (That is another difference with high school: no one takes attendance!) Lectures do not make sense because they offer one way to learn, when students have many learning styles. But they are a reality of college life, at least for now, so it is important that you think more strategically about them.

Do not see yourself as a transcriber or a clerk, but as an engaged intellectual and scholar. If you are a strategic student, you will think of a lecture as the external side of a conversation, with the other going on internally. In other words, a lecture is one side of a conversation between you and the professor. It is rare for a student to have the courage to ask a question in a large lecture. It's intimidating and it might be considered grandstanding. That is really too bad. But just because you don't say anything doesn't mean you have to be passive or inactive. Try to think of the lecture as if it were a discussion between the lecturer's words and your thoughts. In your mind, you ask: "How did that idea connect to the one she just said? What is the relationship between what she is saying and the readings that I did last night or last week? Where is this course going? How are all of these lectures hanging together conceptually? Is she building some kind of larger argument that I'm not seeing yet? She just told a particular story; was that important? Why did she tell that story? What am I supposed to get from that? I'm not sure what that means—should I?"

If you are an engaged student, you will listen actively to the lecture and wonder what it all means. That is the very same kind of thinking that you should apply to reading textbooks, novels, articles, and other materials. *What does it mean?*

Note-taking techniques should reflect this effort to understand, not just to record the presentation. Most notes, in fact, do not record the lecture. They are bullet points down the left margin, followed by simplified summaries of the lecturer's words. I will make no effort here to suggest an alternative. Students have to figure this out for themselves, choosing something that helps them engage with the material, not just record it. There are many worthwhile how-to books that are worth consulting and using.[3] But I will make some suggestions:

▶ Get to the lecture early enough to review some notes and collect your thoughts. You want to "warm up" so that you are ready with questions the lecture should answer. That will make you more focused.

▶ Do not write everything down—or even try.

▶ Step back intellectually and *listen* by not taking notes for a while.

▶ Every minute or two, briefly summarize what you have learned in those minutes.

▶ Find a way to identify lingering questions, by circling a point or with a question mark.

▶ Try splitting the page vertically, with summaries on the left, questions or thoughts on the right.

▶ Do not leave immediately after the lecture is over. Sit and think about what you have seen and heard. Then write down key points and questions for follow-up.

Any exercise like this will help you connect the lecture experience to the wider goals of learning, understanding, and applying the material. Recording the lecture, either in notes or digitally, may be necessary but is entirely insufficient. You need to think about the wider meanings and the connections to other lectures, other lessons, and associated readings. As the memory of the lecture fades, notes will do nothing to advance this thinking if they are not provocative themselves. Do your notes help pose questions? Do they point to concerns or confusion that can be resolved elsewhere, such as during the professor's office hours? As you shuffle away from the lecture hall, are you still engaged in this thinking or have you already moved on intellectually and personally? Better to stop, reflect, and then move on.

Your class notes, therefore, can do far more than record an experience. If taken strategically and self-consciously, your notes set the academic and intellectual agenda for what is to come. By doing this as a strategic student, you will begin to see the connections that the instructor had in mind. Things begin to gel with each other, and because they start making more sense and seem to rely on each other in order to be true, it becomes a lot easier both to memorize and, more importantly, to understand.

The problem with memorizing a whole series of things that do not seem to have any connection is that there is no framework to hold them together, no way to segue from one to the next. It would be *worse* than memorizing the phone book; at least the phone book is in alphabetical order. In that case, you could think, "Well, what names come after C?" That's easy: those that start with D. But it was easy only because you already know the alphabet—that is your organizing framework. Imagine what would happen if you shuffled the listings in the phone book and *then* were asked to memorize it; it would be impossible. There would be no way to connect them and, of course, no way to see any patterns (such as the large number of Smiths).

By self-consciously connecting ideas, both in the way that you think about the material and the way that you take notes about it, you can be a strategic student who begins to see the big picture. When you start understanding the big picture, the little pictures will start fitting in nicely.

Working Hard? Or Working Better?

When I meet with students who are struggling academically (a topic I will cover in Habit #9, *When You Are Failing, Understand Why*), they say to me, "I just have to work harder. I know I wasn't working hard enough, and that's why I did so poorly." On one level, this might be true. There are students who are distracted by too many commitments or by a few activities, like the college newspaper, in an exces-

ADINA GLICKMAN, M.S.W.
ASSOCIATE DIRECTOR, CENTER FOR TEACHING AND LEARNING
STANFORD UNIVERSITY

Every college student has study skills: you wouldn't be in college without them. You've developed some of them intuitively. When life got too busy, you dusted off the academic planner your well-meaning Uncle Bob gave you and began using it to keep track of when things were due. In high school you acquired skills like how to take notes and scan texts.

But the volume, pace, and complexity of college-level material will challenge you to develop new, more sophisticated tools. Although these skills may be just beyond your comfortable range of motion, none of them is impossible to master. Some will make more sense to you and be more useful than others. Others may seem redundant or trivial. Learning is an idiosyncratic endeavor, so work with the study strategies that are most useful to you.

In the ten years that I have offered academic skills coaching to students, 90 percent of my advice on how to improve academic skills has come from students before them who sweated and agonized in their own struggle to self-improve. The other 10 percent of my advice comes from my own efforts in college and graduate school. What follows is a consolidated list of these strategies.

1. Learning

Learning new material is like filling up a partially filled filing cabinet. The files already in the cabinet contain other things you've learned. If your filing system is well organized, you will know where to put the new information. Different disciplines and types of knowledge require different types of organizational structures, so biology and French literature will be organized differently. Before learning new material, consider looking through your filing cabinet. In other words, revisit your current knowledge before learning new material.

To remember something you've learned, you need to understand it on a conceptual level. It's therefore essential to develop self-diagnostic skills to determine whether you truly understand something or are simply recalling facts from memory. One technique for this is "playback" in which you state *in your own words* how an idea functions, what it means, and why it's important, making sure to rephrase *in your own words* any explanation you've been given so that you are building a logical progression. If you can put it into words, it's yours for life.

2. Reading

When it comes to reading, advanced skills require you to indentify which words, phrases, and texts are important to what you're learning. Everything you read will need your critical assessment of its context, scope, and relative importance to your studies. Not every word you read will be equally valuable to you, and it will be your responsibility for determining which ones to focus on.

Reading different types of text will require different strategies. To read strategically, the following tools may help:

❭ Learn in layers. Think of reading as building a house. You can't hang drywall until you've framed with 2 × 4s. Similarly, you can't digest depth and detail until you have created a conceptual framework. Pre-reading—in which you get the "big picture" of the structure and the scope of what's to come—is a good way of building a conceptual framework. When you then read for detail and depth, all of this new information will have something to attach itself to, like drywall attaches to the wood frame.

❭ Formulate meaningful questions. A meaningful question will yield solid answers from your text. Reading is research, and your job before diving into any text is to ask what it is you're looking for, and what you need to know.

❭ Prepare yourself cognitively. Reading provides new information which your brain will attempt to fit together with the information you've already learned. Help this "additive learning" process by considering what you already know about something for a few minutes before reading.

3. Note-Taking

Highlighting sentences and writing snippets in the margins are great starts to imprinting information in your mind, but these notes

continued

won't necessarily help you learn complex material. As with general learning, concepts must become meaningful to you in your own words to become permanent elements of your knowledge base. Your words on a page, documenting your thoughts, interpretations, summaries, and reactions to material, are a personal breadcrumb trail that should lead you back to the aspects of the material you have determined are important.

As with reading, you will need to make decisions about what's important. How do you know if it's important? If someone asked you to explain your notes, the notes would tell you enough to be able to describe what you've heard or read. Taking notes is the beginning of the writing process and can be a great help to you when you want to recall what you were thinking. Notes are your ideas on paper—and doesn't that make them kind of like a first draft?

4. Test-Taking

Exams test your conceptual understanding, not whether you remember how to do a problem similar to the homework. Review your notes within a day of the lecture. You will retain 40 percent more than if you wait a week. When reviewing, interrupt your memorization circuitry and think about what things mean. Continue reviewing course material until you're solid. Over-learning is a waste of time.

5. Time Management

Beyond the basics (like using a planner), successful students use several additional strategies. The most important is planning ahead. If you don't notice ahead of time that you have to travel for an athletic event the same day that you have a physics midterm, it will be your lack of planning and not your knowledge of physics that will have the greatest impact on your exam. Build your daily schedule around classes and meals. Use big chunks of time for immersion in big-picture concepts, and small bits of time for review and organization. Identify the tasks within the assignments. For example, writing a paper may entail generating a reading list, getting call numbers from the library, hunting around the library for the books, reading, thinking, writing, rewriting. If you only think about "writing a paper" as the writing portion, you will underestimate how much time the whole project requires.

> If you are procrastinating, determine exactly what is deterring you and address it. For example, if you are putting off doing a problem set, figure out if it's really the *whole* thing you are avoiding, or just one piece of it that refers to a part of a lecture you didn't understand. Is it the *entire* paper you don't want to write, or are you just immobilized because you don't have a clear thesis?
>
> There are no "right" skills or "right combination" of skills. Your task is to find the right cocktail of strategies that work for you and that work best for specific tasks.

sive, self-destructive way. They may be involved in a serious personal relationship, often for the first time. They may be doing volunteer work and finding that experience to be much more rewarding than sitting down with an organic chemistry textbook. There also are serious student athletes, preoccupied with training, practices, competitions, and road trips. I hardly blame them for making these high priorities. These are important, enriching additions to the academic experience.

There are other students who are distracted, even crippled, by unhealthy problems. They might be addicted to drugs, alcohol, or gambling (the last a growing problem with the availability of online gambling sites). A student easily can be distracted by emotional issues, mental health problems, or physical disability. We will talk about these issues extensively in Habits #9 and #10.

But much of the time when students say that they are not working *hard* enough, it is really that they are not working *well* enough. Most of the successful students that I know are busy people. They have many serious commitments—playing in an orchestra, performing for a dance company, staging a new play, writing for the newspaper, or running a soup kitchen somewhere in the city. But these students have found ways to be very productive in their studies. They use their time in a focused, concentrated, and self-disciplined way. They get more out of each minute and each hour of studying than a less committed student does because they know they must get some assignment or reading done in the 82 minutes they have before rehearsal.

In fact, many of the students who struggle the most are the students with the fewest commitments. They face vast expanses of time, sometimes entire days, without any particular responsibility. They are not sure how to fill that time. They do not have any anchoring or structure. Busy students know they must get the job done now. They cannot just wander. That kind of intentional focus can be very successful.

Figuring out how to be productive when studying is not easy. Again, there are plenty of folks who have thought about this and written many books filled with strategies worth trying. I will warn you that many of these strategies are obvious, but I think it much more important that you experiment with what works for you. When I meet with my freshmen advisees, some for the first time in an extended meeting, they have been in college only a month or two. Yet they already have established study habits that may be difficult to change without deliberate effort. So we have a conversation where I ask: "When do you study? When does that happen? Under what circumstances? Where are you doing this? Are you doing this with anyone?" Most of them are surprised by these questions because they have fallen into a habit without actually giving it any strategic thought.

With self-conscious experimentation, you will find a personalized approach that suits you best. That is why I have no single approach to sell you now. Some people are true night owls. Others need to get up much earlier than they do now. I suspect most teenage college students are in the latter group but do not know it. Some people like to have long stretches of time for studying one particular subject. Others find that very burdensome and boring. I have students who enjoy studying on Friday evenings, although I cannot imagine why. Some study while listening to their iPods or enjoy studying in a coffee shop. Some people study in front of a television, God help them, while others need the absolute quiet of a library stack.

Most likely, when you are new to college, you do not know what is best for you. So vary your location, timing, and sequence from day to day, and see what works. Experiment with different parts of the library to find a place that is not too quiet—or too relaxing. If you are self-conscious and strategic, you will be efficient and capable of learning successfully.

Healthy Mind, Healthy Body

LEORA BROVMAN, Ed.D.

ADVISING DEAN

COLUMBIA UNIVERSITY

What do sleep, good nutrition, and exercise have in common?

They are all characteristics of a successful student!

College students have a unique opportunity to grow, to learn, to develop intellectual skills, to set their own goals, and to develop the final stage of independence that is adulthood. This is a serious undertaking, and the prospects of accomplishing all of this in four years—while having a good time—may seem overwhelming. Students come to college with so many pressures, not least of which is learning self-management.

Having spent many years advising students in their undergraduate studies, I have become convinced of one thing: a healthy body leads to a healthy mind.

Yes, all students remember their parents telling them that breakfast was the most important meal of the day. They remember those lazy days on the couch, watching television, when they should have been outside playing and soaking in the fresh air. But that was only for the elementary or middle school child, not for the young, independent adult away at college, right?

Wrong! There is a strong correlation between one's health and one's ability to engage successfully in academic studies. I often see my students begin each semester engaged, enthusiastic, and healthy. But after a few weeks, their energy is sapped, and they have started falling behind in one or two classes. As the semester continues, the downward spiral does too, and being run down leads to being sick which leads to having to stay in bed which leads to . . . I think you get the picture.

The first and most important task any college student has is to take care of himself. For many students, this is a new and unusual task. They're used to being awakened in the morning, having someone prepare their breakfasts before school and their dinners at night, and having their daily schedules planned out for them in advance. Without all these reminders and preparations, when life is suddenly up to them, students may feel overwhelmed.

continued

With all these new responsibilities, many students feel they don't have the time for eating right, getting enough sleep, or exercise. "After all, I'm at college to study, make good grades, and get a good job!"

How can college students stay well while doing well in school? The key is planning and time management. First, students must set aside time for the tasks of daily living. This includes meals and sleep. Doing laundry, shopping, and physical exercise should also be part of any weekly schedule.

Let's talk for a moment about the importance and value of sleep. Studies show that in order to be productive we all need a good night's sleep, which is best achieved through a regular bedtime and waking-up time. You cannot make up lost sleep. And an all-nighter to prepare for an exam is more likely to put a student in her advisor's office, panicked, an hour after the exam has started, because she overslept! One pre-med student at my institution has realized, after much trial and error, that she accomplishes nothing after midnight. So every night at midnight, she stops studying and goes to bed.

In terms of planning, students should ask what they hope to accomplish, what their academic and intellectual interests are, whether they should study abroad, and what ideas they have for life after college. While there is no doubt that a student's time at college should be somewhat organic, allowing for the unexpected or unanticipated discovery of new academic interests, it is also true that one must plan and think ahead. Using a spreadsheet, laying out a proposed schedule for eight semesters, can be helpful. Don't forget to check your school's core requirements. An easy way to get regular exercise is to include a physical education class each semester. Don't count this as an academic class but, rather, as one of the necessary elements of being a successful student.

Of course, planning ahead and managing your time well do not guarantee success. But if you are organized and thoughtful in how you approach your week, and if you understand and acknowledge that success has many components, you will be on your way to being a successful student.

Go to Bed!

It is very tempting for you as a college student to stay up really late. It is part of the culture and the fun of college to have the freedom, and even the right, to stay up well beyond any reasonable hour. For as long as you can remember—in fact, as long as you have been around—your parents have told you when to go to bed and insisted that you go to sleep. Now that you are out of earshot, you can go to bed whenever you want. Not surprisingly, most of the students that I know stay up to incredibly late hours—sometimes until 2:00, 3:00, or even 4:00 in the morning. And then many of them need a nap in the middle of the afternoon. Naps are the drug of choice for most college students.

The problem: a college student who is not getting to bed is an adolescent who is ignoring the needs of her body and brain. At some point, her cognitive functions are going to decline, probably precipitously.[4] If she woke up at 8:30 AM, by 11:30 PM she will have been awake for 15 hours. It seems a safe assumption that after that point, little or nothing she studies will make sense. She will not be able to remember it or connect it to anything else. When her body craves sleep more than it craves intellectual stimulation, she is wasting her time. Taking a mid-afternoon nap may not help, as she might not get the REM sleep she needs, but it will certainly invite another late bedtime.

If you are more sensible, then you already know that you are staying up too late. Try to recalibrate by front-loading your studies. Some of the most effective—and healthy—students I know make an effort to get everything done by 10:00 PM. They do this by getting up a little earlier than their peers and approaching the "school day" as if it were a "work day," with no breaks and no naps and intense focus. When they are not sitting in class or eating, they are preparing for an upcoming lecture, reviewing notes for a seminar, doing readings and assignments, and generally pushing every minute to pass without waste. This is a difficult regime, but it works.

This routine is especially important for student athletes. Whatever level of competition they face, today's athletes are far more serious and dedicated than ever.[5] They devote dozens of hours each week to lifting weights, practicing, traveling, and competing. Many of them, perhaps even most of them, struggle to balance these demands with academics. But efficient and successful *scholar* athletes succeed by defying their peers, even their teammates, by getting to bed earlier, getting up earlier, and attempting to get in most of their day's studies *before* a late afternoon practice.

There is a very good reason to do this. Consider that a student athlete taxes her body enormously, putting all of her physical resources into movement. For that time, and for as much as several hours afterwards, her body is working and recovering. Under these circumstances, she cannot think at the level she needs to understand and connect information. Her body focuses on repairing muscles and tendons, and restoring oxygen and energy. Not a great time to study.[6] So she is much better off having done her school work beforehand. If she frontloads her work, she can take full advantage of her peak cognitive strength for learning. And then, when she is tired and inattentive, she can turn on the television, text her friends, go on Facebook, and go out for pizza.

✤ Put It in Perspective

Just because you were successful enough in high school to get into a good college does not mean that you know what to do as a college student. Too many bright, extraordinary students think that the challenges of a competitive school can all be met with harder work and greater focus. That is only partly true; if you want to learn, you have to do the work. But many students confuse a work ethic with a clumsy approach to learning that emphasizes memorization and plodding through texts and lectures without thought. Despite their *capacity* for seeing creative connections and for having insight in the face of ambiguity, they fail to study strategically.

To be a strategic, successful student, you need to approach the work ahead with more thought, with a textured search for meaning. This approach calls for asking questions more frequently, taking notes that are more provocative, and having a conversation—aloud when possible, but internally if not—with the material. How does X connect to Y? What is the relationship of Z to this? I am looking at events A, B, and C: how do they fit together? Professors try to give their students the frameworks for analysis and understanding, but each student has to look for those frameworks, and then practice using them over and

➤➤ Taking Exams, Not Measuring Your Worth ◆◆

JOHN P. LOGE, JR.

DEAN OF TIMOTHY DWIGHT COLLEGE

YALE UNIVERSITY

When I ask first-year students for a show of hands if they have experience with lecture courses and with end-of-term examination periods that consist of several hours-long examinations, few hands go up. For almost all freshmen, the first examination period of blue books and monitors can be nerve-wracking and even daunting. All aspects of an academically demanding college take some getting used to, and experience is the best teacher. I remind my students that they will get used to it and that, even better, they will discover resources within themselves that they did not know they had. And, especially in a residential university, freshmen have the good fortune to be surrounded by others in the same boat who care about them.

As my students work hard to finish a term, at the start of each examination period I send the following e-mail:

> Exams are a test of your knowledge and not a test of your identity and personal worth, although it is difficult to make those distinctions sometimes. Keep perspective if you can. Examination period is a difficult time, but it is a finite time. And even this difficult time is an opportunity to look after yourself and others—a cheerful word, some encouragement, a cookie—small things that can mean so much, small things from one human to another.
>
> While taking an exam or writing a paper you might even have fun thinking—putting ideas together, calculating clearly, discovering themes, recalling with good effect, making connections coherently, making connections spontaneously, and finding you have personal resources you did not know you had. All these things are possible. Remember, you will be fine.

over. Once those frameworks are in place, you will find, as a strategic student, that your thoughts and new information can be organized for easier use and recall. Rather than dunking your textbook in blue highlighter ink, you will have a conversation with the author on meaning and importance, while making sure you have not lost the connection to the course and the instructor's expectations and message.

And all of this will be a lot easier if you get some sleep.

Build Integrity to Get into Professional or Graduate School

Most successful students, perhaps not surprisingly, like going to school. They have a hard time stopping, in fact. They recognize their own academic talents, believe they understand the reward system (even if that means obsessing over grades), and hunger for more. They are not fools, either. Looking at the job market, they see that many interesting and worthwhile careers—medicine, the law, business, college teaching—call for more than a bachelor's degree. So they conclude that they want and need a professional or graduate degree.

Those who dream of becoming doctors are especially prominent at many colleges, partly because they take so many courses as preparation and because the profession is so famous. My colleagues at top colleges estimate that 30 to 40 percent of incoming freshmen call themselves "pre-meds." Pre-meds are famously driven and ambitious because they know that the competition to get into medical schools is intense, but their reputation for being cutthroat is exaggerated. Their dedication and even obsession empowers them to become dedicated students, hard-working public servants, and effective research assistants. Because of their prominence in many college cultures, pre-meds offer an interesting and provocative case for showing how your life now—as a college student—can affect your future.

Throughout this book, you have seen stories of pre-meds, some of them in academic trouble, others battling their parents over what the future will hold. The pre-med culture is not always a happy one, as these students debate the wisdom of this choice while coping with the intense challenges of its science and math requirements. Those who are struggling in organic chemistry or physics suffer doubly, as they are burdened both with poor grades and a growing doubt that they can get into medical school at all. This raises tough questions of identity, purpose, and family expectations that have no easy answers.

I am not going to debate the wisdom of this choice here, nor will I discuss whether you *should* go to professional or graduate school. You may be considering this choice, and I will leave that to you, your family, your friends, your career counselors, and your professors. That choice may be just right for you, so let me ask the next question: *How do you get into these schools?*

To answer that, I offer you Habit #7 on the Dean's List, *Build Integrity to Get into Professional or Graduate School*. I will use the case of medical school to make my argument, but understand that this case can be applied to any choice you may be making, such as law, nursing, business, public health, education, or any academic graduate training.

The best way to get into these schools—and into medical schools in particular—is to focus on integrity. College offers you the chance to develop some values and to strengthen others. You can become more committed to public service. You can fortify your work ethic. You can grow emotionally. You can feel closer to God. Here, I will focus on how you can develop your integrity and then use that integrity to get into medical school. Keeping and growing integrity is an important goal because it captures two important pieces to the puzzle of medical school entrance. The first is honesty, and the second is individuality.

By honesty, I mean the strength to tell the truth, to be open, to admit mistakes, to be willing to learn, to ask good questions sparked by an admission of ignorance, and of course, to exercise the good judgment and morality to avoid cheating. It means knowing when "gutting it out" or "just working harder" is not enough, and realizing when help is needed.

By individuality, I mean how you can find a way to express what is true about yourself, learn to be your own person, and find your own path by defining life your own way. This means being imaginative about what you want to do, being courageous enough to do it—on your own, if necessary—and being daring enough to walk where you are not comfortable.

I could argue that, defined this way, a life of integrity is a better life. But I am not going to rely on morality to convince you to act with integrity. I am sure you have better sources for learning what is right and what is wrong: your parents, your community, your faith. And I am not going to say that being your own independent person is superior to being a dependent or attached person. There are many cultures that believe the latter approach strengthens families and communities far better than individualism.

Instead, I am going to argue that *having integrity is a strategically sound approach to the fierce competition of getting into medical or other professional or graduate schools*. To win this competition requires that you set yourself apart from others, distinguishing your talents, achievements, and potential as unique and attractive. You should ask yourself, "If I am to compete against other applicants, what special niche do I fill? In what ways can I bring features to the table that other people do not? How is it that I'm unique?"

I have counseled countless successful pre-meds and pre-law students, and I have helped others with many different ambitions win national competitions for major scholarships like the Marshall and the Fulbright. These students are successful because they embraced a cause or an idea that belonged to them. That deep sense of committed ownership gave them the motivation to work hard and to win the external measures of a full academic life—awards, good grades, and great test scores—as well as the more lasting, internal feelings of accomplishment and the knowledge of really helping others. If you want rewards like these, and want to use them to get into medical or other schools, then consider that such rewards will come more easily to those with a life of integrity.

Be Honest

What does it mean to lead an honest intellectual life? It means embracing the act of learning by admitting what you do not know and feeling no shame for that. In a competitive college, it is easy to be

ANDREW N. SIMMONS, Ph.D.
DIRECTOR OF THE CAREER DEVELOPMENT CENTER
BROWN UNIVERSITY

As an advisor to pre-medical students, I am often asked, "What should I be doing right now to prepare for medical school?" Of course, this kind of open-ended question rarely has a straightforward answer and differs considerably depending upon each individual student's circumstances. More to the point, it is indicative of a belief among many pre-meds that there are some precise but secret strategies that one can employ to gain admission—that there is an absolute right way to win acceptance to medical school. My emphatic and idealistic answer? Be yourself. Find your passion and follow it. You go to college only once, and many schools offer you a wealth of academic and extracurricular opportunities. Why pay all that money just to use college as a stepping-stone to medical school?

To the ears of a concerned and competitive pre-med student, my answer probably sounds quaint and naïve. In the real world, you have to be pragmatic and focused on your goal. Successful applicants to medical school must make a significant commitment to being pre-med in college. There are also some general requirements for admission:

❶ A strong academic record. You need the right balance of depth and breadth of study while building a strong record of achievement in the sciences. But remember: beyond your required courses (which constitute probably a third of your program of studies) you still have ample opportunity to explore other interests. You don't even need to be a science major, though your record in the sciences must be strong.

❷ Good scores on the MCAT. You need competitive scores to get admitted (at least 31–32 with no section below a 10).

❸ Experience showing that you have explored and committed to your career choice and that you have a true desire to enter the medical profession. For the former, you need not spend countless hours observing surgery or suturing bloody wounds. (In most cases, you aren't qualified for the gory work anyway!) But you can observe and shadow physicians or volunteer in an emergency room, hospice, or playroom of a children's hospital. If you are fluent in a foreign language, you may even be able to serve as a translator in a hospital or clinic.

Medicine is an intensive service profession. It is no longer enough to just be a science whiz who tells patients what to do. Medical schools really mean it when they say they are looking for people who have not only scholastic aptitude but also a genuine and mature interest in people of all races, ethnicities, and nationalities. Even with these expectations, you have the latitude to pursue a variety of extracurricular interests. As long as you have explored the medical field and placed yourself in challenging interpersonal situations, particularly those that put you in contact with cultures other than your own, you can spend your time in activities not calculated to increase your chances of admission.

If the core of your academic and experiential background suggests that you will succeed in medical school, you are most of the way there, but admission committees will also want to know what you are passionate about. They will want to know what you decided to do with your college education and why. Use your college years not only to prepare for medical school but also to pursue your passions. This may be the only time you can study abroad, play a team sport, develop musical abilities, become involved in community activism, or study a nonvocational subject that you love. This pursuit of your passions is what liberal learning is all about, and it is what distinguishes outstanding medical school candidates from average ones.

intimidated by the talent and knowledge of those around you. Sometimes you might feel out of place or even unworthy of being among these people who all seem to know more than you do. That's an overstatement, of course, but it is also quite true that many of those around you *do* know more than you. There's not much point in going to a place where you are the smartest or the most knowledgeable; you have nothing to gain. So if you're lucky enough to attend a great college, then you need to celebrate the talent around you, rather than focus on how you compare.

If you can embrace your inexperience and ignorance, you are ready to succeed because you will want to fill yourself intellectually. That curiosity is the foundation of a successful college experience: you will be unafraid of the questions and doubts that fill your mind, that seem to multiply—rather than shrink—with each book, lecture, discussion, and lab. And you can let those questions fly out of your fingers and from your lips and get ready to find the answers yourself.

Sadly, this feeling of inferiority or ignorance is also a moment when things can go wrong. Many students look at the landscape of talent on their campuses and feel not just intimidated but threatened. They begin to see their classmates, not as partners in learning, but as real competitors whose success comes at their expense.[1] Reaching such a conclusion can be tempting if you are taking courses that grade on a curve; this practice implies that there are quotas for good grades, so you had better do whatever is necessary to grab the brass ring. Because the curve is common in science and math courses, succeeding at all costs is a special danger for pre-meds, leading some students to cheat by improperly sharing lab results, copying test answers, plagiarizing, using electronic devices to store answers, and so on.[2]

You know cheating is the wrong choice. It should go without saying that a good person and a smart student does not cheat. By definition. But I'll bet you saw a lot of cheating in high school, and I'm sorry to say you're likely to see more of it in college.[3] Sadly, cheating is becoming more and more common.

Finding numbers to prove these points is difficult, of course. You can't really ask someone if they have cheated or not. If people are dishonest enough to cheat, they also are dishonest enough to lie about whether they have. So a researcher usually asks: "Have you ever *seen* any cheating?" The problem with this question is that most cheating is subtle and hidden. So the answers received become a measure of distrust, probably exaggerating what is really happening—however serious that might be.[4]

Thus, the cycle of suspicion begins. Let's say that in a classroom of 50 students, 1 or 2 of them are cheating on a test. But if you sus-

KAREN BLANK, Ed.D.

DEAN OF STUDIES

BARNARD COLLEGE

Academic integrity is at the heart of the life of a college. To be trusted that the work we do is our own, unless other sources are cited, is a gift.

To cite part of the Barnard Honor Code, academic dishonesty is "to ask for, give, or receive help in examinations or quizzes, to use any papers or books not authorized by the instructor in examinations, or to present others' work as our own."

Students who have been guilty of academic dishonesty say that they were dishonest for one of several reasons. The first of these is ignorance: they don't know the rules. Or maybe life has gotten in the way: they are ill, they're devastated by a breakup with a significant other, they've experienced a family crisis, or they have too much to do. Some students are used to achieving at high levels, and they are afraid that their own work will not be good enough. Despite any good intentions these students have, none of these explanations is an acceptable reason for being dishonest.

First, know the rules. Ask your instructor if you don't know whether lecture notes must be cited in papers or the extent to which collaboration with a classmate on a homework assignment is encouraged or allowed.

Second, if you cannot complete an assignment on time, discuss the options with your teacher, academic advisor, class dean, or member of the counseling service staff. Faculty are often willing to accommodate reasonable needs like extending a deadline if you have been responsible up until the time of a request.

Third, accept that you can't do everything well. Sometimes things are difficult, and we may not do as well as we want. But we also can succeed beyond our wildest dreams. That's life. Acknowledge your weaknesses and take advantage of the academic resources that help students realize their goals.

There are major consequences to academic dishonesty. For students, there are failing grades, probation, suspension, or expulsion.

continued

> For faculty members, there is outrage and a feeling of betrayal, often resulting in more rigidly structured assignments that provide less opportunity for the creativity the instructor had valued previously. And for everyone, academic dishonesty diminishes the gift of trust.

pect cheating is common, you might think that 10 or 20 of your fellow students are cheating. Then your suspicion creates its own reality by tempting you to cheat just to stay even with those that do—or with those only imagined to be cheating.[5] You think that it's not fair that you're trying to do well on an exam or paper when someone else has a leg up. The cheater has an easier path to a better grade than you do, and you are resentful, angry, and distrustful.

To make the problem of cheating more challenging, most students who see cheating do not report it, and those who cheat generally do not get caught. There are ways to catch ethics violations, including increasingly clever online and digital tools, but I think most cheating is undetected.[6] That means that cheaters go unpunished and then gain the advantage, further angering the honest student. The cheater begins to rationalize his behavior. If there is no harm to me or to others, if everyone is doing this, what is wrong with copying a few things from the Internet?

One of the tragedies of cheating is that it perpetuates itself. Once you have pretended to master a subject, if you're asked to build on what you supposedly have learned in the next unit or course, you have little choice but to continue cheating. For a pre-med, this thinking will be disastrous. The pre-med curriculum includes a year of biology, two years of chemistry, a year of physics—all three with laboratories—plus a year of math and a year of English. The sciences and math are unforgiving; if you do not understand concept A, you will never understand concept B, and then you will fail when asked for concept C. So if you cheat on exams in subject A, things are going to get a lot worse in B and C—unless you continue to cheat.

This kind of spiraling disaster is less pronounced in the humanities and the social sciences, but the prevalence of cheating there is no less disturbing. In these disciplines, the primary problem is plagiarism. This is most often the result of students' using the Internet for what they call "research." It seems very easy to go online to search for a particular subject, to find an obscure Web site or citation, and then quickly copy and paste some portion of the information found into a document, claiming ownership of it or just thinking that that is how it is done. Some students plagiarize unintentionally; they know where they got the material, but they do not do a good job of citing it or giving full credit where it is due. Failing to give credit may seem like a trivial offense, but it violates the important principle of authorship. Professional scholars do not make a lot of money, most of them never become famous, and all of them work very hard. Is it fair to them to steal their work without credit?

A pragmatic pre-med might react to this discussion by saying, "So what? I need to get good grades. Physics is not important to being a doctor, so what's wrong with copying a lab report? Everybody else does it; why shouldn't I?" The first answer to this question is obvious: it is wrong. Cheating is morally corrupt; it is a failure to understand that the values of fairness and authorship are more important than advancing personal goals. A cheater is someone who has lost his moral bearings.

This argument does not work very well for a lot of students, unfortunately. For those who decide that it is necessary to cheat, arguments of morality hold little sway. These students either ignore what is right or can no longer recognize that what they are doing is wrong. By the same logic, those pre-meds who have integrity do not cheat in the first place. So morality is not a particularly helpful argument; it is beside the point. To some international students, this debate is confusing. They may not see the problem with sharing data, information, or texts. They think of it as a communal effort, which raises complicated issues about moral relativism.[7]

A more effective argument for the pre-med who is cheating or who is tempted to do so is that such actions are dangerous and self-destructive. In their effort to gain credentials and superior records of achievement, cheating pre-meds have forgotten that they are training to save lives. Physicians are not ordinary professionals. They are entrusted with the health and safety of society. As surgeons, as pediatricians, as oncologists, doctors are entrusted with our lives and those of our loved ones. A student who has cheated to enter this profession is playing with fire.

A physician has to make hundreds of judgments every day that have a profound effect on her patients. Someone who does not know what she is doing and tries to cover it up is a danger to those patients. A physician who is not fully competent because she cheated her way to her degree is a threat to the people who have trusted her.

Cheaters are the kinds of people who cannot admit to a mistake or confess to ignorance. They try to cover up, and that is self-destructive. Medical schools always ask colleges if applicants were involved in cheating, even for the most minor of violations. And they usually flush those candidates from the pool. When they can choose from so many applicants, why should they take a cheater?

Most of the cheating cases I know involve a student who is in trouble academically and, in desperation, does something he or she would never do normally, like copy a lab report late at night. These students rationalize their actions—"It's no big deal, just a small report," "I worked on this with her, so the results are mine, too," "The professor wanted us to work together"—but they know these are weak defenses. If the threat of hurting or killing your medical career before it begins can make you pause at this moment, ask for help. Get an extension. See the professor and tell her you are lost. Drop the course and take it another time. Seek out an academic advisor. Or just go for a walk to clear your mind and remind yourself that honest ignorance and confusion is at the root of real learning.

Then go back to work and do the learning for yourself.

Be Yourself

You may be as relieved, as I am, to move on to something more positive than cheating. Let me oblige.

So let's consider the task of the admissions committee of a professional school so that we can understand how another form of integrity—individuality—can help you persuade the members of that committee to let you in. An admissions committee must construct a class, not just admit a random group of applicants. That class needs to reflect diversity, just as it should represent excellence. The committee wants to admit, and then educate, a group of men and women who will embody that institution's values, learn critical skills, and then represent the school with honor, humanity, and effectiveness.[8]

This means that medical schools are not looking for just one kind of student. This recruitment challenge is faced equally by other graduate programs like law and business schools. Medical schools want a variety of perspectives and a mix of life experiences and academic talents among their students.[9] Put more bluntly, they are not going to just admit biology majors who have taken the same classes, conducted similar research, and had the same limited clinical experience. The members of such a class would all look the same. This would be both painfully boring and counter to their school's mission. Students lacking perspective and cultural sensitivity, for example, would likely be clumsy doctors who do not represent their medical school with any distinction.

If medical schools need a diverse class, what does that mean to you, the pre-med? It means that you should *not* do what everyone else is doing. For example, at Johns Hopkins that means avoiding the larger health-related majors—biology, neuroscience, and public health—*unless* you are genuinely interested in the subject matter. If you did major in biology at Hopkins, imagine how difficult it will be to separate yourself from the dozens of other Hopkins bio majors, as well as the bio majors from every other school. Admission to medical school would then come down to a war of numbers—namely, GPA and MCAT scores—which you might not win.

You certainly would not win that war if you had chosen your major solely on the basis of some preconception of what a pre-med curriculum looks like. Instead, you would most likely be a resentful learner and earn poor grades because you did not enjoy the material you had to master. I have seen this happen hundreds of times, including in most cases of students who have done so poorly as to be put on academic probation or suspension.

This is why I offer an alternative vision for successful admission to medical school, one built on integrity and individuality. Rather than asking you to do what you *think* you should do, I am asking you to do what you *want* to do, and so create your own path to distinctiveness. I am not arguing that being distinctive is just a better state, although I believe it is. Instead, I am saying that it is *strategically savvy* to create distance and differences between you and your competition. By building an intellectual and personal life that is uniquely your own, you are becoming competitive and distinctive without any further effort.

Let me tell a story. As we discussed her first-term courses, a pre-med freshman told me she was considering a neuroscience major with a minor in African studies. I asked her to explain her interest in the latter. She began an animated description of her travels to Africa, her work with AIDS victims, and her interest in medical missionary work. I then asked why she wanted neuroscience as a major. "I'm pretty good at it, it's kind of interesting, and med schools like science majors," she said. I confirmed that medical schools need to be sure you understand and excel at the sciences, but then I suggested she turn this plan on its head.

"Since you're not very committed to neuroscience, how about doing a major in African studies, while completing the pre-med requirements on the side?" She looked at me, thunderstruck. "Really? I can do that?" I explained how she could take a more balanced course schedule, taking sciences and African studies classes simultaneously. To this, she could add language study, such as Kiswahili or Arabic, and spend a summer or semester studying abroad in Africa.

I did not need to convince her that this would be a more interesting way through college. The interest in Africa was hers, not mine, and deeply felt. Instead, I had to convince her of the strategic utility of this choice. I first pointed out that she was likely to learn more in African studies courses because she was highly motivated. That would yield better grades and a higher GPA, a critical weapon in the war of numbers.

Second, I argued that if she did this, she would look different in the applicant pool from the much more numerous neuroscience majors. Johns Hopkins has hundreds of those, but perhaps fewer than a dozen African studies majors, only a few of whom want to be doctors. Medical schools like to see applicants who have studied abroad, and if she added clinical work while she was in Africa, that would show both cultural risk-taking and commitment to medical care. These thoughts were a revelation to her, and she left my office rethinking her plans so quickly that you could almost hear the gears turning inside her head. Whatever major she ultimately chose, she had gained a new perspective on the competitive advantages of distinguishing herself from others.

Making the choice to be different may be strategically sound, but it can be difficult. That student's expectations and those of her parents posed real obstacles to the imaginative leap into another path. In Habit #2, *Build an Adult Relationship with Your Parents*, I discuss how a student may need to build some habits that create emotional separation from her parents. This would give her the room she needs to make this decision. It would be more helpful, of course, if her parents also "got it" and appreciated the strategic advantage of distinctiveness. But here, I will make the point that choosing to be different is also an act of character-building, an investment in the kind of integrity that will remain attractive throughout a student's career and life.

Rather simply, it is the right thing to do.

✣ Put It in Perspective

Thinking of yourself as pre-professional, preparing for specific graduate training, can be wise and sensible. You see plenty of evidence that a bachelor's degree is necessary but often insufficient to work in important and possibly lucrative careers. But there are dangers to this thinking and planning. Pre-professionals, particularly pre-meds, can easily conclude that their college experience is a means to an end, no more. That not only is a disservice to the richer rewards of college life, but it can also create terrible pressures. Students who have this outlook feel compelled to get good grades and also worry about what others will think of them generally. And that can lead to finding an excuse for cheating, ignoring the immorality and dangers, just as it creates a culture that bypasses individuality for "safer," more well-worn routes to professional or graduate school admission.

These pressures and dangers fall on pre-meds especially hard, and that is why I have focused on their case in this chapter. They have created a fabric of expectations about themselves that can be comforting

Being Pre-Med
A Dream or a Nightmare?

SUE WASIOLEK, J.D., L.L.M., Ed.D.
DEAN OF STUDENTS
DUKE UNIVERSITY

Having worked in student affairs for almost 30 years, I'm often asked how I chose to become a dean of students. My answer? "I was pre-med." Here's my story.

Everything screamed at me to drop pre-med—my advisor, my friends, my grades. But I didn't listen. I had always wanted to be a doctor, and the fact that my grades were horrific and that I didn't enjoy my science classes seemed irrelevant. Surely a medical school would recognize my work ethic and my unwavering desire to help people.

So I just kept taking chemistry, calculus, physics, and biology, making C's and D's, but never ever giving up. I thought there had to be more to being a good doctor than just grades.

I applied to seven medical schools, with a realistic chance of being admitted to just one. Well, on the day I returned to campus after winter break and checked my mailbox, I found my first and most significant rejection letter—from my safety school. It was at that moment that I realized that I wasn't going to be a doctor, at least not as soon as I had hoped.

Plan B was to go on to graduate school, improve my grades, and then reapply. What I didn't understand was that my poor grades really weren't what graduate schools were looking for either. Nonetheless, I applied to a graduate program at my undergraduate institution in health administration. What a perfect plan—show my interest and proficiency in health care before reapplying to medical school. I literally talked my way into graduate school and promised the program that I would not let them down. And I didn't (at least not in the classroom). I did very well, having learned how to study and better manage my time. I graduated and began a job in health care, only to learn that I didn't like the environment. I simply hated working in a health care facility. At that point I *finally* gave up my medical school dream and found my way to a career in college administration.

My story has a happy ending. I have since completed two law degrees and a doctorate in education. I continue to feel a need to go to school, probably because I robbed myself of a meaningful and enjoyable undergraduate academic experience.

I've tried to listen a little bit better to the "screaming" since being pre-med. Time in the classroom—as well as time pursuing a career—should never be "work." It should be enjoyable and inspiring. If it is not, make a change, even if it means giving up a life-long dream.

because those expectations offer a clear path into an otherwise uncertain future. But this fabric can suffocate as well. Because the path appears to be clear, many pre-meds lose any academic imagination that they might have had. They might enjoy the advantages of clarity, but this comes at the expense of seeing alternative ways of achieving the same goal, and they certainly rule out other professional options. So they choose paths that are well-worn, most obviously by majoring in a program like biology and gathering credentials, such as conducting research that they think will yield a seat in a medical school of their choice.

I hope better for you: I hope that you will make these choices with integrity, and that if you do major in biology and do lab research, or whatever course you think best prepares you for study after college, you will do so because of an honest interest in the discipline and an enthusiasm for its approach to discovery. If you truly love what you are doing, you will succeed and thrive. A pre-med who is motivated by this love for science will drink in the research culture and revel in the intellectual challenges of cutting-edge science. But for many others, these traditional choices do not fit their passions, interests, or skills. If they pursue a science major, they often face real and repeated academic problems—failed courses, frustration, unmet requirements, or just unaccustomed mediocrity—and their confidence is replaced by doubt and anxiety. Not getting into medical school is the least of their problems.

There should be another way, another set of paths to the goal of being a doctor, paths that do not take so many victims or define "success" so narrowly as a biology major with a high GPA. I believe that, as a student with ambitions for higher degrees, you can find a better way by building an intellectual life and integrity defined by honesty and individualism. Some of this means doing all you can to avoid cheating and get the help you need when you need it. That will mean a life lived honestly. But a larger part of this means finding your own way, guided by a sense of self and ownership over your life.

Learn from Diversity at Home and Abroad

There's no doubt about it: college will change the way you view the world. As a freshman, newly graduated from high school, you are likely to arrive on campus a bit perplexed, a bit worried, and probably very naïve about the world and its people. Yet we know that the world of the 21st century is more complex, diverse, and globally integrated than ever. The economic collapse of 2008 provided absolute proof of global interdependence, as international banking, credit, and insurance problems infected economies all over the world. Every day, America herself becomes culturally richer as her international population changes. So it makes sense to rise to this challenge of understanding a wider culture if your college experience can be a success. And that is why Habit #8 on the Dean's List is *Learn from Diversity at Home and Abroad.*

The challenge of international interdependence is not new. For millennia, people have been trading goods with each other, moving across borders, emigrating, traveling for pleasure, getting an education elsewhere, and generally finding new challenges that new cultures, politics, and economies present to them. Nevertheless, our interdependence and the scale of our interaction are intensely pronounced today.[1] We are profoundly affected by each other. The most obvious, terrible example of this was the events of September 11, 2001, when Saudi Arabians flew planes into the Twin Towers and killed thousands of people from dozens of countries all over the world. It was as terrible as it was fitting for the global age of commerce and interaction that the terrorists attacked the *World Trade* Center.

As the world becomes interdependent and cultural competence more important, colleges are changing too, bringing this global and ethnic complexity home to campus. More and more students of color attend college, and women are rapidly overtaking men as the largest group in college.[2] Most colleges have an explicit strategy, tempered by the limits of the law, to further diversify their student body. And those that succeed create a cultural brew that is exciting, educational, and challenging.

These histories, demographics, and today's global conditions should suggest to you that a critical part of your education should be an understanding of "the other"—those peoples you do not know, who do not look like you, and/or do not live with you.[3] I like this term, "the other," because it could include people who sit across from you in class or the people who live far away, in another land. And that is why this habit on the Dean's List covers two interrelated topics: understanding and appreciating diversity on campus, and exposing yourself to cultural understanding—and misunderstanding—elsewhere in the world.

How difficult these challenges are to you, emotionally and intellectually, will depend on who you are and what you have experienced, of course. You may have had the good fortune to travel abroad, or you might live in a heterogeneous community. If not, you may have more difficulty. But exposure to diversity does not necessarily make someone tolerant, respectful, or understanding. It can be hard, even if you have traveled internationally, to really understand any new environment. You probably visited some place for just a few days, and you were with your family. If you spent more time overseas, or if you study abroad in college, you might live or socialize only with other Americans, perhaps in an English-speaking country. You might feel good about being abroad, but you may have stayed in a protective bubble. Likewise, you can live on a campus rich with many different peoples, faiths, and viewpoints, but if you do not actively engage with them, you may be building new prejudices or magnifying others. By failing to engage these people more directly in an open and understanding dialogue, you can shut off ways to cooperate and build mutual respect.

So it's not enough to be around diversity or to go overseas. You have to connect.

This has always been the tension for students belonging to ethnic organizations on campus such as the Filipino Students Association, the Korean American Students Association, the Black Student Union, and others. On the one hand, participation in such organizations might cloister groups from one another, making conversation less likely. On the other, college is a critical time for students to form their own identity, including their ethnic identity, so these groups contribute to that important development.

Reaching out can involve a leap between groups or to new people, and that is not easy. I made my own initial attempt at this my freshman year. With my lunch tray in hand, I sat down one day with a group of black women in the Commons dining room. I asked them directly, and a bit clumsily, why they were sitting by themselves. I wondered aloud why their lives seemed so separate from mine. They were gracious but equally direct. That separation was real, they said, not imagined or self-imposed. Their lives and their interests were so different from mine that I probably would not understand them. The conversation continued on a variety of related topics, as when I asked one of them about the *Ebony* magazine she had, about what the images meant to her.

That conversation was an opening I did not fully appreciate or really exploit. I did not really understand all I was hearing, and there was no obvious format or educational setting to gain that understanding. My attempt was laudable, I suppose, but inadequate. So my vivid memory of that conversation nearly 30 years ago is laced with regret and a sense of lost opportunity, feelings I do not want you to have. I know now that my feelings of confusion, artifice, unease, and discomfort from that conversation—feelings that did not encourage further exploration—were natural and necessary. How could I expect to be comfortable outside my comfort zone? Students have to be uneasy and open to acknowledging ignorance to find the motivation to learn. And that is a difficult challenge to meet, especially when you are so young.

Difficult or not, meeting this challenge is a worthy endeavor, and completely necessary in a heterogeneous, integrated world and a rich, successful college career. So what do you do? I would argue there are three steps to take, none of them simple: build awareness, seek education, and initiate dialogue.[4]

Open Your Eyes

Many students coming to good colleges are sophisticated enough to be keenly aware of the issues of identity, prejudice, and cultural misunderstanding. To some degree, they have faced them as they have grown. Their parents, I am sure, have coped with these issues. A student may be a member of a minority community, so she has lived these experiences. Awareness comes from experience outside your family too. It could be simple, from attending a concert filled with new music or eating food you have not tried before. You might pay closer attention to the media's coverage of stories of racial and ethnic conflict.

Awareness can and should sharpen your empathy, the ability to connect with people and their experiences and feelings. This is never an easy task, but it begins by being mindful that you may not understand what others are feeling and what they are going through. You begin by appreciating that your vantage point is not the only one that exists, and that many people see the very same thing differently than you do.

In the great Japanese film *Rashomon*, directed by Akira Kurosawa, a samurai and his wife, traveling through a forest, are attacked by a bandit. The samurai is killed. Kurosawa famously tells the story from the vantage points of each of the people in the experience: the bandit, the widow, a woodsman, and even the dead samurai (through a psychic). No story aligns with the others; there is no clear, truthful narrative. Every participant tells a different story, often to their own self-interest. The movie ends with confusion and without resolution.

Kurosawa's insight is profound. We often see the world through different eyes, imagining truth to suit our experience, understanding, and prejudices. Awareness begins with an appreciation of this insight, that others see things differently than you do.

Learning through Diversity

RAIMA EVAN, Ph.D.

ASSISTANT DEAN

BRYN MAWR COLLEGE

Diversity. You've gone through workshops at your high school about it. You've had teachers assign novels and poems by writers with points of view very different from your own. You've volunteered in your community. You've even chosen a college or university where you're living and learning side by side with people from all over the United States and the world. Now you just want to get on with your college life.

Sounds good, but what happens when some of the people on your hall are talking in a language you don't understand? What happens when the girls next door are playing music that you can't stand? What happens when you assume that on the weekends, your roommate will want to go out for dinner and see a movie but she shows no interest? What happens when the boy next door to you is transitioning to become a girl?

Living in a diverse community isn't always easy. In fact, much of the time, diversity requires a certain amount of adjustment that can sometimes feel like a strain. On the other hand, living among people who are just like you—whatever that means—might not only be pretty boring but would also deny you the experience of encountering difference and learning from it. Going to college isn't just about book learning. It's about experiential learning, and that happens right on your hall every day.

As a dean, I've found that the unseen diversity issues are often the ones that students have the most trouble understanding. Differences stemming from socioeconomic class, for instance, can be challenging for students because they don't necessarily understand the class background of their friends. While students may already have some sense of the importance of being sensitive about differences pertaining to race, religion, and gender, they may not appreciate how class differences can shape behaviors in a college setting. As a result, some students may assume that their friends would jump at the chance to go skiing on the weekend or shopping at the local mall, and they may feel upset when they do not.

continued

Class differences can affect many kinds of behaviors, not just those related to discretionary spending. First-generation students may feel intimidated by titles such as "professor" and "dean," and they may feel uncomfortable about seeing a professor during office hours, asking an instructor for an extension on a paper, or talking to a dean about getting a tutor, even though plenty of other students are asking for help from these same sources. It may be hard for them to think about applying for a summer internship or applying to graduate school if they don't have someone at home who can help them through the process.

Of course, there are certainly first-generation students who are adept at getting the help they need, just as there are students with parents who have advanced degrees who don't know how to get help even when it is offered. But if you're feeling unsure about how to make full use of the resources at your college because there's a part of you that feels uncomfortable about being in a college environment at all, find someone approachable to talk to. Ask an upper-class student who knows the system at your school. Ask a professor or advisor whom you have come to know, a coach that you see almost every day, or the person in the admissions office who emailed you when you were applying to the college as a high school senior. It doesn't matter to whom you first reach out; the important thing is that you reach out to someone who can answer your questions or point you to someone else who can.

Of course, what diversity means to you is different from what it means to your roommate. And that's a good thing, even if it can lead to some complicated conversations about what holiday decorations can be put up on the walls and for how long. Compromises have to be made, and compromises mean that both parties have to give up something they would prefer not to give up. What feels natural to you is apt to feel strange to somebody else, and vice versa. But feeling strange is part of being in this world, and getting along with strangers is how you end up making friends.

Diversify Your Education Portfolio

A second step is education. Your college curriculum should help, of course. Johns Hopkins recently cataloged the number of courses available on campus that dealt either explicitly or implicitly with racism, internationalism, and issues between cultures. The number of these courses was astonishingly large, nearly half of the full humanities and social sciences curriculum. That was a very comforting exercise, as it showed the faculty's wide and deep commitment to understanding the history of racism, conflicts between ethnic groups and religious groups, the origins of misunderstanding, conflict, and war. In the spring of 2009, for example, the university offered "The Sociology of Privilege," and "Space, Place, Poverty, and Race." While many students do often miss the point of these courses, it is important to offer discomforting courses that help students understand difficult histories, the sociology of racism, and gender inequalities.

But do not think that these opportunities will reconcile differences or make it easier to talk to each other. Learning comes from debate, and debate can create uncomfortable conflict. So a diverse education should be filled with difficulty, challenge, and confrontation—mediated by the civility of a safe, respectful environment. You should think of making these lessons a central goal of your college life, to include them in your personal definition of being "learned," and so to define success by better understanding these conflicts.

My own effort to do this as an undergraduate came late—but not too late. As I sat watching the film *Gandhi* when it was released in late 1982, I became overwhelmed with the depth of my ignorance of his story. His life in South Africa and then in India seemed completely alien to me, and I wondered how I could have missed this in my education. An idea grew slowly, not blossoming for another year, that I had focused too much of my studies on the European experience; it was what I knew. As my dissatisfaction with my Euro-centric education grew, I started focusing on Gandhi for inspiration. During the summer before my junior year, I applied for a Fulbright Scholarship to India and made Gandhi's life in South Africa the subject of my college senior thesis.

But it was not until I spent that Fulbright year in India that I really understood what I had been missing. Great swaths of the human experience had been outside my reach, particularly the giant tapestry of South Asia. Unfolding before me, India challenged me to learn quickly and intensely about her history, culture, and religions. I had given little thought to Islam beyond the impact of conflict with Europe, and now could see how varied Muslims were. I knew little or nothing about Buddhism and Hinduism. I did not even know Jainism existed.

So the *Gandhi* film had started my awareness of "the other" in Asia, and my Yale studies began to address this deficit—but only with full immersion during a year in India did I become better educated. Your own journey may require as many steps, maybe more.

Start a Conversation

If you do succeed in making the understanding of diversity a priority, there is one more step toward mutual understanding and respect: dialogue. The act of dialogue is an important one because it shows a willingness to reach out, a willingness to understand, and mutual self-respect. It also gives a student from one vantage point the chance to show a student from another that he has learned something, showing raised awareness and deeper learning. This can be an astonishing moment for the other student, who may have assumed that the first student's ignorance was profound and that there was no basis for a conversation. Even better, if both students have done their homework, they can both be equally and appropriately surprised.

But where do these dialogues happen? How does this conversation begin?

Recognizing that a conversation like this cannot be forced, you should look for a place of healthy community and exchange. This could be in the classroom, in a discussion section, or in a seminar, encouraged by a faculty member interested in applying the course to the reality of personal exchange. It could begin in a student activity where you are working together to achieve a particular goal. It might happen on the playing field or on the basketball court. It could start when a group of volunteers get together to help local children learn math skills. It could be during a gathering hosted by an interfaith center. And, of course, it could and should happen in student housing.

I am not suggesting that a frank discussion about race or diversity be the first conversation. I never did talk to those black classmates again, probably because we had not built any foundation of common interest or goals before we began our intense conversation. We needed something to agree upon or accomplish together, such as staging a play, before pondering things about which we would disagree. We needed to develop trust, empathy, and a sense of mutual commitment and involvement. And then we would be free to tackle difficult issues.

That does not always happen. Even when a student has friends of many backgrounds, he or she might be reluctant to engage in that conversation. Once again, this underscores the importance of awareness and education. For example, a white student might not be aware that many black students feel that other people think they should not be there. Black students often believe that whites are passing judgment on them, thinking them to be undeserving of a seat in a prestigious college. They worry about asking questions or participating at all, for fear that admitting ignorance—a crucial step to learning—would make them look stupid. Claude Steele and Joshua Aronson call this "stereotype threat."[5]

Over several years I had conversations with a struggling African American woman who seemed to think that wherever she was, people were looking at her and judging her. Wherever she went, she felt she had to represent her race. Rather than being an individual student with problems and challenges, she carried the burden of proving the worthiness of her race. That was a terrible burden, one she could not carry, and one that was at the root of her academic struggles. She never did overcome this and many other challenges, and sadly, she left the university.

But imagine if she had had a conversation with her white friends about this perception. If she or her friends had had the courage to ask tough questions and struggle with difficult answers, she might have found her anxieties lessened. It may be true that black students receive greater, unfair scrutiny. But perhaps not to the extent she imagined, and not with the intention of crippling her self-confidence.

So I urge you to be emotionally daring. After you have made friends with somebody who is different, try asking her tough questions about how she feels about her life. Ask her how she feels about her relationship with other peoples and races. You can begin the process of appreciating life from her vantage point. And that will lead to deeper understanding and cultural respect, an important goal of any successful college education.

Study Abroad

Meeting the challenge of diversity at home is important, but it is not enough. The days when Americans could disregard the world as unimportant, if such days ever existed, are over. But I think the arguments for exposing students to world travel and to study abroad are common and a bit preachy. So let me identify the excuses you might make to avoid study abroad, and we will see how to answer those.[6]

First, you might think about the opportunity costs. The one or two semesters of junior year that could be slated for study abroad may be the heart of your college education. At that point, you will be hitting your stride intellectually and socially. You have lots of friends. You are taking interesting seminars, not big lecture courses. You are conducting original research. Maybe you are a leader of a campus group or captain of the volleyball team. Just at that moment when you are at the pinnacle of a college education, someone suggests that you go as far away from campus as possible for study in Beijing, Jakarta, London, Rome, or Buenos Aires. Ridiculous! Just as you have gotten your feet under you, you are asked to fall down again.

Second, you might be scared—a common feeling. However much you have studied a foreign language, it is intimidating to go where people do not speak English. You cannot communicate your feelings, concerns, or ideas as easily as you can in your mother tongue. You also face the scary possibility of eating strange food every day. You will not know where you are, so you might feel stupid or lost. You could violate local customs or social norms, looking clumsy when you want to be sophisticated. You are concerned about feeling alienated, misunderstood, distant, strange, and detached in a foreign land.

Third, you are too broke and confused to go abroad. When the dollar is weak, foreign tuition and living expenses are high. The costs of travel, particularly air travel, can seem prohibitive. If you and your family think of study abroad as an inflated form of tourism, then it

Step Outside Your Own World

JANET A. TIGHE, Ph.D.
DEAN OF FRESHMEN and DIRECTOR OF ACADEMIC ADVISING
COLLEGE OF ARTS AND SCIENCES
UNIVERSITY OF PENNSYLVANIA

Study abroad is a big part of the undergraduate experience at my university. For some students, it is the traditional semester or year at another college or university. For others, it is a summer program abroad. And for a small but growing group, it is an internship or experiential learning situation. Deciding which of these experiences is right for you involves some exploration. It is also one of those decisions in which good advising can make a real difference. These conversations about overseas study will probably involve several types of advisors, including those who specialize in study abroad, career counseling, and academics.

The place to start these conversations is with yourself. Spend a little time thinking about *why* you want to study abroad (as opposed to *where*). The destination question is crucial, and study abroad advisors will be of invaluable help with it, but it is important to recognize that this decision isn't the place to start. The decision on studying abroad is not like planning a vacation. Destination matters, but the decision needs to be informed by a much broader set of factors. In today's globalized, interconnected society, you must consider studying abroad in concert with your other life goals. You must ask a much wider range of questions, both practical and philosophical.

As you articulate why you want to study abroad, consider how the experience will fit into your larger educational plan. At most schools, an academic advisor can help answer questions such as how the study abroad experience will help you fulfill your major requirement. Athletes, some science students, and those pursuing pre-medical school may need to consider when and for how long they can be away from campus. There are also practical questions that need answers. Can I afford study abroad financially? Will my financial aid package apply? Are there other forms of aid? How will this experience appear on my transcript? Again, study abroad and

continued

academic advisors can be a big help. These advisors can also assist you in figuring out eligibility questions. It is not unusual for institutions abroad to require students to have a certain level of language proficiency or a minimum GPA.

Finally, keep in mind that globalization works in multiple ways: you can meet people from other countries, with other cultural experiences, on your own campus. Look around campus for ways to experience the rich diversity of cultures that make up our world. Whether you decide to study abroad as a part of your undergraduate education or to explore other cultures without leaving campus, make sure you avail yourself of one of the great experiences of college life—stepping outside your own world.

would also be an unnecessary luxury, especially in trying economic times. There are confusing logistics, too. "How would I get there? Who would I live with? Where would I get fed? Would I be safe? Could I stay healthy?"

Fourth, you have requirements to complete, and you are accustomed to doing this in a familiar academic environment. So you wonder if studying abroad is going to fit academically. You say to yourself: "On campus, there's a very clear path to graduation. All these courses are taught by the faculty at my college. They hand out letter grades. The transcript is normal. I have a seamless academic experience. It might not be an easy one, but at least it is predictable. If I go to the University of London, what will happen? How will they grade or evaluate me? How will this affect my future? What kind of class work would you do when you're there? How do they teach people there? Do they write the same kind of papers? What about exams? Do they expect differently of me? Do they expect more of me?"

No wonder that most students decide *not* to study abroad. They reason that it is just too complicated, too difficult, too scary, too expensive—too something.

These anxieties are real, but they overshadow the far greater benefits that will come from living overseas.[7] First, note that the first word of "study abroad" is "study." So you should think of the experience as a logical way to extend your current studies, a new venue that might allow you to learn something you could not in the States. That is especially true if you enjoy doing your own research. One Johns Hopkins student went to the Orkney Islands, off the coast of Scotland, to examine folk music traditions. He played in bands and talked to countless Scottish musicians about what influenced their work. Another student traveled to the jungles of Madagascar for a summer. She spent nights in the pitch black listening for the calls of frogs for an environmental project on habitat destruction. Others lived for a semester in Belgium studying human rights trials, they looked at Australian geology, or they explored traditional medicine in China. Whether these destinations are exotic or not does not really matter. What does matter is that they are intensely effective classrooms to learn certain lessons that years on a campus in Boston, Chicago, or Baltimore cannot teach.

Second, experiences overseas, by their very novelty, are richer, brighter, and more intense. Sure, this can be disorienting and even a little frightening. But the intensity of the experience will make it more memorable, more provocative, and more lasting than anything you could get at home. For a long time after I returned from a year in India, if I sat quietly, I could reconstruct *every day* that I had spent on the subcontinent. It was an astonishing exercise, taking about a half hour to quickly think through all of the different experiences I had, in order, and to reconstruct all the faces I saw and the ideas that whirled through my head. It was like watching a year-long video at high speed, a video vividly colored, filled with unusual sights and sounds, smells and tastes.

This high-definition film was not just memorable; it was provocative. I would struggle to make sense of what I was seeing, combating and embracing feelings that I was having. A whole new set of political, historical, and sociological questions would tumble at me at a blistering pace. My head would reel from all the things that I had to make sense of in any given time. All I really needed to do was open my eyes in the morning, and the learning would begin.

While a foreign experience is not easy, and should not be, getting there can be. Every college will have an office responsible for study abroad. Think of visiting it like going into store without an obligation to buy. You should ask a few basic questions: "Where could I go? If I speak Spanish or German, but only a little, are there good programs for me? I'd really like to go to Barcelona, but how?" The number of choices will be bewildering, so a good advisor is a must. Over the last 20 years, American and foreign universities have launched hundreds of programs to accommodate the many different kinds of needs, interests, and levels of fluency of American students who want to spend time abroad.[8] A good study abroad office will walk you through the process of finding the right program, and they should challenge you to be a little more daring than you had expected to be when you first walked in. Listen very carefully to that advice.

A study abroad office will also help you through the logistics, including pre-clearance of courses you will take. They will show you how to dovetail these with your major and minor requirements. They can even help with the special needs of a pre-medical student or students in engineering, the natural sciences and other fields whose curricula are more regimented and inflexible. They might suggest, for example, that a pre-med take a summer course or two in the basic sciences to free up a term that might otherwise be spent on campus. They can reassure you that the courses that you take overseas will count toward your major, minor, or second major. They will explain the challenges of financing such an experience, pointing out that financial aid usually follows students and/or suggesting scholarships to ease the burden. They may caution you to avoid especially expensive locations. Given limited means, you may not necessarily enjoy all that those places have to offer. There may be other countries, particularly in the developing world, where your dollar will go a lot farther, and the experience may be richer and more provocative, in any case.

Once you are there, you should prepare for the fun and challenge of being surprised. You cannot anticipate all that will happen, and that unpredictability heightens your senses and sharpens the mind. A sharp mind and a quick tongue will be particularly useful when you discover, unexpectedly, that you will be representing the United States. As soon as people find out you're an American, they will want to talk to you. They will want to know more about Hollywood or what it is like to live in New York—the two most obvious places on the American map to a foreigner. They may ask you about favorite musicians or movies. But mostly, they will talk politics and foreign policy, especially

U.S. involvement in Iraq, Afghanistan, and the Middle East. You might find yourself defending the United States on issues and policies with which they do not even agree. I call this defensive patriotism. Students may agree with critics of American policies, but they begin thinking, "What business is it of theirs? America should do what it wants."

These arguments and feelings are just a few among the many that will challenge your identity and worldview. Stepping outside a familiar culture is an odd and disorienting exercise. But in its intensity and strangeness, the experience has unique power to teach. That is the enduring value of study abroad.

❖ *Put It in Perspective*

The best reason to go to college is that it will disrupt everything you think you know. Your professors will make every effort to push you off balance, to challenge how you think, and to openly question your values and presuppositions. They will do that with demanding rigor that you should expect at a competitive institution. Likewise, your exceptionally talented classmates will upset your concept of the "normal" and introduce you more richly to the idea of "the other." Are you the normal one? Or are they? Perhaps that is a useless, patronizing term. You could be "the other" to them just as they are to you. The richer that tapestry, which is made possible by the institution's power to attract great students from all over the world, the more provocative and disruptive it will be. You will meet people from places that you did not know existed, and they will say things you cannot understand. You have gone to a strange country, even if it looks just like an American college.

This disruption can be scary. You might not be sure what to make of it. You may be uncertain how to behave. You might be tempted to retreat to a smaller group of homogenous friends or shut down the input. But you should resist this temptation by countering it with the curiosity that should be powering your entire education. Ask questions, take related courses, and study abroad. Talk to international students and other ethnic groups. What do they care about? What are they thinking? How do you reconcile this with what you think? Students need to understand that diversity and difference are identical. College

Diversity on Campus and Abroad

SUSAN MARINE, Ph.D.
ASSISTANT DEAN OF HARVARD COLLEGE and
DIRECTOR OF THE HARVARD COLLEGE WOMEN'S CENTER
HARVARD UNIVERSITY

A funny thing happens during the beginning of your college experience. You'll find yourself being herded, probably by an earnest upper-classmate, from one party to another, through a whirlwind of campus tours, '80s dances, and perhaps even an ice cream social. These events, superfluously entertaining though they may seem, are often designed to help you meet many different people in a very short period of time. As September turns to October and the parties turn to three squares a day in the dining hall, it will be all too easy to find yourself always sitting at a table with people who look, talk, dress, and even think... *exactly like you!* If you see this happening, run, don't walk, to another table (being careful, of course, not to drop your tray). Do so knowing that one of the most profoundly meaningful aspects of the selective American liberal arts college you're fortunate to attend is the painstakingly thoughtful manner by which the diverse cohort of students known as "your class" has been assembled by the admissions office.

The buzzword *diversity* gets bandied about quite a bit these days, but the true meaning and value of engaging with difference lies in how it helps to expand your capacity to think and feel about others in a more open, nuanced, and constructive way. It's nice to attend campus functions, but being informed about other customs, geopolitical systems, environmental challenges, cultural norms, and areas of contested belief—firsthand from those who have lived them—will enrich your experience by giving you insight into the way that your own culture might be grappling with surface tensions of its own.

Studying abroad will afford you the opportunity to leap headlong into the exhilarating skill known as "navigating the unfamiliar," but making a concerted effort to really know your college peers who are from different worlds will pay off immeasurably. All this, and all you had to do was change tables. Or roommates. Or chairs in your first-year seminar. To get the most of college, make it your mission to surround yourself with people with whom you can participate in conducting the reverent and uniquely humbling symphony of human difference.

promotes difference to provoke awareness, education, and dialogue—not to make the place look interesting and colorful.

These challenges are fundamental to a great education in an interdependent, conflicted and complex world. An education will not be complete or successful, and your world citizenship will be in doubt, if you do not face "the other" and learn what that means.

When You Are Failing, Understand Why

Matthew was a first-year student at Johns Hopkins University. His record from high school looked a lot like the records of his Hopkins classmates. He took difficult courses, and he aced them. He volunteered in his community, and he won awards for it. He was captain of the varsity tennis and soccer teams. His scores on SATs were stellar, and he arrived with 15 college credits from Advanced Placement exams. He was smart and articulate. He was the pride of his family and of his Texas hometown.

And Matthew then earned a 1.60 GPA in his first term at Hopkins.

How did this happen? He rarely went to class. He didn't study at all, or very much. He hung out with friends and played video games. He was unmotivated and detached. He lied to his parents on how things were going. In fact, it is amazing he did not fail every class. He must have earned the two D's and three C's on brains and momentum.

More incredibly, Matthew's story is not unique. It is a surprising secret about life at even the best colleges that a lot of students struggle academically. Some wobble as they go, earning poor grades and sometimes failing courses. Others meet disaster, failing every course and risking expulsion every term. Some never graduate at all. Just because these students attend a great school—Stanford or Harvard or Hopkins—does not give them a special coat of armor against failure. To the contrary. These are students for whom academic achievement has defined their identity, and now they face the scary reality that something is very wrong, perhaps with themselves. In this chapter, I will talk about the situations and causes for this kind of academic struggle.[1] It is as important to talk about failure—more important, really—as it is to consider success. Anyone can handle success.

So let us start by discussing the shock of the thought that failure is a possibility. It is a stunning and surprising idea that good college students fail. It seems beyond imagination that a student who had managed to get into a top school could actually fail out of one. But, in fact, the record of academic achievement, excellence, commitment, and hard work that were prerequisites to getting into a top college may not be enough to prevent these students from having difficulty once they are there. Ironically, their preparation might not be preparation enough—or it may be beside the point, if there are other reasons for their struggles.

The prospect of poor performance can be nightmarish. Most college students derive much of their self-esteem from academic success. But if they are struggling, when they look in the mirror they see someone they never imagined: someone getting D's or even F's, when they have never seen a C before. A series of difficult, tough emotions will hit them at that moment: "How did this happen? What is wrong with me? How could I have done this? What will my parents say? What can I admit to my friends, to my family? Is this shameful or common or what? Am I not as smart as I thought I was? And if I'm not smart, then what am I?"

More negative, confused thoughts crowd their minds: "I've spent most of my life impressing teachers; they all think I was great. I got great recommendations. I got fantastic grades. Here I am at a top college, and now I can't seem to cut it. I got straight A's in science in high school, and yet I can't seem to do better than a B on any given assignment, and I seem to mostly be getting C's. My test scores are near the median or the mean, sometimes well below that, not the top. I've made lots of plans based on a successful record at this college. I was supposed to get a high GPA and get into the medical school of my choice. Now I can't even seem to pass calculus, let alone chemistry. Is it possible that I'm not supposed to be a doctor? Is there a chance I got into this college by mistake, some kind of terrible typographical error? How am I going to get out of this mess? Am I going to be able to clean up my record? Am I going to be able to go on to major in biology? Am I even going to graduate?"

These increasingly panicked questions are completely natural and understandable. No one goes to college with the expectation that he or she is going to do poorly. So, when you get your first poor grade on an exam, it is a shocking, terrible moment. How is this possible? It is also distracts you from the more important mission of focusing on learning, not grades. Poor grades overshadow everything, making it impossible to have a deeper view of your college education. So, you need to do something to restore an engaged life of learning.

But how?

For some, struggling academically can be traumatic and disabling. Strong students have lived most of their lives in the sunshine of their teachers' approval. With poor grades, they feel banished to a dark, hidden cave, far from the smiling beneficence of the professor. To make matters worse, they may not even know this professor. He or she may appear to be an intimidating, unknowable, and now displeased intellectual god who hands down grades without caring what impact they will have. Feeling like an anonymous victim deserving of punishment adds imaginary problems to the real, making further failures more likely.

Many of the college students I know spin into self-criticism and struggle to pull out of that. They suffer from depression and other forms of mental illness—a powerful problem on college campuses today.[2] And this makes the situation much worse, as they find themselves unmotivated to get out of bed, to go to class, to stay focused, to learn.

For others, failure may be less dramatic, a simple bump in the road. Perhaps a student had every intention of preparing for an exam, but he was distracted by other issues: a breakup with a girlfriend, a loss on an athletic field, problems with a roommate. More commonly, he may have made a poor choice of coursework, finding the course boring and himself unmotivated to learn. I will discuss this at greater length shortly.

Another student may have a particularly bad semester, more like a jarring pothole in the road than a bump. This could be the result of a more serious, but passing, external event such as the death of a beloved grandparent, her parents' divorce or loss of a job. In these cases, her semester's grades may be wildly different from any previous ones. A student who normally earns A's and B's is suddenly getting C's and D's, and then finds herself on academic probation and out of good standing.

Whatever the severity of struggles you might face, whether it is a single crash on one test, or a whole pattern of failures that leads to academic probation or even dismissal, you need to consider the possibility of failure. We all fail, after all, at one thing or another. These failures can be minor, such as not doing a job well or offending a friend, or severe, such as losing a job or ending a marriage. Big or small, our failures must get our attention, and we must carry on after that. No one deserves to be crippled by mistakes, even very serious ones. So learning how to cope with failure is a powerful life tool.

It may be counterintuitive on a competitive campus, but the ability to discuss failure can help you build closer relationships and a more meaningful sense of community. Misery loves company, it has been famously observed. More people face real academic failure than you might imagine. All students worry about the possibility, and all but a rare few will experience some form of failure and disappointment. The struggling student therefore shares good company in this challenge. He might feel alone in these feelings, but those feelings are everywhere. Discussing them will draw him closer to his friends, who are fighting the same anxieties and self-doubts.

In the pages that follow I discuss at length the many and multiple causes for academic struggles. That list is surprisingly long, and it can be complicated because several of these causes can intersect with one another. They feed and complement each other. Collectively, they cause problems that might not have been serious individually. For many years at Johns Hopkins, we tried to identify variables like these so we could predict who might go on academic probation to get students help before it was too late. That exercise proved to be futile because there are so many variables at work, variables that mix with each other in so many different ways.[3] But the complexity of that problem does not let us off the hook.

The complexity should not prevent you from thinking about what causes failure, either. If you are doing badly, you will need to use your own skills and intelligence, with the help of others like academic ad-

KAREN BLANK, Ed.D.

DEAN OF STUDIES

BARNARD COLLEGE

Most students associate failure with poor grades, but my definition of failure includes not taking advantage of the extraordinary resources and opportunities that are offered on campuses: the faculty members with office hours to discuss ideas and answer questions and the advisors and counselors who support and challenge students to grow. Unfortunately, too many students at highly selective colleges consider themselves to be self-sufficient and find it hard to ask for help. They don't realize that asking for help is actually a sign of strength, not weakness.

My definition of failure also includes failing to interact with classmates whose backgrounds and views are different from our own. Students who can overcome fears and recognize the rewards of embracing others have gone a long way toward preventing future failures.

Failure is inevitable in all parts of life, especially when we are courageous enough to take risks. We must not despair because of failure or allow failure to define us. Addressing our failures—and becoming a better person because of them—is one of the most powerful lessons of the college experience.

visors and counselors, to figure it out: "What happened? What went wrong?" The first step to making things right is determining what is wrong. That process is always distressing and even embarrassing. I have sat with many students, sometimes with their parents, as we try to figure this out. Sometimes the student cries, sometimes the parents do. I offer plenty of tissues, a drink of water, patience, and reassurance. Whether the problem is grave or simple, this conversation has to take place. And that begins with developing the ability—the habit—of assessing what is going wrong. So, Habit #9 on the Dean's List is *When You Are Failing, Understand Why.*

As you can imagine, traveling through the desert of failed expectations will not be pleasant, but it will be important. Those who have made this journey are better people, in many ways, than those for whom everything is easy. They are more modest, more forgiving, more understanding and empathetic, and more mature than those who have not faced the challenge. And where better for you to face your limitations, when better to learn how to cope and then triumph, than a place where you are making the transition from teenager to adult?

There are four broad reasons for academic struggles that we examine below:

❶ lack of motivation
❷ poor time management
❸ weak study skills and talent
❹ poor mental and physical health

Feeling Unmotivated

Let me start with the most important of all the reasons for academic problems, though the hardest to fix: lack of motivation. It might seem puzzling that students going to a good college—students who have generally gotten a lot of satisfaction from their academic success—find it difficult to be motivated by certain subjects. Yet it is a common problem that has several explanations of its own.

First, some students are burned out. They don't have the intellectual energy to climb another mountain. Such burnout stems, in part, from the intense pressure they have experienced just to get into college. Driven in high school to create a superior resumé, jammed with activities and littered with high grades, yesterday's prep student may be today's stressed-out, burned-out freshman.[4] She is exhausted from the travel to college, with little left in the tank. I have seen many students who feel that getting into Hopkins was enough, and when they relax, they fail.

A related problem is the preoccupation with grades, as discussed in Habit #1, *Focus on Learning, Not on Grades*. If you are interested only in getting good grades, your motivation is very thin. This is a common mindset: many top students are motivated only by the goal of good grades, a focus that can strip them of the desire to learn for its own sake, for gaining knowledge and wisdom. And that might not be enough for you, not enough to push you to work and learn. The whole enterprise can become quite hollow and uninteresting. It may even be unchallenging for the exceptional student, who begins doing poorly in class, ironically, because getting A's is so easy to do. By mastering what is needed to earn an A and not having an interest in anything more than that, he simply falls apart.

An equally profound motivational problem is the desire to please others rather than yourself. Many students figure out quickly that the key to good grades is to discover what makes the instructor, teacher, or professor happy. After all, they are the ones making the evaluation and handing out the grades. So their pleasure seems to be the highest issue at hand; if you can make them happy, you win a good grade and can move on. That exercise can also seem hollow or elusive, particularly if you do not know your professor. How can you please someone you do not know? Since college instructors are more difficult to know than the high school teachers who knew you well, this can be daunting to you if you think that pleasing the teacher is the key to good grades.

More importantly, being motivated by the desire to please your parents may cause more problems. (I talk about this at greater length in Habit #2, *Build an Adult Relationship with Your Parents.*) We have all been trained since infancy to please our parents. They are the ones, after all, who gave us a hug or said "Good job!" when we did something worthy of their approval. And the opposite is true. We were scolded or punished if we did things they didn't like. This is how it should be. In fact, this is how we learn right from wrong, for example. But pleasing our parents is deep in the psyche. We have been conditioned most of our lives to listen to them and try to do what they tell us.

Of course, teenagers can and should figure out how to handle this need for parental approval. There are other reasons for living, of course. Eliminating this need would—and should—be impossible, as there is always an appropriate place in a student's life for a parent's opinion. But the act of pushing away often reaches a crescendo in late adolescence—precisely when you are going to college.

On the other hand, you may not want to separate from your parents. Many students of your generation are comfortably intertwined emotionally. "Millennials" are famously connected to their parents, consulting them on all matters and remaining in constant touch by phone, text, and e-mail.[5] The end result is a complicated and contradictory mix of feelings and instincts regarding parents. You want to please them, but you don't. You want to tell them to go away and mind their own business, but you don't. You feel that you should show them your grades as usual, but you're afraid. This ambivalent and problematic mix of feelings creates problems with the motivation you need to work hard. If you start to rebel against your parents, and they provide the main motivation for your studies, you may begin to slip and fall.

Whatever the mix of factors that anchor—or undermine—your motivation to study and learn, losing this motivation can be terrible. This is a problem that has plagued many pre-meds, whose motivations might be thin or misplaced. Perhaps they want to be doctors to please their parents. Or they do not really understand the profession. Or maybe they are young people experiencing the uncertainties of a shifting life.

If this weak ambition is tested with a few poor grades, an unpleasant experience with a research professor, the difficulty of getting a clinical internship, or just a disturbing conversation with another pre-med, a student with little motivation begins to crumble. She thinks, "I've always wanted to be a doctor, or at least I thought I did, and now I'm not really sure. Now I am finding organic chemistry not only difficult, but stupid and pointless." That attitude, however understandable, is a recipe for disaster as she disconnects from the course, ignoring her work, and feeling resentful.

A freshman pre-med advisee of mine named Brian came to my office because he had failed nearly every one of his fall semester courses. These were science courses, the kind in which he had enjoyed success throughout high school. He admitted to me that he took them at Hopkins because he assumed that when he came to college, his easy mastery would continue. In fact, college sciences can be far more aggressive, serious, and complicated than they are at the high school level. But Brian was not really interested in the science, only in the grades he had enjoyed. And his interest in medical school was not based on any deeper appreciation of the profession. His motivations were thin indeed.

Brian began to hate the materials in front of him. He would read some of the textbook and be consumed with resentment. "I can't believe I have to read this stuff. I can't stand even the words I'm reading. I can't believe I'm sitting in this course. I can't believe I have to figure this out. It is just so boring." The intellectual challenge and the richness of the academic experience were now lost on him. He was not thinking about whether he had learned anything new. He had appreciated nothing about the physical sciences. None of that was important. The incentive to get easy, good grades proved as empty as it really is. That motivation, unconnected to real learning, undermined his efforts in the long run. He was left with an empty mission: to earn good grades. That was not enough, so he failed out. He had forgotten how hard he worked to get into college, and how privileged he was to be in college at all.

A lack of motivation is a grave and dangerous place for pre-meds. If they think of their studies only as a means to an end—good grades and medical school admission—they will lack the commitment to excel in the very courses that stand in their way. Finding no real interest in the subject matter, they begin to tank. This is made more likely because many pre-meds take the required courses in chemistry, biology, math, and so on *only because they are required*. They do not want to take these courses; they have to. Life is filled with things we must do. We have to pay bills. We have to pay taxes. We have to go grocery shopping. But we do not have to take academic courses we do not want to take.

Some students have trouble seeing their own lack of motivation. They use passive aggression because they do not want to tell their parents that they do not want to be a doctor. Rather than having an honest, albeit scary, conversation about their future, they stop doing the work necessary to get good grades. As their transcript deteriorates, filled with terrible grades and many repeated courses, they build an increasingly strong case that they should not be going to medical school. They are saying to their parents, "Look, I earned a D in organic chemistry. You can't go to med school with a D. Can't I do something else?" It can be a desperate moment, as the child begs the parent to be released from this contract.

Setting aside the case of pre-meds, students who take courses just because they must are in real peril. Let us say that you sign up for a

European medieval history course because that is required for a major in international studies. You do not really want to learn anything more about European politics or history. Maybe you have done enough of that in high school, or maybe you are just not interested in the Middle Ages. Imagine the resentment that you will have toward that course. Resentment is a powerful, destructive emotion. And it can spill in many directions, creating anger toward a system you will blame for "forcing" you to do things to fulfill choices *you* made. You might be frustrated with the instructor, who keeps giving you poor grades— which you deserve. Worse, you start hating the material, which has no stake in this. So you procrastinate, deluding yourself into thinking you do not need to understand it, and refusing to do the work.

Without motivation, learning has no energy. The educational experience collapses. You do not and will not learn. And the inevitable result is trouble.

Managing Time Poorly

One of the most important changes from high school to college that you will experience is that you have so much time on your own. High school students usually arrive at the school at 8:00 in the morning, and they stay there until 3:00 in the afternoon. All day, every day, they move from class to class, and teachers instruct them in the material. Teachers do a lot of supervision and give a lot of feedback. High school students answer a lot of questions in class, and there is an ongoing discussion of the curriculum and emphasis on its mastery.

High schools have a clear framework for learning. The experience is very regular, predictable, and disciplined. Even students without self-discipline will learn something every day. To sustain this momentum of learning, the high school experience has two features not found in college.

First, high school teachers can require assignments that are due nearly every day. These regular assignments reinforce the expectation that students will complete tasks in a timely way. In other words, there is a disciplined structure in place for managing time. College classes, with few exceptions—perhaps in a language or a writing course—have many fewer assignments, spread out over a 15-week semester. Nor-

Learning to Fail Successfully

LEAH BLATT GLASSER, Ph.D.
DEAN OF FIRST-YEAR STUDIES and LECTURER IN ENGLISH
MOUNT HOLYOKE COLLEGE

In the least conspicuous corner of my office hangs a poster entitled "Freshman Counseling." I inherited it from my predecessor as she gleefully departed. The image, in Dungeons and Dragons style, is daunting.* A tall guard, perhaps the executioner himself, stands masked and towering above a meek first-year student. The guard is holding the end of a long chain around the student's neck; on the other side of the desk sits the homely and obese dean in hooded medieval garb, hunched over, with feather pen in hand, skeptically awaiting the student's explanation. A book called *Career Paths* leans against the leg of the gothic desk.

On the first day of classes one semester, this poster, merely a source of amusement for me on my busiest days, took on new meaning. A student—let us call her Emily—entered my office with her head hanging low. She quite deliberately avoided looking at me as she gripped the letter outlining her poor performance and the terms of academic probation. Emily was already shrugging her shoulders and expressing despair, shame, and apology, even before reaching the seat on the other side of my desk. She glanced over at the poster. Ironically, the ominous image put her at ease, and we had a good laugh for a moment. "I feel just like that kid," she said. Over the course of the next six months, Emily learned how to get rid of the executioner and the chain around her neck, the one *she* had conjured up in her imagination as a result of her failure.

In my role as academic dean, I frequently meet with students on probation who have not yet experienced failure and are consequently paralyzed academically. One of the most pivotal skills for a student who wishes to succeed in the academic arena is the ability to fail well.

"Good failing" requires the strength to make use of a self-generated

---

* The poster, one of a series funded by the Coca-Cola Company, was team-painted by the brothers Greg and Tim Hildebrandt, illustrators and animators who were well known for fantasy art. The posters were created in the 1970s when the Hildebrandts' illustrations of Tolkien's work were popular.

mess. As Anne Lamott explains in *Bird by Bird*, "Perfectionism is the voice of the oppressor, the enemy of the people. It will keep you cramped and insane your whole life." She urges her writers to "go ahead and make big scrawls and mistakes. Perfectionism is a mean, frozen form of idealism, while messes are the artist's true friend. . . . We need to make messes in order to find out who we are and why we are here."* After the mess, learning can begin, and this is precisely what the students I work with discover. Learning how to fail can be more valuable than the lessons learned in the courses in which students ultimately earn A's. The courage to rethink a failed piece of work, to write, rewrite, inquire, and respond to the comments and questions of a critical reader is crucial for anyone aiming to excel in college.

More often than not, students on academic probation resisted turning in an imperfect paper, completing a flawed exam, or appearing in class because they were paralyzed by the fear of criticism. In short, they are bad at failing.

A good example of "bad failing" is the pattern Emily confessed to as she sat in shame during our first meeting. In her first semester, she had been surprised by her low grades (not yet F's) and had subsequently internalized them as symbols of her inadequacies rather than as opportunities for growth. While on probation, Emily learned that criticism is the best gift college can provide. Failure can and should be the key impetus for success. I asked Emily which of the courses from her first semester was her favorite. "Great Books," a first-year writing-intensive seminar, was her favorite even though she had earned a C– in the course. When her first paper came back with exclamation points and question marks in the margins, and the words "we need to meet" at the top of the first page, Emily hid. In her mind, the professor was the judgmental figure behind the big desk in my poster, and only some guard pulling her along with a chain could have gotten her to that office. Avoiding the professor was her way of erasing the reality of those margin-filled papers. It was as if she had convinced herself that if she ignored the comments on her papers, they would not really be there. She dutifully continued to hand in her assignments, and each one was worse than the one

* Anne Lamott, *Bird by Bird* (New York: Doubleday, 1995), pp. 28–32.

continued

before. Her final grade seemed to her something tragic from which she might never recover. Literature was, after all, the field in which she hoped to major.

A decision had to be made now about whether to continue into the second semester of the seminar with the same teacher. "How will you feel if you drop it?" I asked. "Will you miss the discussions and the readings? Were you excited about what you were learning even though the grades were low? Tell me about what you learned." Emily went on for 30 minutes, describing details about what intrigued her and how these texts related to the books she had just picked up for her second semester courses. We determined together that Emily would stay in the course, but that she would no longer be invisible. She would make use of her failure as a vehicle for success. She agreed to meet with her professor on a regular basis, and she learned what it meant to visit a professor during office hours. This became a new strategy for all of her courses, and the transformation yielded remarkable results.

At the end of the semester, the two of us chatted about what had happened to her, or rather, what she had made happen, and we glanced up at the gothic poster on my corner wall. "You know," she said, "the best thing about probation is getting rid of the chains that hold you back."

A version of this essay appeared as a commentary in the *Chronicle of Higher Education* 55, no. 34 (May 1, 2009).

mally, weeks will go by without an assignment due, leaving students unaccountable until a mid-term exam.

Another feature of high school that cannot be found in college: parents are around. Parents get constant feedback from students, from teachers, and from principals. They read report cards. They see how many classes you have missed. They monitor your progress every step of the way. That commitment and interest are probably among the reasons you are in a top college at all. If your parents were not interested in your education, you would be sunk. But when you leave home for college, without that oversight, you lose that framework. While there may be a few commuter students, everyone else is living away from home, often for the very first time. Without your parents around, there is no one to look over your shoulder and say, "Have you done your homework?" "You can't go out; you haven't done your homework yet." Or, "You can't go to the movies with your friends; you've got that essay to write for Mrs. Jones."

So, without the oversight of parents, without the instruction from daily classes, and without the involvement of teachers who know you well, you are on your own—for better and for worse. Your classes now meet every other day or even once a week. Your professors trust you to learn the material outside of class. And there is no one to keep you focused and to turn off the lights when you need sleep. With your time unstructured and unsupervised, you are likely to let your school work float without direction or focus.

This would a disastrous excess of freedom were it not for the other obligations of life—eating, bathing, washing clothes—and the commitments from other activities and obligations. For example, student athletes have practices, travel, and games that give their lives framework, discipline, and regularity. They have coaches who want them to stay out of trouble, keep their academic eligibility, and succeed athletically. This culture, particularly in NCAA Division III schools, usually supports a healthy culture of academic success. Athletes can make very good students. They realize rather quickly that they have very little time to waste. When they can grab an hour or two in between activities, class, or practice, they grab it and study with keen focus. They do not waste it. And, of course, student athletes who do not appreciate this are the first people to lose their eligibility and fail out of school. Other activities create similar structure for nonathletes. They could have rehearsals for orchestra, for a singing group, or for a drama group. They might belong to clubs that have meetings and offer activities at specific times during the week.

Naturally, these activities can consume too much time. College athletes can be too committed to training and competing. Campus newspaper editors can spend too many late nights putting out the paper. Fraternities may demand too many "rush" activities of a freshman who would love to join. But these are stories of excess. For the most part, and certainly in contrast to high school, a college student's time is her own. How she manages that time will have a crucial effect on whether she learns and succeeds—or does not.

Finally, there is a large group of students who waste their time completely. The Internet is the primary reason for this, drawing students in for hours of surfing, watching YouTube, updating Facebook pages, e-mailing or tweeting friends, and gambling. This last one is highly troubling, as many students I know compound the problem of wasted time with financial risk. But Facebook is rapidly becoming the most powerful destroyer of productive time, though I'm sure it will be succeeded soon by another version of social media that's even more time consuming. Other students fail to get involved in anything interesting or productive—I am always amazed at the number of uninvolved freshmen, the same people who overloaded on activities to impress college admission deans—and so their days have no anchor at all. What should take them three hours to do now takes six, some of which is spent on the trivial.

Of course, it is fine to do juvenile things, to communicate, and to have downtime. Playing video games and watching TV and movies, along with these other distractions, provide a healthy and needed break from the intensity of academic work in a competitive college. But all of these activities have addicting qualities that many students cannot resist. They are more fun, and more exciting, than studying. That is especially true if a student has made poor choices of courses and does not care for the material. Such activities are a real danger for students, even a cancer, taking them away from more meaningful activities with direct human contact and away from their work. Failing to control their power is a guaranteed act of self-destruction.

Weak Study Skills and Talent

One might expect that students at good colleges have sharpened their skills for learning and studying. Didn't they get admitted because of that? In fact, students vary a lot in their ability to be effective learners, and those with poor study skills have a lot of struggles, particularly in the first year. On one end of this spectrum are students who come from highly selective, extremely competitive prep schools. These schools include Andover in Massachusetts, Exeter in New Hampshire, Riverdale in New York, and Sidwell Friends in Washington, DC. Some of these schools, like St. Paul's or Deerfield, have a residential compo-

Time to Fail

JOHN T. O'KEEFE, Ph.D.

DIRECTOR OF ADVISING AND
ACADEMIC SUPPORT SERVICES and CLASS DEAN
WELLESLEY COLLEGE

There is never enough time to do our best. If fact, it can seem to many students that there is only time enough to fail. Often, there is the sense that just a little more time to prepare or study or write would prevent failure. Students may feel that hectic schedules and the many demands on their time inevitably produce poor work and poor grades. With failures cascading one upon another as the semester comes to an ugly close, students can feel time passing all too rapidly. What can follow then is a loss of control—over time, work, expectations, and prospects.

Better time management is one simple answer to this issue, but the diagnosis is usually much easier than the cure. There are lots of excellent strategies for managing time: realizing how you spend time now, careful scheduling, using a planner, prioritizing in advance, and so on. These tools can work well and can help you make choices that will give you balance in your work. There may not be enough time in the day to succeed perfectly at every task you face, but good time management can help you succeed at the things that are most important.

Refocusing on your principal goals is one way to regain control over an unraveling situation. It is not easy to look beyond the most immediate needs when assignments and exams are pressing, but keep in mind that college isn't about demonstrating perfection, but about learning. If you're able to articulate something about the knowledge or skills you've acquired even in the middle of what feels like helpless floundering, you are on your way to redeeming yourself after failure. There may not be time for perfection, but there is time for real achievement, however modest. Managing your time better and acknowledging your achievements can turn a sense of failure into a recognition that you are moving forward.

nent; their students have an added advantage to the rigorous training they receive because they are already accustomed to living independently from their parents. Many independent schools and some public magnet schools offer an education which requires managing many hours of studying; students with this kind of background find it much easier to handle the open landscape of college.

But many other students in top colleges come from far less rigorous programs. That does not make them less deserving, but it does make them less prepared for the demands of college. Competitive colleges would not have the richness of experience, the geographic reach, nor the economic diversity they now enjoy if they did not accept students outside elite prep and public schools. Outside of these selective schools, there is much more variation in how well prepared students are for independent learning outside the classroom.

So, within a given class at any college, students will differ considerably in how well they know how to study and to manage their time. If you found your high school undemanding and you only studied a few hours a week, you may not realize how much time you waste when you sit down to study. You may not have very good note-taking skills. If you have not been asked to write many papers, your writing skills may be quite weak. And the challenge is that many students are not aware of these weaknesses, at least not right away.

One of the only predictors of good grades at Johns Hopkins is the number of hours a week a student is accustomed to studying. Because Hopkins has such smart students, many of them will say they sailed through high school on fewer than 10 hours' study a week. If freshmen continue that practice in college, they will have a problem adjusting to the college environment, where they need to study somewhere between 20 and 30 hours a week on their own. When you have to double the amount of time that you need to study, that can be a shock. If you have to triple the time, that can be terrible. You may have the focus, the motivation, and the work ethic to do more, but if you do not know what to do, then much of your new effort will be wasted.

More often than not, this lack of preparation results in B-level grades. That might be disappointing for students with high expectations and long histories of A-level work, and they may simply adjust to that reality and make efforts to be more efficient and effective over time. But on occasion, students' study skills are so poor that they contribute to another set of issues that can really cause a student to have trouble.

A related—but much more delicate—explanation for academic struggles is talent.[6] A lack of talent can cause serious difficulties. I enter this discussion with some trepidation. We all acknowledge that some people are more talented than others, but since education can be seen as an equalizer, you might also think that support and hard work can overcome a lack of talent. That seems like a very American concept, where a national sense of equality is grounded in learning. Still, we celebrate those among us who excel, and we think at least some of that success is rooted in talent.

Perhaps a better phrase for "talent" is "getting it." In my experience, for a given subject, there are students who "get it" and those that do not. For example, learning a foreign language certainly requires discipline, persistence, and hard work. But you may not "get it." College may be too late in your life for you to have retained the natural skill to construct a new linguistic framework.

The inability to "get it," to have natural skills in addition to learned skills, is most pronounced in math and the sciences. This is the only explanation I can find for the fact that some students really struggle with these subjects, but not for lack of trying. These students work really hard. They are focused and dedicated, often to a fault and to the exclusion of healthy, balanced distractions. They are also intelligent, capable of learning at a sophisticated, intense level. But for whatever reason, they just cannot see the world as a chemist does, for example. They cannot connect the concepts in a chemistry course like organic chemistry, which demands application of key ideas to new problems—not simple memorization.

I have had plenty of students come to me perplexed about their poor grades. They report their long hours, and they think that they just need to work harder. We discuss the likelihood that they are inefficient workers, focusing on learning by rote rather than problem-solving. If that does not explain the problem, we will go through a long list of other possibilities. But if we exhaust those theories, I have to ask gently, "Is it possible that you are just not 'good' at this? Do you have to be good at this? Is it possible you'd be better at something else?" Those questions are fraught with peril for any advisor, as it might sound like a condemnation. But I am trying to suggest that their intelligence and effort might be better spent studying another subject. When you decide on a particular subject, it is important that you get satisfaction from it—at least in part because you are good at it. You should not have to struggle with the mastery of its concepts; they should come relatively easily. You "get it." When asked to perform in that field, you don't need to expend Herculean effort for mediocre results. Success, in part, comes from inside you. But the reverse must also be true. If you do not "get it," you will face more than your share of difficulties.

Unhealthy, Unhappy, Unsuccessful

The final main reason students struggle in their classes is poor physical and mental health. Physically, students lead challenging, even punishing lives. Some of them are athletes and push themselves to excel, but often too hard and without regard to leaving sufficient energy for intellectual work. All students try to take full advantage of their young systems to live a life that is, quite frankly, self-abusive. They get very little sleep, finally knocking off at 2:00 or 3:00 in the morning. They experiment with or use drugs. They smoke, although smoking has lost its cachet as the traditional college partner of studying and coffee drinking. They often eat poorly, despite the best efforts of a school to offer healthy alternatives through its meal plan. They may not get enough exercise.

More commonly, students have drinking problems. Binge drinking and alcohol abuse are at all-time highs among those of college age,[7] despite the fact that the drinking age is supposed to make access to alcohol impossible for at least half of the student population. Everyone except state legislators knows that the 21-year-old drinking age is a joke. Students have started drinking in high school—sometimes before that.[8] They continue those habits, and expand them, into their college years. Alcohol is a necessity at college parties, and many students take pride in recounting stories of drinking until they black out. Of course, not every drinker is an abusive drinker; most students are not. Nevertheless, use or abuse of alcohol does not make the academic enterprise easier, affecting memory, recall, and stamina.

Doubt, Disillusionment, Disappointment, and Despair
Confronting Freshman Anxieties

JULIE LYTHCOTT-HAIMS, J.D.
DEAN OF FRESHMEN AND UNDERGRADUATE ADVISING and
ASSOCIATE VICE PROVOST FOR UNDERGRADUATE EDUCATION
STANFORD UNIVERSITY

A common quip on our campus is that Stanford students are like ducks—calm on the surface but paddling like mad underneath in order to get where they are going. Like any population of intelligent, ambitious high-achievers, our students work very hard. And things don't always go their way. But Stanford students seem to think they are supposed to act relaxed and upbeat all the time, even when they are really feeling quite the opposite. Deliberately hiding negative emotions is a lonely enterprise, and it's hard work to boot. It doesn't take a clinical psychologist to know that no matter how well this works for ducks, it is not so great for people. It's okay to admit it when things aren't going so well.

In early January, 16 weeks after freshmen begin their Stanford undergraduate experience, we gather them for "Mid Year Convocation," an event that offers a careful examination not of their hopes and ideals but of their worst fears. Unlike the frenzied hoopla of orientation, winter quarter is a good time to reach first-year students. They have a set of grades under their belts and a quarter's worth of experiences fresh in their memories, and we know that many and perhaps most are feeling to a greater or lesser extent that things are not going quite as planned.

Some students worry about not measuring up academically, harboring the typical "I am the admissions mistake" doubts and fears. Some are feeling like outsiders, not yet having found academic, extracurricular, and social niches. Some are disappointed because coveted opportunities have eluded them (and they are accustomed to achieving most things they seek). Some worry that Stanford seems to have fallen short of their expectations. Some fear their dreams of being a doctor have evaporated because they outright failed O-Chem. And the duck syndrome means that to the extent

continued

they are facing a struggle, they struggle alone, wondering "what is wrong with me?" while everyone else appears to be high-achieving and relaxed.

Our aim with Mid Year Convocation is to surface feelings of doubt, disillusionment, disappointment, and even despair, and to dispel the sense of outsider status associated with these emotions. Coupled with the goal of normalizing these feelings, we aim to instill in the freshmen a sense of ownership of the matter—to help them understand that acknowledging their concerns and seeking out support and resources is the healthy thing to do. The stars of the event are the upperclassmen, whose narratives reveal that Stanford students often struggle. Embedded in the narratives are the numerous resources and supports the campus offers. Failure can happen to anyone, even to those for whom you might least expect it.

Here are some of those upperclassman narratives from the past few years.

Sophia: The Pre-Med Who Failed Organic Chemistry

Chemistry 33 was challenging in a way I had never known; it required me to think in an entirely new way, to imagine how molecules I'd never seen behaved and interacted. I tried doing the reading, but got lost in all the details. I thought everything would work out in the end. I'd ace the final or pull through with a great grade in section.

Two days before the beginning of summer break after taking the final, I got an e-mail from the Registrar. I had flat-out failed Chemistry 33. I felt stupid—hundreds of other students did fine in organic chemistry; why not me? Clearly, I wasn't cut out for medical school; I even wondered whether I was cut out for Stanford at all.

When I returned to school for sophomore year I started taking advantage of one of Stanford's most amazing resources—its people. I talked to a mentor about the importance of finding what it is you are passionate about. I made an appointment to talk with a professor at the medical school who had taught my Alternative Spring Break class. We ended up talking about why he chose to go into medicine and the effect it has had on his life. I felt my desire to become a doctor beginning to stir again.

I re-took Chemistry 33 during my sophomore year. I attended every outreach session, and all of my section leader's office hours. I joined a study group to go over problem sets. I met with a learning specialist to talk about how I could maximize my ability to study chemistry. Maybe most importantly, I was honest with myself and with my parents about how challenging I found this course. I got frustrated a lot, but something told me to keep going. That March I received a B.

I am now a first-year medical student at Stanford. The first year of medical school is a lot like my first year as an undergraduate. I am trying to figure out who I am and who I want to be, what my interests are, and how I can get to where I want to go. I am back to knocking on professor's doors, trying to find out about research projects and different fields of medicine. Many of the resources I take advantage of are similar to those I sought help from as an undergraduate—my advisors, the career center, my classmates, and my family.

For better or for worse, I still grapple with my fear of failure. I am not always positive that I'll make it, but I am positive that I will keep trying because I am no longer afraid to ask for help. Sometimes failure can teach you a lot.

Alex: Is Psychology a "Real" Major?

My first year, I took a fascinating course in psychology. Throughout the quarter, I found myself looking forward to each week's readings and even ventured into the normally untouched supplementary readings. By quarter's end, I had decided that psychology was the path for me.

However, my conviction did not remain steadfast for long. For the rest of my freshman year, I received a barrage of both intended and unintended condescension from my peers: "Psychology's not a real major." "Psych classes are so easy." "You don't learn anything useful from Psych." By sophomore year, I was ready to find my calling in a "real" major.

My passion for psychology was reaffirmed when I took two higher-level psychology courses later in my sophomore year. These courses completely reshaped the way I viewed and judged human interactions, relationships, and life in general. The fact that I took away so much from them convinced me that I had chosen the right major for myself all along.

It can sometimes be difficult to stand up to the seemingly ubiquitous pressure to choose a "real" major. Fortunately, I had stumbled

continued

upon amazing resources and people at Stanford that supported me the whole way. Some of my professors helped solidify my interest in the field. Most professors are very willing to set aside time to talk to a student who displays genuine interest in their discipline.

Ultimately, majors don't matter. What matters is that you learn to be passionate about something and then be disciplined enough to see it through. Once you do that, you've proven the more important point: that you can not only educate yourself, but you care enough to do so. All majors at Stanford teach you the necessary critical thinking and analytical skills that will serve you well on the job. To my surprise as a newly graduated college student, I found that companies like Google do not care if you majored in English, or economics, or psychology. They care that you are dedicated and passionate about what you do, and that this passion will also carry over to the work you do later in life.

Kelsey: The Self-Doubting Superstar

A superstar. That was my label in high school. I was the best of the best. I graduated second in a class of 600, and I was the pride and honor of my teachers, my parents, my family, and my peers. However, my first year at Stanford got off to a rocky start because my ego caused me to hide my fears and doubts deeply within myself.

Looking back, I realize that I simply failed to adequately manage my time. I only had two to three hours of class a day, something unheard of in high school, but instead of taking advantage of my valuable time, I procrastinated like never before. The work piled up. Thirty pages of reading behind schedule turned into 200 over a week and a half. I slowly drowned in the stress of readings and problem sets. I started loathing my courses not because they were boring, but because I simply could not handle the workload.

When I asked other students how they were doing, they said things like, "Oh, I'm loving this class. I'm caught up with the reading and I already started my paper," or "Yeah, I'm already done with the problem set for next week." I felt frustrated and incompetent. Everyone seemed to be able to read faster, to type faster, to study harder, and to simply perform better than me. I wondered why I was no longer a superstar. But I was asking the wrong question.

After receiving a C– on my first college paper, I felt humiliated and worthless, and that I had failed miserably.

I no longer felt like myself, no longer the successful young man that had arrived only two weeks prior, but instead, a defeated dimwit who could not even achieve mediocrity. I closed myself in a bubble of despair and panic. I was too proud to talk to anyone about how I was feeling from fear of being judged or looked down upon. These feelings lasted throughout the term. My fear of failure was so great that I actually gave up writing my final core humanities paper altogether.

My self-doubt spilled over into my other classes. I was doing so poorly that I was unsure if I would return to Stanford for winter quarter.

Surprisingly, when I returned home for winter break, instead of receiving me with remorse, my family welcomed me home with open arms and with an aura of celebration. Over the break I rested physically, emotionally, and mentally and felt a new spirit within me. I found a stronger person that I had allowed to remain dormant. In January I returned to Stanford ready to redeem myself.

I took advantage of my campus resources and scheduled an appointment with an academic advisor at the Undergraduate Advising Programs Office. I learned how to manage my time and how to handle the workload while still enjoying time for myself. I met with dorm staff and kept them posted on my progress. I even scheduled an appointment with a counselor at Counseling and Psychological Services and learned that I just experienced something common among freshmen. With that good news, I was ready to get back on my feet.

Over the next few weeks I continued to improve in my classes and to adjust to life at Stanford. That quarter I grew to love living at Stanford and earned better grades. When the 10 weeks came to an end I knew I could hold my own and make it on the Farm.

None of my accomplishments would have been possible without help from my advisors, professors, friends, and family. Succeeding in college is not easy. Success consists of very hard work and dedication, but you deserve to be here and are just as capable of making it as anyone. For students who struggle, help is available. All you need to do is ask.

continued

Wilson: The Student Who Flunked Out

At one point or another, we all fail. Whether it's during your 4 years in college or whether it's 10 years down the road, failure is an inevitability. I was the first graduate of my high school to ever go to a school as highly ranked as Stanford. I had perfect grades, played two sports, had great test scores, and was extremely involved in extracurricular activities. But immediately upon arriving on campus, I started to feel like I was not as smart as I had once thought I was.

For a long time I thrived on being excellent at everything. And all of a sudden, that was no longer possible. At Stanford (and, as I later learned, in life in general), there was always someone who was better or smarter than I was. By winter quarter of sophomore year, my motivation had dwindled. So I stopped going to classes. For the first time in my life, I wasn't passing a class. I just wasn't doing what I was supposed to be doing. And I wasn't asking myself, "Could I have worked harder?" or "Did I really take advantage of all the resources I had available to me? Could I have read more, or gone to office hours, or studied up on some of the things that I didn't really understand in the library? Did I really put forth the effort required to get the results that I wanted?" For all of these questions, the answer was "No."

But see, I didn't see my situation that way. Instead, I thought I just wasn't as good as the next girl or guy in my classes. When I started to doubt myself, my behavior followed suit. I partied on weeknights. I missed more classes and failed more tests. By spring quarter of that year, I was drinking or doing drugs every day. Every single day.

Stanford could tell that things weren't right with me, and they suspended me for a year.

I didn't tell my parents for months, because I had totally let them down. I did tell my grandmother, and she said, "What's in the past is in the past. What's in the future is uncertain. Today is all you've got. Do what you have to do today, and forget about all the rest of that stuff."

And so for a year I worked, audited classes, and desperately tried to get back into Stanford. I took things one day at a time. I worked on one problem at a time, because in all honesty, my situation did not look good. Eventually I returned to school committed to doing better. And life is awesome right now. My grades are great, too. But I don't even care about that stuff. Because grades are someone else's measure of my success. Forget about other people's standards. Forget about what other people are doing. Do what you know is right. Do what you want to do. Do what's going to make you happy. Because doing that so far has gotten you to where you are today. The only reason that I "failed" was because I stopped holding myself to my own standards and started measuring myself by everyone else's standards. If you feel like you just have to get an A in a class, then do what you've got to do to get that A. But it is my humblest recommendation that you take just one step back, realize there's more to life than some professor's evaluation of you, and just go to bed at night a better person in some way than you were when you woke up. Look for those day-to-day challenges, and tackle them. Because the days add up, and one day you'll be able to look at yourself in the mirror and know that you're successful, regardless of your GPA, or your parents' opinion, how much money you're making, or what the gossipers say. You can do it.

While young, college students push themselves so hard that they are unusually vulnerable to diseases. They do not get enough sleep. They also live in close quarters. Public health officials, I am sure, despair at dormitories.[9] They are like Petri dishes for bacteria and viruses. So students suffer from a steady stream of colds, flu, mononucleosis, and many other common problems. If a student is academically vulnerable already, getting sick can make a bad situation a disaster. The same would be true for injury, though there are usually services available to those students, such as note-taking and classroom accommodations.

By far, however, the greatest danger to a student's success and academic standing is poor mental health. There is a quiet desperation on college campuses today as growing numbers of students battle depression, eating disorders, anxiety, and many other emotional challenges. This is a world that most other students do not see, but it is quite real and an enormous challenge to students, families, faculty, and administrators. Counseling offices have become extraordinarily important in this battle for better mental health, and the number of students they see seems to grow without end.

I have had countless conversations with these students. They are disconnected, uninterested, detached. Their levels of anxiety range from fears of failure or of social situations that trap them in their room, to simple test anxiety that trips them up in exams, even when they are fully prepared. They have crippling addictions to gambling, online games, or alcohol. Sometimes these are new problems, perhaps triggered by a serious loss or failure, like the death of a parent or unexpected difficulty in a critical course. Other times, these are problems they have faced much of their lives, so they are accustomed to therapy and medications. Whatever the mix of problems, it is heartbreaking to sit across from someone so promising and smart who must battle demons no one deserves. More often than not, when such conditions are untreated, the first casualty is academic failure, which compounds the problem.

♣ Put It in Perspective

This discussion has offered a contrast in tone and content from the other chapters. Here, we have focused on failure and its causes, as I encourage you to develop the habit of self-assessment when you're struggling. I have grouped the reasons for academic struggles into four wide categories: lack of motivation, poor time management, weak study skills and talent, and poor mental and physical health. These four often work in tandem or combination, one leading to another. Depression, for example, will by definition cripple anyone's motivation. Someone with little talent for a subject will get discouraged, start avoiding the subject, fall behind, and then fail. Or a student might be perfectly well motivated but devote so much time to Facebook that she falls behind. The list of causes for academic struggle is thus long and interrelated.

For the next habit, we will discuss what to do about these problems. But before we do, I want to return to the challenge of encountering failure. It is akin to being in a car accident. As you drive, you acknowledge the possibility of collision. You take precautions, such as navigating carefully or judging your speed appropriately. But you do not spend a lot of time thinking about this; you have confidence in your abilities, and you expect to get where you are going without delay or costs or conflict. Then you hit something. If you are lucky, the accident is minor; no one is hurt, and the damage is to the cars only. If you are not,

➤➤ The Highs and the Lows of the First Year ◄◄

THOMAS N. CHIAROLANZIO, M.A.

ASSOCIATE DEAN, GEORGETOWN COLLEGE

GEORGETOWN UNIVERSITY

The post-Thanksgiving period is probably one of the most stressful times for our first-year students. The work has piled up, and only a few days of class remain before study days and exams and final papers. Some students tend to procrastinate, believing there is ample time to get everything done and still pull off the good grades they're used to getting.

After advising students at Georgetown for over 13 years, I have witnessed all types of behaviors and excuses about not keeping up with the work. One year, I received several emails from professors concerned about one student, whom I'll call Sean, who had been missing class and was falling behind on assignments. A graduate of a strong public high school in the Midwest, Sean had completed several AP classes, earned 4's and 5's on most of the exams, scored high on entrance exams, and earned solid grades. Based on his high school transcript and the glowing recommendations written on his behalf, Sean should have been able to handle the work at Georgetown. I immediately contacted him to express my concerns and ask that he see me the next day.

In our meeting, Sean admitted to struggling in his two classes that required extensive reading and paper writing. He came clean about missing class and falling behind, and said he had hoped to catch up over the Thanksgiving break. I appreciated his honesty while expressing my worries about his behavior.

I encouraged Sean to reach out to his professors for help. We also discussed time management and the help our Academic Resource Center could provide. Finally, I let Sean know about potential outcomes if he did not pass his classes, including academic probation and suspension. When Sean left my office, I had an uneasy feeling because I was not confident he would follow my advice. I e-mailed his professors to let them know of our meeting and my instructions. Unfortunately, my hunch came true, as Sean did not reach out to his professors and tried to go it alone. He finished the semester with one D and one F.

continued

I received a furious phone call from Sean's father right before the winter holiday. How could Sean wind up with such poor grades without his father knowing? Why didn't Georgetown do something to prevent this? It was one of those hold-the-phone-away-from-your-ear moments. Eventually, I let him know that Sean had to give permission for me to answer his questions. I explained that the deans would be reviewing Sean's overall record in early January to determine his status.

Sean was asked to provide the Dean's Office with an explanation about his performance in the fall and to elaborate on why he should not be suspended for the spring term. He wrote a letter promising that next semester would be different. We allowed him to return but placed him on academic probation and provided conditions for his probation. Despite his best intentions, Sean was ultimately suspended after he again fell behind on assignments and received poor grades during the spring semester.

For Sean, the first year of college was the most difficult year of his life. He had never struggled like this before and had never thought that after his first year he would be returning home. While away from school during his probationary period, Sean got a job and committed himself to it. He read in his spare time, and realized that he had let go of a wonderful opportunity. After spending seven months away, Sean was ready to return to Georgetown. He returned with motivation, dedication, and renewed energy. He found his courses interesting, stayed on top of his assignments, and received positive feedback from his professors. He was more mature, understood what his limitations were, and genuinely seemed to want to be a Georgetown student again. He changed some old habits, and whenever he felt that he might fall behind, he would talk to his professors. Sean mastered his courses and earned three A's and a B. After the term ended, I talked with him and asked him what he thought triggered the success. He said he just hadn't been ready to tackle college-level work right after high school.

I don't believe Sean felt that he deserved to be at Georgetown, and he may have been burned out from working so hard in high school. Time away from academic life was the best thing for him. When he returned, he was more mature, more motivated, and truly wanted to learn. He wanted to earn an education when he was ready. Fortunately, Sean's self-esteem was not so damaged that he couldn't recover. Virtually every student can succeed even if, at times, the goal is blurred. It just may take some time.

car and drivers can be damaged seriously. The accident itself, however serious, has an unreal quality to it. It has an unexpected nature. The attention you are getting and the inconvenience you have caused and suffered seem strange and incomprehensible. You may not understand what happened, or you might be clearly to blame. The emotions swirl, from shame to anger to dismay to anxiety to regret. It is a mess you never expected as you left your driveway that morning.

A student at a good college is a great driver with a spotless record. She worked hard and enjoyed the approval and admiration of many: teachers, parents, siblings, fellow students, maybe others. She could get from starting point A to destination B so easily. She understood where to go and how to get there and enjoyed the pleasures of always doing that with predictable success. And now that record is fading, crumbling, or shattered.

Poor grades, sometimes rare, sometimes common, reflect a deeper problem in learning. Struggling students lose their grip on an identity shaped by success and outcomes everyone could see. Sometimes they can forgive themselves, but it is difficult because the stakes are high and the problem so unforeseen.

Facing failure is grim work for anyone, but it seems especially strange and terrible to a student who expected to continue being the "best of the best." The seriousness of the situation depends, again, on how you defined success—and so, failure—to begin with. I have argued that if you measure success with grades or simple outcomes like admission to a specific graduate school, then you will be devastated when those measurements fall short. If, on the other hand, you think of the infinite ways to learn, to be engaged intellectually, then you will not be so dependent on those fickle ways to be successful. You can be disappointed when you did not get the grade you wanted from a course, but your ability to see what you *did* learn will ease that pain.

Cope with Failure by Rebuilding and Forgiving

Recovering from our failures is the greatest challenge we face at any time of life. Ironically, the failures themselves feed a feeling that they cannot be overcome. But successfully recovering from our mistakes and weaknesses can be enormously rewarding and satisfying, like a cool drink after a hot day without water. Figuring out how to rebound from disaster is a vital skill, one you will rely upon all of your life. In the more immediate future, if you've had academic struggles, you need to regain your footing to rediscover the importance of learning and earning a degree. You'll want to move on to new challenges; college should be a step in that progress, not a barrier. That is why Habit #10 on the Dean's List is *Cope with Failure by Rebuilding and Forgiving*.

When faced with the challenge of rebounding, you can make choices. The most critical choice is to get help. This chapter is an effort to give you that help, so I appreciate that you are reading this. But reading will do little beyond provoking thought or discussion. To make this real, to move on to success, you need the support of family, friends, mentors, counselors, and others. Those people can give you ideas, skills, and inspiration. They can help you find willpower to change when yours is lacking. Any investment you can make in open and honest relationships with those around you, especially with your parents, will yield great rewards when your reserve of willpower is low.

Ultimately, however, the willpower, the desire for change and improvement, is for you to choose. I offer the following suggestions—organized to parallel the diagnoses from Habit #9 (lack of motivation, poor time management, weak study skills or lack of talent, and poor health)—with the knowledge that advice can only go so far. You must internalize it, embrace it, and have a clear feeling that you can move on and ultimately succeed.

Find Motivation in New Places

A lack of motivation is a difficult handicap to overcome, but it's critical to restarting your intellectual engine. A student with little motivation approaches her studies with a sense of obligation rather than a sense of joy. She crams things into her head because she knows she must, rather than absorbing things because she wants to understand them.

But how do you shift from an unhealthy or weak motivation to one that is more positive and internalized? This begins with tearing down some of the barriers standing between you and a healthier attitude toward your education. If you take a look at Habit #5, *Understand That Majors and Careers Are Not the Same Thing*, you will see the argument that the majors that students choose in college have nothing (or little) to do with their later careers or professions. There are, of course, some exceptions to this. But for most colleges, it is difficult to draw a line between academic study and professional development. One area of academic study is just as legitimate and potentially as professionally useful as any other, particularly in a liberal arts environment. This is a very liberating idea, relieving you of the pressure of choosing one over another, and eliminating the worry that if you choose poorly, you've ruined your future.

If you are not prejudiced against any particular area of study, you can enjoy success in unexpected quarters. Any area of study can offer you great intellectual joys, provided that it suits your needs and fulfills your sense of curiosity. *You can recapture your motivation for hard work and success by finding an area of study that fits you.* You must find a major, a minor, and other academic programs that really excite you intellectually, and set aside all other considerations, particularly those judgments about the "usefulness," "marketability," or popularity of a particular field of study. If you favor an academic program for its intellectual pleasures, then you will find the internal desire to learn. You will just want to learn more.

Recapturing motivation, then, begins with a deliberate effort to rekindle an innate sense of curiosity. Once you have given yourself the luxury of choice and have unplugged the expectations of others and of yourself, you will be free to explore, to find things that are interesting to you.

I always caution students about how they define *interesting*, a term at the heart of intellectual motivation. Naturally, when we make the judgment that something is interesting, it is based on previous knowledge. Otherwise, there would be no basis for the label. For example, knowing a little bit about ancient history could make a student interested in systems of governance, philosophical questions, and the art work of classical Greece. Because he has a framework upon which to make sense of Greece—he knows where it is located, roughly what timeframe we are considering, and the critical role that Greece played in the development of Western civilization—he has a basis for understanding that something set in the classical period would be interesting and important.

Another subject, say economics, might seem very dull to him. But before he makes that call, he should consider why it seems dull to him at that moment. It is possible, of course, that his judgment is based on a full and fair exposure to the subject. He has taken a few economics courses, attended a brown bag lecture, and followed the news in *Forbes* and the *Wall Street Journal*. He takes his pulse. Nothing. Truly dull.

It is equally possible that he does not know what he is talking about. He either thinks it could be boring, perhaps from a rumor, or he is intimidated by the work it will take to see if economics is worthwhile. His initial ignorance is a barrier to learning anything more.

A senior at Hopkins once told me that she would never have thought of becoming a sociology major if she had not stumbled onto a course, thanks to university distribution requirements. She took the course, and somewhat by accident, she found the questions that were being discussed very interesting. They resonated with her. If she had just chosen her required courses off a menu, she might never have learned that. She would have seen the word *sociology*, not understood what it meant or what researchers in the field discover, and then moved on. It is like a large menu at a Chinese restaurant. There are a number of choices that seem very familiar. You might choose to order those, avoiding a whole set of dishes that seem mysterious and potentially risky.

Choosing course work and majors is much more important than choosing a meal, but having higher stakes does not mean that these choices should be conservative. In fact, early in college and early in every semester, choosing courses is easier than picking Chinese dishes off that menu. When you order a strange entree, you will not know whether you like it, or even what it looks like, until it arrives at your table—and then it is too late. Choosing courses is more like taking small samples from a buffet, and even then, you are not committed to "eating" them. In the first week or two of classes, you can sit in on a class for the entire period or even just a few minutes to sample what that course will taste like.

But there are many other tools you can use to explore and find something that excites and motivates you—at very little cost. One of my favorite suggestions is to go to the university bookstore. College and university bookstores have an entire section, perhaps a whole floor, dedicated to textbooks and other readings from the entire curriculum. Most students see this resource in its most obvious role, a place where you go to buy books for the courses you are taking. But I also see it as a place for previewing those very courses, which can be done not only at the beginning of the term but at any time during the term. Most stores simply leave those leftover books on the shelf until they decide to either store them or return them to the publisher.

So if you are curious about what anthropology is all about, you should go to the anthropology section of the bookstore. You can pull some of these books off of the shelf, sit down on the floor, and read them for a few minutes. You can grab a lot of them and try different areas. You could glance at them as you would magazines on a rack in an airport. You should get a sense of the field, and the courses offered within it, simply by looking at what the department considers important enough to put on a syllabus. If you find that an hour has flown by before you look up, then anthropology might be your thing.

You can also make a deliberate effort to look at areas that you do *not* think are interesting. Since you probably do not fully understand all the disciplines—no one does—your impressions may be wrong. When you pick up a textbook on archaeology or on earth sciences, you may find yourself completely entranced by the text. You should not fight those feelings. They are the beginnings of a flame of learning. You want to build that flame and encourage it, whether you've been struggling academically or not. So, going to the bookstore can be an excellent way to get a sense, in a matter of minutes or at most a few hours, of the full academic range of choices that could really excite and motivate you to excellence.

Another option for exploration, again at relatively little cost, is to surf the Web sites of the various academic departments. This may be a more obvious suggestion to a digital generation, but it is stunning to learn from unmotivated students that they did not think of doing this— or did not make the effort if they did. In many cases, department Web sites are not designed to market a given subject, although they may be used to recruit graduate students. Most of these sites are straightforward, with links to faculty, research, courses, and so on. They are not written in a way that is designed to sell anything. But that has great merits. If you are wondering whether political science is a good fit for you, it is important to know the normal world of political scientists, not some slick version of that (if that is possible!).

A "normal" political science Web site can show you which individual political scientists belong to the department. No two political science departments are alike because they each have a different mix of faculty members, with varying areas of expertise, research agendas, and seniority. Naturally, faculty cannot offer courses in areas that they know nothing about. So, unless you are still looking for colleges or plan to transfer, there is little point in knowing about the discipline generally. You need to know about *your* college's department and decide whether what it has to offer is interesting to you.

A third way to explore, and to rediscover motivation, is to talk to people. The most obvious people are those students who are particularly interested in their studies. It is possible that their interests will match yours, though you should remember that just because you are friends with someone does not mean your academic tastes are compatible. But if other students can share their love of a discipline and of that faculty with you, that love may be infectious—so it's worth a try. They can report on whether faculty in that department are especially engaged, caring, and accessible. They can say whether classes are small, interactive, and fun. You can do this more systematically by examining course evaluations compiled by the college. Any department with a great reputation deserves a second look, irrespective of subject matter. And it could be a perfect, motivating choice for you.

Another group of people to talk to are the faculty themselves. You might be surprised by how few students do this, mostly because they think such a meeting is contrived and because the faculty intimidate them. But if you do not know what sociologists do, you should ask a sociologist. Like all professionals, they would be happy to tell you about themselves and their field. This conversation should not focus on requirements. There is no point for you to look at requirements until you are convinced that your curiosity will be satisfied by this course of study. Seeing the world through the lens of obligation and requirements may have gotten you in trouble in the first place. So you should stay away from requirements and think about what it is that you want to learn.

Examining the curriculum and the faculty in greater detail should help you decide on an interesting course of study. But what if it does not? You have some other options. Many students are so goal-oriented that they must see professional merit in a subject matter for it to have interest. Yet these can be the same students who do not know what they want to do, so logically nothing has interest for them. Those students need career counseling, an invaluable experience that can help them think systematically about their options. Meeting working professionals and alumni doing something "interesting" can have the same effect. If some of the choices they learn about excite them, then students can try to create connections between the career and their major. (Here I use "create" deliberately, as I have already argued that such connections are weak. But if seeing stronger connections helps to get you jump-started, please do so.) Such conversations, counseling sessions, and research may also help a struggling student see how important her degree will be to a new life. She may see how the skills and perspective she'd get from a college education will push her career forward. Seeing the value of her education, then, she can regain momentum and motivation.

Another option for reigniting curiosity is to leave college—for just a while. This may seem heretical to those who expect a simple road to graduation and happiness. But when a student is really struggling academically, he has already veered off that road. Leaving college can give him time to gain the maturity and self-discipline he needs. There is nothing like working as a waiter or, as one of my advisees did, at a glass factory to cause one to quickly realize that a bachelor's degree is a very good idea. But that is a negative lesson: the student is faced with some terrible alternative (like the dangers of a glass factory), and so he returns to school for no other reason than to avoid pain or humiliation.

A temporary departure from college should involve something more enriching and stimulating. That might mean volunteering somewhere, even part-time, perhaps at a soup kitchen, to spark questions: Why are these guys homeless? How did they get here? Why isn't there more help for them? Do they deserve that help?

If possible, such volunteerism could be international. You could spend a summer, for example, working as a volunteer in a village in El Salvador. You would find great inspiration by learning from and helping the villagers, sharing their lives, eating their food, and communicating with them. You could then return to college to learn more Spanish, examine Central American politics, find out about the sociology of Latin families, discover the history of Catholicism in the Americas, study the economics of farming, or, from a concern about the health of the people you met, work to become a physician, a nurse, or a dentist. You may not have found inspiration in a book or a classroom, but you might in the faces of children that you see on the streets of San Salvador.

Or if you travel for fun and interest, you might discover an interest while looking off the deck of a boat and wondering about the marine life below, or perhaps while standing in a museum or in a garden, perhaps in Paris, Florence, or Beijing. These experiences will help you find the motivation to learn, which will push you to work hard. The reward will be the success of an enriched life—oh, and better grades too.

Manage Your Time Well

As we have seen, students may also struggle in their studies because they lack good time management skills. This exacerbates the problem discussed above. When you are not interested in learning something, studying becomes a painful chore to be avoided—the very root of procrastination. That is understandable and human. All of us would rather spend time in more pleasurable activities. But let us set that issue aside and suppose that you have found a subject that you do want to learn, but it requires mastery of something that may not be quite as stimulating. For example, if you are interested in biology, you cannot avoid a number of related subjects like physics, whose mastery is fundamental to biology. And you may find studying physics a real chore.

So what do you do when you would rather do nothing than study what you must? Simply and literally do nothing. You will be tempted to text a friend, call your mother, turn on the television, or read a newspaper. Fight that temptation, if you can. Just sit there, staring into space, doing nothing. Do not eat or drink or sleep. Nothing. After about five or six minutes of this, you will be consumed with boredom. And faced with the choice between the agony of nothing and the challenge—albeit unwelcome challenge—of physics, you know what you will do. Get to work.

Still, time management is not just about avoiding procrastination. It is about actively managing the way that you spend your most precious resource. One of the best ways of doing this is to analyze how you actually spend your day. This is done is two steps. In step one, you can estimate what you do during a given week. Start a spreadsheet, either one you create or one provided by an advising office, then list every half-hour down the left column and the seven days across the top row. For each half-hour slot, write down what you think you *should* be doing during that time. Write down everything: when to go to class, when to practice and eat, when to meet with other students, how long to spend online or on Facebook, and how long to sleep. Nothing should be left out, including time to exercise, to have fun, to watch television, and so on. Somewhere in there, you will need to insert 25 to 35 hours devoted to studying outside of class work and laboratory work.

In step two of this exercise, take a similar time grid with you wherever you go over the week that follows and document exactly what you *really* do. Naturally, this real-time diary will not resemble the planned diary. None of us is perfectly efficient. All of us get bored and distracted, and life is full of the unexpected and unplanned—thank goodness. But the degree to which you have veered from the ideal is the point of this exercise. How much more than you imagined did you spend talking to friends? Updating your Facebook page? Playing video games? Surfing the Internet or gambling online? Watching movies? How far are you from the ideal?

No one can or should be fully efficient. That is not the purpose of college. Many of our distractions are important, but it is a matter of degree. The most successful students, those who have fully embraced the experience and have many accomplishments and good grades to show for it, have been very busy—but have made every effort to be efficient. They manage themselves consciously and strategically. Several days a week, for example, they might get up a little early to study or review notes before they go to class. If they have an hour between classes, they will sit down to study rather than getting a cup of coffee and chatting or staring into space.

Some successful students that I know think of the daylight hours like their parents do, as the hours to do a job. Most working people stay focused on their job all day long because they want to or they must. Naturally, everyone takes time to call their spouse, do a little Web browsing, schedule a doctor's appointment, and enjoy lunch with a colleague. But for the most part, professionals will stay focused on the task at hand between 9:00 and 5:00, often much longer.

This idea runs counter to a deeply engrained student culture, in which most students get started with their studies at 7:00 PM and then study straight through until after midnight. It can be nice to be part of a campus culture, but this part of the culture is not helping the struggling student. If you don't get to work before dinner, you've made completely inefficient use of the hours before the sun goes down. If you average three hours of class a day, then you have wasted eight hours of daylight without doing anything academic. That is quite simply poor time management, and it can lead to serious academic distress. So it would be better for you to think of your studies as a job. You can get the job done and then enjoy what remains of the evening.

Develop Better Study Skills

When you are really struggling, you need to consider the possibility that you may not have the necessary skills or knowledge to succeed in particular courses. In that case, you have to face three distinct and difficult possibilities: that you are not prepared, that you lack understanding, or that you may not have the talent. By the first, I mean that your high school preparation has not fully equipped you to do well in college. That is unfortunate, of course. But since no one can go back and fix that, we will focus on improving study skills as a reasonable substitute. The second possibility is that you do not understand what you are supposed to learn. Fixing that is a matter of more aggressive instruction. This is where tutoring comes into play. The third possibility—lacking the talent to succeed—is tough to imagine, let alone consider seriously. But if you have excellent study skills and you work hard but are still not understanding the material, the only remaining explanation is that your talents do not fit that subject very well.

Let us take these one at a time.

Compensating for Inadequate Preparation

The first issue is inadequate high school preparation. Unfortunately, there are a variety of ways in which you may have been poorly served by your high school. For example, you may not be a very good writer. Maybe your teachers had you write short 3-page papers, most of them summaries. But your college essays are supposed to be 8 to 15 pages, and on occasion much longer. You realize you know little about how to structure a paper like that. You're not sure how to argue a point, build a thesis, or cite your sources. Maybe you have the basic skills down but don't know how to put the rest of it together. That can be a serious problem that may not have an impact immediately, especially if you avoid writing-intensive classes and stick to courses that have midterms and finals.

There may be other legacies from high school. Perhaps the foreign language instruction there was inadequate or even incompetent—a sadly common problem for my advisees. Maybe you were not pushed hard on your math skills, perhaps because you were the best student in class. This may reflect a wider problem, that your high school was not particularly rigorous. Whatever the reason, if parts of your education are just not there, that will be a special challenge when your classmates have a stronger background. These are realities for which no student should apologize, nor is it helpful to blame those high school teachers. But the recovering student must acknowledge these realities, compensate for them, and be aggressively honest about what he or she can handle and cannot. Any good college will allow that student to take a slower route to a similar destination, but remedying the problem begins with acknowledging a weak background and the need to take that slower route.

In fact, a more serious legacy from a weak background is a lack of study skills, not an insufficient depth of knowledge. Freshmen at Johns Hopkins voice this concern all the time. They did not know that college was going to be this much work, and they are not sure how to cope with it. Adjusting to a new academic schedule with a great deal of rigor is an enormous challenge for them. So what to do?

If you are struggling because you have poor study skills, it is worthwhile to review Habit #6, *Don't Just Work Hard—Work Smart*. When reviewing the insights in that chapter, you should focus on the basics: preparing fully for class, writing papers well enough in advance, and giving yourself the time to be thoughtful about what you're learning. You need to pay attention to note-taking skills. Your notes should be more useful and more thought-provoking than a simple transcription of what is going on. You may want to think about how you read. Are you trying to consume every word? (You shouldn't.) Are you only reading from beginning to end? (That is not necessarily a good idea, unless the book is fiction.) You need to be self-conscious about how you are approaching textbooks and other readings. It may help here to get a coach. Your college is likely to have a program that assigns you a study coach who can meet with you to review strategies, map out time management, and strengthen specific skills like note-taking.

In college, you are not likely to get daily assignments that provide

Rebuild Those Study Skills

SUE BROWN, Ph.D.

RESIDENT DEAN OF FRESHMEN, HARVARD COLLEGE

HARVARD UNIVERSITY

One of the hardest parts of my work as resident dean of freshmen is counseling first-year students with unsatisfactory midterm grade reports. In ideal cases, students recognize exactly what went wrong and articulate a clear plan for improving their grades and ensuring that it never happens again. They are glad that it happened early, since it gives them the opportunity to be more proactive going forward.

For most students, though, this type of insight comes all too slowly. They've always done well, and now they are looking at a D or even an F. *How can this be?* Perhaps they did poorly on their first chemistry midterm. *But I always did well in high school in the sciences. Chemistry was my favorite subject!* That may be true, but taking college-level science exams (or exams in any college-level subject) involves skills and strategies that are very different from those that made their high school careers such a success. I suggest that my students view this as an opportunity to take inventory of their study skills and to make adjustments to enhance and improve them. Making changes is tricky for many students. The students are reluctant to let go of their existing study strategies because these strategies have been thoroughly tested and they work. *They got me into college, didn't they?*

Taking stock of your study skills is a lot like cleaning out the closet. Each strategy is like a favorite shirt or pair of shoes. Of course, you keep the ones that you still wear and tweak them if necessary (sew on a button or get some new laces). What about the ones that don't fit anymore, or that are torn and old and faded? *But that was my favorite shirt in junior high school! I won the kickball championship in those shoes!* No matter how attached you are, they aren't much use to you now. It's time to let them go (or at least put them in storage), and make room for new stuff.

How do you take stock of study skills? Check out your college's study resources. Ask your instructors what studying advice they

continued

have for students taking their class. Ask other students who did well in the courses you're taking how they engaged with the material. Talk to your academic advisor. Do these things early, before your first term gets under way. And be sure to take out your list on a regular basis and repeat this process. You'll quickly learn to adapt your tools and strategies to any class you take. (And who knows, you may finally get motivated to clean out your closet.)

you with a steady feedback loop from your instructors. Those daily assignments and regular deadlines may have been an annoying feature of high school life, but they did keep you on track and alerted you, your parents, and your teacher to problems. Every day in high school, you were slowly gaining the skills needed for larger exams and other challenges. But in college, you will find that you rarely are asked to do any assignment daily. That is why it is important to do the extra work or the optional problem sets available in a course like calculus or physics, to practice and to give yourself feedback. You could do these with another student, if you like. Together, the two of you can compare how you each solved a problem, appreciate if there are multiple ways to solve it, and simply get positive feedback as you practice.

In college, you need to have self-discipline and consistency to master and understand many of the required skills and most of the useful concepts. The need for that kind of daily work may be obvious for a language class. But in chemistry, without any written assignments and with only one or two midterms scattered through the semester, you may think that it is enough to just read the textbook and take notes in class. In fact, what you must do is work on problems, the kinds of problems you will find on the exam.

Learning to Understand

A second problem related to weak skills is a lack of simple understanding. Let us assume that you are hard working, self-disciplined, and reasonably skilled in your study habits. But you still do not understand what is happening in a course. This is a common problem in physics and organic chemistry, where you are likely to find many students who are motivated and hard working but who still perform poorly. These two classes are especially befuddling because instructors are trying to show their students a new way to think, to solve problems, and to become scientific. Often, you can meet this challenge by simply diving into the material and working and reworking problems—again and again and again. But there is a point at which that can be unproductive and even self-destructive.

If, despite these efforts, you still do not get what is going on in the course, you really have only one choice: admit that you need help. A lot of students have too much pride to admit this. They have enjoyed individual achievement for so long that they cannot imagine the teamwork needed for successful learning. They have gotten by on hard work and native intelligence so regularly that an admission of confusion would be a hurtful blow to their self-esteem. I can offer no wisdom except this: *Get over it.* We all need help throughout our lives, starting with the help we get from our parents. It is preposterous and empirically wrong to imagine a life of complete independence. The process of learning highly sophisticated concepts and skills demands a community effort. Students who need help should get help!

But where?

Incredibly, most of the students I know never consider asking for help from their professors. These are the same students who became superstars in prep school because of their strong relationships with teachers. But because they see their current "teachers" as intimidating and distant, they have trouble imagining the conversation in which they ask for help. Certainly, there are some people in academia who are unwelcoming and difficult. But most instructors are committed to their subject matter, and they want to do a good job teaching it to others. They are in their profession because they love the subject matter and believe it is important. They want you to enter into their world and respect it. And they also know that even the best-intentioned of students cannot enter that world without some basic understanding. It is their mission to provide that framework of understanding.

Professors try to do this in many arenas, with the classroom only the most obvious. Struggling students cannot rely on the classroom alone to make it happen, as their poor grades testify. Yet they rarely consider going to a professor's office hours, a courtesy found in every college and university. My colleagues at Johns Hopkins observe with some pain, and even a sense of rejection, that they hold office hours, but no one ever shows up. They find this peculiar, especially when they have classes that number in the hundreds. "Where is everybody?" they wonder. Some of that is their fault. Their office hours may be too early in the morning or conflict with other classes, and students simply cannot show up. Perhaps some instructors are not welcoming or friendly. But most of the time, the problem is that students do not think of the value of office hours, and they are not sure what they would do if they did go.

Let me offer some suggestions on this problem. Imagine a student walking into a professor's office. The professor's desk is a mess, her book shelves jammed. She is staring intently at her computer screen. "Professor Harris? I'm David Russell . . . from your biochemistry class?" She looks up, registering no recognition. David is disappointed, only partly understanding that the instructor of a 200-person lecture course is not going to recognize anyone in particular.

But now what? What does he say—"I'm not doing well in your course, can you help me"? That is not going to work. David will get some sympathy but get no further in understanding the material that has been troubling him. She might suggest that he go to section, do extra problems, see someone at the Tutoring Center. But he knew all of that already. David will thank her and leave, unlikely to admit to another instructor that he is struggling.

Before David comes to that conclusion, he should consider Dr. Harris's point of view. She is busy writing up results of an experiment she has been working on for months. Perhaps tenure is in the balance. She knows she has office hours, but no one ever comes to them, so she is ensconced in her work. Then David arrives. She struggles to focus on him and searches her memory quickly for his face. David seems familiar, the one ferociously taking notes in the fourth row on the left. But he has never introduced himself, let alone spoken to her. So she cannot remember his name. Next, she waits for him to ask a question, but he only tells her he is in trouble. She already knows that a lot of folks struggle with biochemistry; that is not news. She waits longer for something specific to help him with. David looks pained and embarrassed, and she sympathizes. She fills the silence he has left with suggestions like seeing her teaching assistant or getting tutoring. Eventually, she gives up and finds a way to end the meeting. David goes, and she is left uncomfortable, regretting she could not help. Then she gets back to work and forgets about it—and about him.

Now imagine a different conversation. This time, David has come prepared. His notes from the readings and class have left room for him to write questions in the column or at least a large question mark. He has taken the time to go back through his notes, compiling these questions on a separate sheet. He also has brought back the midterm, circling key areas of a problem he missed but still does not get. He is ready. He has an agenda, a list of questions, specific references that he does not understand. By focusing Professor Harris's attention on a specific set of questions, David will get much more insight into the material. He also has shown a great deal of effort and of respect to the subject and to her, which professors like Dr. Harris always greatly appreciate. Creating this goodwill is very important. Now he can get eager help on a regular basis because he has learned how to get that help and has shown that he is ready to learn. David is showing himself and the instructor that he is an active participant in a community of learners, committed to exploration, understanding, and education.

You can use this same approach with teaching assistants. TAs are an invaluable resource. But since you are struggling, it will not be enough for you to simply go to sections and ask a few questions or engage in group discussion. You need to do more. Like instructors, most TAs have office hours. Because they are young scholars, trying to find their way and to learn important teaching skills, they are often even more willing to spend extra time with a student than the instructor is. Again, it helps to appreciate their take on their relationship with students. They are at a different professional stage than the instructor, and that can serve your needs even better. They are committed to figuring out how to explain to you a concept they mastered only a few years before but one that now seems obvious, even self-explanatory. Given their inexperience, they will make mistakes, but those are usually more than compensated for by their enthusiasm and their determination to get it right.

There is a point at which these two resources, the instructor and the

TA, exhaust themselves, even under the ideal circumstances of good-will and affectionate dedication. This comes from simple mathematics and the limits of time. If a student is struggling in class, it is very likely that many others are too. Those students will be looking for help and answers to questions—if they know what is best for them—which can quickly use up the time and energy of instructor and TA. This is when it is necessary (though it should not be the trigger) to use tutoring services. Every college offers a variety of tutoring services. There might be one-on-one tutoring, group tutoring, and/or drop-in tutoring.

Group tutoring can be a very good approach to untangling your academic questions; you feel part of a larger community of people who are struggling and who are confused. It is very reassuring to know that, even at a top college, there are other people who are having trouble understanding course material. Furthermore, other students may think of questions that you may not have framed but need to know the answer to. So a group setting can be especially helpful.

For those who are more timid or even embarrassed by their academic struggles, an individual tutor may be a good answer. That individual will go step-by-step through questions or problems. Preparing for this meeting is just as important as the meeting itself. Just as they would for an instructor or a TA, students need to bring to their tutors sets of questions and specific problems that are causing difficulty. Students may identify certain problem sets, for example, and pick out specific questions that a tutor would address.

Finding What You Do Have Talent For

A final, darker reason behind a student's apparent lack of skills is that he or she does not have talent for the subject or subjects that gives the most difficulty. I write this with some hesitation, so let me be clear from the start. I am not suggesting that any student lacks native intelligence or that there is something wrong with him or her. But something is just not fitting, clicking, or working despite all efforts—those of the student, the instructor, the TA, the tutor, or the advisor. The student still cannot pass a certain course or set of courses. I knew a student who took linear algebra *four* times, each time trying to absolve the D or F that he got the previous time. Four times to be reminded of failure. Four semesters of coursework lost forever. For *half* of his college experience, he kept taking this same course, trying to climb a mountain that he clearly could not climb.

Yet he stubbornly held on to this idea because he needed that requirement for a particular major that he refused to abandon. He could have made other academic choices that would have precluded the necessity for linear algebra, but he refused. He thought that a particular major would serve his needs, namely, to get into medical school when the pattern of repeating a course was knocking huge holes in his boat—and should be avoided if at all possible, medical schools say emphatically. This young man needed to face the reality that this subject was not for him. No amount of hard work would overcome the fact that he was simply not talented in this particular area.

Of course, each of us experiences this to one degree or another. I do not mean to suggest that a student either has great talent in a subject or no talent at all. Our talents all live on a scaled gradation. But it can be difficult for students to take on subjects for which they have little aptitude, even when their hard work makes up for some of that deficiency. Sometimes it is simply better to do something at which you excel. Because excellence comes with less effort, you can use your time and energies in other ways. Rather than struggling through a subject that poses difficulties for you, you can enroll in courses that suit your talents and enjoy them because they provide positive feedback as you go. And you have time to enjoy other parts of college life.

Guiding a student through the possibility that he or she lacks aptitude for a particular subject is very awkward and difficult. If a student comes to college as a pre-med, but then suffers failure or difficulty in a string of pre-med requirements, an academic advisor is obligated to broach the subject. "Is it possible," the advisor asks gently, "that this is not for you?" Perhaps there is another way to medical school, spreading out the requirements and majoring outside the sciences. "Why don't you take the difficult pre-med courses one at a time rather than two or three at a time? Let's spread out the work so that each semester you can focus your energy on one course. By providing extra, focused time and energy you should be able to overcome quite a bit of this problem."

But it may be better to just avoid subjects altogether for which you have little talent. You should try a different subject, a different class, a different major. You should explore to find something that you are good at. And then you will find that your lack of calculus skills is completely irrelevant. You are not taking calculus any longer, and you never will again. You simply are avoiding what you are not good at.

Now, there may be subjects you *must* overcome to get to where you want to be. Perhaps, within the wider constellation of courses needed for a major, there are just a couple for which you have little talent. Then you must mitigate this by taking things slowly, one course at a time, spreading uncomfortable requirements out, and getting lots and lots of help as you go.

Most important, you must forgive yourself. It can be very difficult for any student who has gained great emotional satisfaction from academics to realize that there are some subjects for which she has little or no talent. It is an admission of limitation that many talented students are not willing to do. But as you grow in maturity, you will need to be more forgiving of yourself—or at least you *should* be. You should acknowledge that there are some things that you are good at and some things that you are not. Try to maximize opportunities in areas in which you thrive, and try to minimize involvement in those in which you do not. But when you are facing difficult areas, try to do so with a sense of humor. Acknowledge that we all have our limitations. And when we must overcome those limitations, we just need to ask for help and support.

Take Care of Your Health

The rise of mental health problems on college campuses is disturbing and saddening.[1] It seems wrong that students should have to struggle with these challenges at a time of life when they should be embracing the newness of intellectual flowering, discovering worlds unimagined, and growing from adolescence to adulthood. It is possible, of course, that mental health problems have not increased as much as our *awareness* of those problems has. That debate is academic; whatever the cause of the upward trend, it is unacceptable. Indeed, it is hard to know which is more troubling—that so many students suffer, or that so many students who are suffering do little or nothing about it. And suffering in silence is one of the reasons why there is a high correlation between academic distress and mental health difficulties.

Universities and colleges across the nation have made efforts to address these problems, primarily by developing elaborate, large, and sophisticated counseling centers.[2] These centers are staffed with trained professionals, most of them with doctorates, some of them holding psychiatric degrees. Counseling centers are convenient to the student body, offering appointments, drop-ins, crisis consulting, and 24/7 emergency response. Their services are usually "free," included in tuition. As a practical matter, these centers cannot see patients for extended periods of time. But most students find relief and resolution in six or seven meetings. If the situation is more serious and requires longer-term care or medication, a counseling center can refer the student to a professional in the neighborhood or the city. So help is available.

The problem is that students do not always take advantage of these services.[3] The reasons for this failure to get help, I think, are similar to the barriers to visiting Advising, asking for tutoring or just getting answers to academic questions. All of these require students to admit weakness and need—an admission they think runs counter to the merciless competition at a top college. They think that people will think less of them and begin to doubt their abilities, their worth, or even the wisdom of their being at that college in the first place. After all, when you have gained admission to one of the best programs in the country, it carries with it the cachet of accomplishment. And with that comes the cloak of invulnerability.

Of course, this is complete nonsense. Everyone has problems. Some problems are more intense than others, but all of us need help from time to time throughout our lives. More often than not, we need help when we least expected needing it. And college is such a time, as students strive for independence—not dependence on others for help.

No one goes to college thinking that he is going to have to spend a lot of time in therapy, although this may be changing because of the availability of therapy and drugs at an earlier age. In the past, students with mental health issues would have done poorly in high school and would never have been admitted to a top program.[4] Now that they are able to cope with their problems and achieve academic results, they are joining the academic elite. But from my informal view, those same students are reluctant to get help at the college level. Perhaps they think that college gives them a chance to start over, and it does—but only in part. Outside the view of their parents, these students sometimes stop taking medications and have no one taking them to therapy.

I am not suggesting that students with prior problems are the only students needing help. Far from it. Students from all parts of life and with many medical backgrounds battle emotional problems, some quite serious. Some mental health issues, such as bipolar disorder, become manifest when a person is 18 or 19.[5] Depression is more common still. It is a tragic consistency that many students whose transcripts are awash with D's and F's are handicapped by depression. They find it almost impossible to get past this struggle, to focus fully on their studies. Some of them cannot get out of bed to go to class in the morning because their emotional paralysis is so intense. If they do get up, they have difficulty concentrating. They are too distracted by the problems that they face.

In addition to depression, some students must cope with grief. They may be grieving the loss of a close romantic relationship or the death of a treasured uncle, a beloved grandmother, or worse, a parent. The father of one of my advisees had been killed in the Twin Towers on 9/11. The son insisted that he was okay. He was adamant that he wanted to remain enrolled and that there were no issues that he had to cope with. We advised him to take a leave of absence. Coping with the loss of a parent was bad enough, but to have that be part of a national and horrible tragedy was much worse. He refused. Not surprisingly, he failed out. The following semester he did take our advice and went home to heal.

Healing, of course, is the most important thing a student can do under the circumstances of depression, grief, or emotional devastation. It makes little or no sense to try to succeed in a rigorous academic environment while being hobbled by serious mental illness. The same can be said of physical illness or injury, and this does happen on occasion. A student breaks a leg or hand, or suffers mononucleosis or another debilitating physical disease that requires an extended rehabilitation to recuperate. But physical illnesses or injuries are much more obvious than mental health issues, and people appreciate the need for treating them.

Sometimes, healing can occur simultaneously with your studies. Rigorous, regular therapy at the college's counseling center is critical here. A disabilities services office can accommodate an injured student with extended time on exams or note-taking services. Help from an advising office is crucial, too, as the personnel here can help manage coursework, both in the short and the long run. This might mean a reduced course load, timely withdrawal from difficult courses, reordering the sequence and timing of difficult requirements, and the occasional Incomplete for a course to be finished after the term. But heal students must, and they should do what they must to heal.

Take a Break

Many students who are dismissed for academic reasons throw themselves at the mercy of an advisor or dean, hoping to get another chance to improve their standing. That's understandable. These college students, among the best in the world, cannot conceive of involuntary time out of school. They never have had an extended period of time, other than a summer, away from school. Schooling has defined their lives: it is what they know; it is what they do best. It has a rhythm and a pattern with which they are familiar. And of course, they enjoy the company and social life that surrounds their education. Most of their friends are classmates who would continue their schooling, magnifying a sense of failure and a feeling of being left behind.

While such a student's peers seem to be doing just fine, chugging right along to a four-year graduation, she is facing physical or mental challenges that she never thought would cripple her ability to excel. Now she is facing eight months or more away from the environment in which she has usually thrived. This is a painful experience. Students facing this prospect feel that it may be impossible to return to a normal life, restart their educational plans, and go on to fulfill the dreams that have been building for many years. And if a student is undergoing depression and some other emotional challenge, this only makes matters worse.

Take Care of Your Mental Health

MARCELLE CHRISTIAN HOLMES, Ph.D.
ASSOCIATE DEAN OF STUDENTS and DEAN OF WOMEN
LICENSED CLINICAL PSYCHOLOGIST
POMONA COLLEGE

If you are struggling with a psychological condition such as depression, anxiety, or an eating disorder, *you are not alone.* Many students start college worried, anxious, or with obsessive thoughts. Many also come to school with a history of antidepressant use and psychotherapy, and possibly even hospitalizations or substance abuse. Some students also start college with a history of difficult family situations. If this describes you, there are some steps that you should consider taking. Being proactive about your (own) health is the best advice for success in college.

First, *learn the symptoms* of some of the more common mental health issues, including depression. Symptoms of depression include eating more or less than usual, weight gain or loss, feeling sad and crying, inability to sleep or sleeping too much, difficulty concentrating, and thoughts of suicide or death. If you are feeling anxious, there are several different kinds of anxiety disorders. Generalized anxiety disorder is marked by constant worrisome thoughts, often accompanied by physical symptoms of anxiety (such as muscle tension, headache, or stomachache). Other anxiety disorders include post-traumatic stress disorder, which can occur after a traumatic event, and obsessive-compulsive disorder, characterized by persistent intrusive thoughts or compulsions to perform certain ritualistic behaviors. Symptoms of eating disorders include an excessive preoccupation with weight and body image, refusal to maintain a normal body weight, excessive exercising, eating large quantities of food, and vomiting or using laxatives in order to prevent weight gain. You may have experienced some of these symptoms in high school. Learning that they are in fact symptoms of a treatable psychological problem is the first step in receiving the help you may need.

If you've experienced these symptoms, you may think that things will be different once you're in college. However, you may discover that your coping resources are coming up short in the first few days and weeks away from home. The minor concerns that you may have dealt with in high school might start to mushroom, and if you have not laid the proper groundwork, you may find yourself sinking deeply into the quicksand. *Assuming that your problems will magically go away just because you're away at college could be a costly mistake.* The stresses of adjusting to a new environment, making new friends, taking classes, and coping with new responsibilities might make things worse for you. Although some problems might indeed resolve themselves over time with little effort on your part, others might require hard work.

Next, *identify your campus mental health resources early, and use them if you need help.* Research the policies for receiving help from the college counseling center. On many campuses, counseling is free or is offered at a substantially reduced charge. Here are some questions to ask: Does the center offer individual and group therapy? What are the center's privacy policies? Do you need health insurance to be seen there? If so, are there programs that help students pay for insurance? How many sessions do most students attend before they start to feel better? Is there a session limit at the counseling center? What are the credentials of the therapists there? If you think you would work best with a female therapist, how many women are on the staff? If you think you would work best with a therapist of color, are there any Latino, African American, Asian American, or Native American therapists on the staff? Is there a psychiatrist on staff, in case you need refills of your prescription medication? Getting solid answers to these questions now can help prepare you for the possibility that you might need to use campus counseling resources later.

As you look into the counseling resources, *organize your medical or counseling records or have them transferred directly to the counseling center.* Many students enter college unsure of the precise name of that prescription they were on in the 10th grade. Finding out what worked (or didn't work) for you in the past is helpful information for a potential counselor. You also might want to ask your parents a few questions about any past therapy or about your family mental health history. Filling in the blanks of your personal and family medical and psychological health history will help your therapist help you.

continued

Familiarize yourself with some of the administrators and policies listed in your student handbook. There may be an administrator or dean dedicated to helping first-year students, or a dean who specializes in working with students of color. There may be a disability coordinator whose job it is to help you if, due to your mental health condition, you need to miss a few days of class or are so anxious that you have difficulty finishing assignments. Connecting with these people, even if it is only a casual conversation during your first month of college, can help you put a face to the name in the handbook. Learn your university's leave policies in case you ever need to take some time off. With whom should you speak if you'd like to take a leave of absence for a semester or perhaps a year? What do you need to do in order to return? Many students decide to take a leave of absence for a semester or for a year if they find that the stresses of college are overwhelming to them. There is no shame in taking a break to learn better coping skills or to seek therapy at home. Use this time—if you need it—to get stronger. Then you can return to campus and complete your educational goals.

Throughout my time as a professor, as a psychotherapist in college counseling centers and private practice, and as a dean, I have seen many students with psychological conditions successfully graduate college. They have subsequently secured fulfilling jobs, graduate school opportunities, and other rewarding pursuits after college. Your path might be a little different from other students, but being proactive about your mental health, open to the resources that exist to help you, and prepared for potential setbacks, is a formula for success.

But experience has shown those of us in Advising that a leave of absence, voluntary or not, can be the best strategy for the long-term success of a struggling student. Students need to get away to reset their priorities if they lack a full commitment to their education. They may need to think about their sense of self-discipline and sense of purpose. They may need to get away from friends who influence them in unhealthy ways. And they may need to take care of their health.

The many students that I have required to leave college for a while have, almost without exception, returned much healthier, recommitted, and reenergized. They realize that their education is critical to the success that they want. They understand that they need to work hard but also that they need to work well. With time away, they see that they need a change of direction, a new set of courses, a new major, and even a reconstruction of their career dreams and plans. They may discover, as the glassworks student did, that many jobs that do not require higher education are dangerous, draining, or unpleasant—or all three—and that they should concentrate on their studies, get the job done, and graduate.

None of these lessons is easy to learn while in college. There are too many intellectual demands, too many pressures, too many obligations, not enough time, and not enough sleep to allow for this kind of thoughtful reevaluation and rededication. It is simply impossible to study *and* recuperate from one condition or another at the same time. My student athletes understand this particularly well. They know you cannot rejoin the team on the field if you are injured. They need to nurse that injury and get back into strong health before rejoining the team. This is exactly why a leave of absence can be enormously helpful. Without all the obligations, distractions, and work involved in studying at a top college, the struggling student can focus on the personal and regain the strength to learn and succeed.

✤ Put It in Perspective

If you have struggled, there is one thing you must do as you recover from those difficulties, something more difficult than healing: *you must forgive yourself.*

Failure and struggle are an inevitable and natural part of life. No one can go from cradle to grave without experiencing a wide variety of significant and daunting challenges. Some of those challenges are the consequence of our own choices, mistakes we make, miscalculations we suffer in our personal lives and our professional plans. But, while it is a cliché to note that everyone makes mistakes, why does everyone have such difficulty forgiving themselves? If mistakes are a natural part of life, why can't forgiveness be the same?

In college, forgiveness begins—though it won't end—by abandoning the need for perfection, measured by straight A's, and replacing it with an understanding of our limitations and a deeper commitment

JOHN T. O'KEEFE, Ph.D.
DIRECTOR OF ADVISING AND
ACADEMIC SUPPORT SERVICES and CLASS DEAN
WELLESLEY COLLEGE

From time to time, students at Wellesley College put on a program called "My Favorite Failure." They invite faculty and staff members to tell their stories of personal failures, what lessons they learned, and how they gained some perspective on these dismal moments. The program illustrates vividly that even the best of us experience failure. Sometimes, the best in us can be produced by failure.

My own favorite failure is the F emblazoned on my college transcript. I was an excellent student in high school and got into a competitive college, where I was set to study architecture, a field I had settled on early in my childhood. That F was the low point of a steadily declining academic record that began in my first year in college. I was failing design studio, and there could be no clearer repudiation of my plans to become an architect and of my self-identity as academically gifted.

Many students face similar circumstances, although usually not with such a seemingly dramatic notation on a transcript. It's more often a grade on a test, or a comment from an instructor in office hours, or a case of writer's block. What is the "failure" embedded in these moments? It's not so much these external signs, but the inner conviction that we have lost our way, that the plans we had for ourselves turn out to be misguided. Even more challenging, the self we thought we knew turns out to be someone else.

The external markers of failure are important to identify, but just as important is to examine the factors that affect failure. While these are intensely disappointing experiences, they actually are exactly what a liberal arts education is supposed to produce. Many of our top colleges pride themselves on instilling a sense of self-examination and a readiness to question assumptions in their students, helping them start a process of lifelong learning that will keep their minds and spirits alive long after graduation. It was the F on my transcript that taught me that (and, in fairness to my many excellent teachers and advisors in college, they had been trying to help me learn that lesson in gentler ways all along). It took that F to make me look at the choices I had made and to question whether they were really right for me. In fact, they were not, and I went on to change schools and majors, and to build new career plans. Failure isn't fun, but it is an essential part of learning. Out of failure comes success.

to learning. This is very difficult for the better college student, who draws identity, motivation, power, and adoration from perfectionism. These students are intensely competitive. They take their cues and derive their self-esteem from the approval of others. But students who struggle understand the limitations of this world. They can begin to see that the approval of others is not nearly as important as one's own approval of the life he has chosen and the work that he does. And they can see that the pursuit of learning can never fail—whenever and whatever we learn, we are successful.

Students who find a place in their hearts to forgive themselves are the better for it; they understand their fallibilities, and they do their best to cope with them or to minimize them. They realize that life can be a series of experiences we choose consciously, and that we work hard to do what we can to succeed within that framework. When hard work is not enough, they learn to ask for help. When they fail, they learn from that, forgive themselves, and move on. They appreciate that a perfect outcome cannot be reached and that perfect grades could not measure that anyway.

They say, "What I need to think about is the broader value of my education. I need to think about why I'm here and to rededicate myself to creating a learned life, a life of engagement and curiosity." That life does not require perfection, and it chooses the learning *process* over measured *outcomes*. It requires a mind that is alive and ready to learn, not one that remembers everything, nor one that functions as everyone else's does.

If you can put your struggles in this light, and forgive yourself for missteps and inherent imperfection, you will gain something far more valuable and lasting than a high GPA.

You will gain wisdom.

Plan Boldly for Life after College

Images of life after college color the most critical choices students face: where to go to school, what major to choose, what coursework is needed, and others. Fears and dreams of the world beyond fall like a shadow over an academic culture that would prefer the full attention of every young person within its walls. But that is impossible. An American college education is an investment, and a very expensive one at that, likely to pass a yearly cost of $50,000 soon, if it hasn't already. Students and their parents constantly think and talk about what the student will do next. If there is uncertainty about the future, that is the subject of endless speculation. Or if the student has settled on a particular dream (lawyer and doctor being the most common, it seems), then every choice and every grade affects the likelihood of that dream's fulfillment.

Here, I will make no effort to dismiss these anxieties and plans. They are too important. Other academics might consider these distractions from the study of legitimate and important ideas, concepts, and discoveries. And we all agree that college is a precious place and that the years spent there should be savored and enjoyed. But I know, from thousands of conversations, that thoughts of what happens next always linger in a college student's mind.[1] Therefore, I want to embrace this problem so that you can be focused on wider missions beyond professional preparation, such as becoming a learned, cultured, and sophisticated world citizen. I hope that a more open, structured discussion of the issues about life after college will help put them in perspective, not in a box to be ignored. And that is why the final habit of a highly successful student, Habit #11 on the Dean's List, is *Plan Boldly for Life after College.*

This strategic discussion has four parts to it:

❶ "I have always wanted to be a ___": Why do we say that?
❷ Appreciating the unpredictable nature of career development
❸ Building tools for navigating the unpredictable
❹ Setting shorter-term goals, including public service

"I've Always Wanted to Be a Doctor"

Asking young people what they want to be when they grow up seems like an innocent question. In some ways, it is. We are inviting them to dream of possibility, to fantasize about great adventures, and to pretend to be grown up. In other ways, it is not. Adulthood has many responsibilities and challenges that children cannot imagine, but we are asking them to try. Still, it is mostly a way to begin conversation, like asking, "How are you?"

The problem is that many young people think they need to *answer* the question. "I don't know" does not seem to satisfy anyone, even if that answer is both honest and accurate. So, they often come up with something. Some, we know, are unlikely fantasies—"I'm going to play second base for the Yankees," or "I want to be an astronaut on a mission to Mars," or "I want to drive a fire truck"—but there are others that seem plausible, even attractive. The most obvious: "I want to be a lawyer," or "I want to be a doctor." And with one of these simple answers, the young person has satisfied many needs at once, giving instant certainty to an unknowable future, while comforting everyone by picking a career that is supposed to be the perfect combination of education, prestige, and money.

If you have answered that question this way, you probably have been sincere and correct. You might have had a powerful experience at a hospital in the hands of a healer or worked at a clinic. You might have seen a TV drama featuring a brilliant attorney defending some benighted soul or an intern at a law firm. And that might be OK. After all, we do need talented doctors and, yes, lawyers. You're welcome to join those professions, of course, and it's a worthy dream.

But I am more troubled by the reaction of parents and other adults. Many parents interpret these dreams as a contract, as a quick solution to many anxieties about their children's future and security. We should know better. As a father, I am equally guilty of crafting dreams for my children—"You'd be a great ___," or "You know, you can turn that talent into a job as a ___"—but I have to catch myself. First, my kids are still children, an appropriately long way from learning their full talents, interests, or professional needs. And second, I should not be sending them signals that the future is so simple. I want to be reassuring that everything will be fine in the misty future, but I do not want them to fear uncertainty either.

Parents like me join a growing chorus of teachers, advisors, relatives, admissions counselors, and friends who ask you, "What will you do when you grow up?" with greater urgency as time passes, and as you keep moving through school. We worry about your rapidly approaching future. Will you have a job that can be counted on and a career people will respect? We have asked another form of this same question—namely, "What's your major?"—if we think that will make a difference in the future. Really, this is just another way of asking, "Are you going to be OK?"

While our concerns about your future may be understandable, by asking these questions we are creating serious problems for you. First, we are demanding an answer from you, reinforcing the false idea that an answer will somehow make the future clearer and more secure. Just saying "I want to be a doctor" does not make that a guaranteed outcome, nor does it make the profession the best fit for you. There are lots of reasons why that could be true or false, and asking you is not helping you figure it out. We're just pressuring you into making a choice before you are ready. In effect, by asking the career or major questions, we are subduing our anxieties by transferring them to you. That question is doing you no favors.

Second, when we ask those questions, we may be making you feel obligated to "the Plan" that takes you from here to fulfilling that specific dream: you've got to take this course, attend that college, do that research, volunteer at that clinic, go to that medical school, become that specialist. When we ask, you answer; then we plan, and now you're obligated to stick to "the Plan." What started as a question motivated by concern long ago has now manifested itself in academic choices and realities—not all of them pleasant or well suited.

So couldn't the answer—shouldn't the answer—have been, "I don't know"?

The Uncertainty of Careers

Some people can answer the career question when they are seven years old. They embrace that future enthusiastically, pursue an education to reach professional school, gain the training they need, and go on to have full and successful careers—always true to the dream they grabbed at age seven. But most of us are not like that. Most people I know or have met, including hundreds or thousands of alumni from prestigious universities, could not have predicted where they have arrived professionally—and still do not know if they are "there." They tell countless variations of a story in which they met someone unexpectedly who loved his job, or they moved to a new town and stumbled onto a job listing, or they got a call from a family connection who heard they were around, or they read a book or saw a lecture that inspired them, or they realized that they had talent in marketing, not medicine, after helping a friend promote a new business venture.

These same people chuckle at "the Plan" that they had had as high schoolers and undergraduates, or at least smile at their own ignorance and naïveté. For example, I loved the documentaries of undersea explorer and inventor Jacques Cousteau. I was inspired by his courage and his beautifully articulated concerns for dying oceans. I imagined myself as a marine biologist, diving deep underwater for discovery and advocacy, just like my hero. It was a good and noble dream, one that made me apply to Yale to become a biology major. The problem was (a) I was not a very good science student, and (b) deep-water diving scared me. Faced with the prospect of being an incompetent and terrified oceanographer, I abandoned "the Plan."

My story of discovering that my plan was a lousy fit is a common one: you can ask your parents, relatives, or neighbors. Sure, some of those people chose their path early. But most will say they spent a lot of time bouncing around, buffeted by doubt and taken in unexpected directions—not all of them pleasant. They probably had to do what was needed to pay the bills, feed their children (like you), and get on with life. And that doesn't always follow a script. Their early twenties might have been especially tough, as the financial necessities of rent and college debt battled with the idealism of perfect freedom and the desire for fun. Just as things looked promising, an unsupportive supervisor or an unlucky break derailed the current plan, leaving them grasping for something new.

This is not a pretty picture. You will be tempted to say, "Oh, that won't be me. I'm going to be a lawyer, not some loser who can't figure out what to do." I would like to suggest an alternative reaction, one that is difficult but has many rewards: *embrace the uncertainty*. There is a second side to the coin with uncertainty on it. And that is freedom. Since uncertainty is more likely than clarity, since serendipity seems more powerful than planning, we can choose to approach the future with fear and the illusion of control, or we can enjoy the ride and celebrate the freedom.

Consider for a moment the cost borne by previous generations to win the luxury of uncertainty and freedom. College students have the freedom to make almost any professional choice, however bewildering that might be, because their families have sacrificed. These families worked hard, and they live in a society that allows and then rewards excellence in both genders and for all races and ethnicities—though not equally, of course. That represents a profound shift in the human experience, where class, race, and gender were insurmountable barriers to choosing a career. Even the word "career" is a luxury: people for countless centuries did what was needed or dictated to survive day to day.

Maybe these freedoms are too new. Perhaps we give in to quick answers because they are comforting, and the alternative is too bewildering and uncertain. But the great power of a college education is to jump—or be pushed—*out* of a comfortable place, into a new world of strange ideas, conflicting values, and unpredictable outcomes. And just because it is a scary place does not mean we should not embrace it.

Making Good Mistakes

ANYA BERNSTEIN, Ph.D.

DIRECTOR OF UNDERGRADUATE STUDIES and SENIOR LECTURER

COMMITTEE ON DEGREES IN SOCIAL STUDIES

HARVARD UNIVERSITY

For many college students, senior year is the first time in their lives when they have not had a path to follow. After elementary school comes middle school. After middle school comes high school. Apply to college, get in. Take courses, choose a major, become involved in extracurricular activities, do an internship or two, and perhaps write a senior thesis. At each stage, the student has concrete tasks to accomplish: write this paper, study for this test, fill out this application. Life after college isn't like that.

Many students view the lack of a path as something to fear. What if I make a mistake? What if I take a job or start a professional degree that I don't like?

I encourage students to make mistakes in the years after college. Their degree from a first-rate university gives them a good start. They don't have to settle on a career right away. Instead, they can try different things—things they won't be able to do later on once they have started a career, like foreign travel and volunteer work. Mistakes made in the year after college can help people make good decisions later.

One of my former students spent three months after college living and working for a nongovernmental organization in Uganda. She hated it. She came home and told me, "Now I know that I never want to live in a place where there are rats again." Another former student spent her first year interning at a nonprofit in Boston. She learned that she really liked researching and writing, but that she didn't like fundraising, and she wasn't very good at it.

For most people, the process of determining what career to follow and how to live one's life is a process of trial and error, and that is a healthy thing. I worry about students who have their entire lives planned out at age 20. They know what graduate school they want to attend, they know where they want to work, and they know where they want to live. While it eases their minds in the short term, this certainty may be less valuable to students than the lessons about themselves and about life that they can learn through a few good mistakes.

Finding Your Way

Embracing unpredictability after college does not require resigning yourself to fate. Naturally, there is much that cannot be controlled. But there are ways to navigate or to channel the raging river. I recommend getting some career management tools. These are not precise instruments, given the unknown variables, but they can filter out some of the noise, allowing you to make better decisions and to keep an open mind that is both systematic and skeptical.[2]

Career centers at every top college offer a number of ways for you to begin figuring out who you are and where you are going. You can take a variety of tests, like the Myers-Briggs personality test or the Strong Interest test, to create a self-profile that counselors can help you analyze. It is pretty simple and straightforward to do: you make an appointment, take the test, see a counselor, do some research, and give it more thought. You can do it again if you need to or as you move through college. Your perspective will change, and your values and preferences will evolve. You will see this advice a hundred times, draped all over campuses and built into every advising publication coming from your college. I am not a career specialist, and there are many ready resources to understand this process.

So I will ask a different question: Why do students rarely take advantage of the career centers at their colleges and the skills that they teach? Students' use of such a center is often limited to polishing a resumé or to signing up for campus job interviews. They might stop by a career fair, though generally to learn about professions they already are considering, not new ones about which they know nothing. The resources for helping you prepare for the *decades* ahead are the most underused on campus, in contrast to those resources you need to succeed in the four years you will be in college: the library, the faculty, teaching assistants, academic advisors and others.

In fact, ignoring career services echoes the general trend of giving careers little or no serious thought. College students apply their incredible talent, great intelligence, and impeccable work habits to academic assignments, of course. But they apply few or none of these to the question of what they will do *after* graduating. They have spent years thinking about where to go to college and how to get in. They have taken SAT prep courses, toured campuses all around the country, and devoted countless hours to completing applications—all to get into college. Then, once they are there, they expend little or no effort on thinking about the problem of what to do after that. The thinking they do is panicked, informed by rumor, limited by ignorance, and clouded by family expectations. They tend to stumble onto a choice or fall back on the "famous" professions, and consider the job done.

Why? Why not apply the same rigor to the questions about the future? Is doing nothing simply surrendering to unpredictability and serendipity? Or is it just laziness? Or avoidance?

Avoidance is understandable. Considering what the future holds can be scary, and that seems to explain why career centers are underused. But looking carefully at alternatives is worthwhile, if only to avoid the possibility that your plan does not fit you. The possible careers of a talented and learned student are endless. And that is the problem. Coming out of a strong liberal arts college, you may have no way to limit your choices. The options are so many that you are bewildered, and you are likely to find refuge in choices others are making around you, or in professions you have heard of or just seen portrayed on TV.

But what if you were to find something that matched your passions and values? What if you saw a shorter list of choices that research suggests someone like you might find satisfying and successful? Wouldn't it help to make the freedom you earned less frightening and more manageable?

So let us say for a moment that you see the value in a more systematic and focused process, the kind that a good career counselor can help develop. Then what? The next challenge is to keep an open mind about its results. By definition, this process is going to offer ideas you had not considered before. Otherwise, there would be little point to it. The critical test, then, is what you do with those ideas. Do you look at them dismissively? "Oh, I couldn't do *that*." Or, "That looks incredibly boring." Alternatively, you might say, "Hmmm. Interesting. What does that mean?" That would open a line of questioning and of research that might result in provocative choices. You might talk to an alumnus doing that type of work, or set up an internship with an alumna in the profession.

A story might help. Years ago, a young woman took my advice to do a self-assessment at the Career Center—to her credit. She went online and took a battery of tests. Then she came storming back into my office, ready to attack my suggestion. "You wasted my time," she said. "This test, among other things, suggests that I should be a landscape architect. Are you kidding me?" I asked her, "Do you know anything about landscape architecture?" She paused and admitted she did not. I then listed the various tasks such a professional does: work with clients, understand the science of soils and plants, develop creative and artistic plans, market the business, supervise employees, and appreciate the beauty of nature. The profession, then, combines science, art, business, and personal relations. And you get to work outside!

She did not become a landscape architect—at least, not yet! She probably thought it was not a fancy enough career to merit the attention of a Johns Hopkins graduate. But the conversation did surprise her. It did make her think twice about dismissing something before giving it thought and a chance. She began to think with a disciplined, open mind. She began to see some merit in limiting choices carefully and based on good data and personalized counseling, not on rumor or lazy selections. I have no objection, on the face of it, to anyone's becoming a doctor or lawyer. But I do object when people make those choices because they lack the imagination or discipline to consider anything else.

What to Do If You Are Still Lost

Sometimes, this strategy of self-assessment and counseling does not work. You may be disciplined and systematic, getting counseling and talking to alumni, approaching the choices with an open mind—and you still may have no idea what to do. Or you may appreciate that even if you could know what to do, that answer might or should or will change as you get older. As graduation accelerates toward you, you feel that you have the right to panic. That is understandable.

Here is a simple solution: think short term. If you take as a given that life has too many paths to count, you might also see that this gets worse as time stretches further out. So you could work backwards. The shorter the time frame, the more predictable the future, and the more realizable the plan. If you can settle on a short-term plan, try to have faith that the future will take care of itself. And that faith has a strong foundation in the superb education you will have just gotten.

There are many attractive short-term alternatives for a recent college graduate. Three of them help extend the life many undergraduates have led in public service, teaching, and international travel. This generation of college students is admirable for many reasons, but their commitment to public service is inspirational and impressive. Recent Johns Hopkins students started a foundation for tribal people in South India, created a nonprofit to educate college students about Africa, dug water wells in rural South Africa, organized conferences on national security, and helped Baltimore City develop healthier housing for the poor. The list goes on and on, including more usual kinds of volunteerism like tutoring school children and caring for the elderly. So, in the short run, recent graduates can become part of one of the many superb public service programs, notably the Peace Corps and AmeriCorps. Some students balk at the long time commitment, but what is their hurry? Public service projects, like teaching opportunities, are among the few jobs where someone straight out of college has any real responsibility or authority. Participants get to work immediately, and that work helps people from day one.

Teaching is a form of public service, of course, but it draws special attention from the recent graduates of top colleges. Anyone who enjoyed the success that got them into a good college owes much of that to an amazing chain of women and men who taught them, from preschool through AP Chemistry. Most students are intensely aware of this debt, and many of them want to repay it by teaching themselves. That makes sense. Aside from their parents and adults in their families, teachers have been the most consistent and effective role models for students. You know what teachers do—or you think you do. There is less mystery to their jobs, and the payoff is immediate. It's good to get a reality check on this profession: the hours are long, the pay is small and the bureaucracy tedious, the demands are enormous. But teaching is a great option for people coming out of college, particularly if their long-range plans are murky. There are teaching programs such as Teach for America, as well as programs in cities like New York, to harness young talent. Or you could apply to one of the many independent schools that hire faculty straight out of college.

For a smaller number, especially graduates with language training or study abroad experience, the possibility of international travel after college is enticing. Such travel might be as brief as the classic backpacking trip on European trains, but there are many other options for more meaningful, long-term travel. Some of these overlap with the public service and teaching options above. Peace Corps volunteers do a lot of teaching, for example. But other options include academic research and/or coursework at a foreign institution. This can be funded by the Fulbright Scholarship, for example. Unlike the Rhodes or Marshall scholarships, which are very limited in number (though worthwhile, of course), the Fulbright has well over 600 opportunities all around the world. The program grows each year to include more possibilities like English teaching assistantships.

Since there are not enough scholarships to satisfy all the demands for international travel, you can consider internships with multinationals, management training programs for corporations with foreign offices, and jobs with international primary and secondary schools.

These three options may be obvious, and you may find them unsatisfying. Consider another way to make short-term choices: set new goals. Most graduates from good colleges burn with ambition. They hunger for prestige, for money, for position, for respect. They worked hard to earn a spot in a great school with an eye toward a special future, however defined or undefined. So they are eager to begin getting something done and getting somewhere. But what if you cannot figure out, quite yet, where that "somewhere" is? One alternative is to put those unspecified ambitions on hold, if temporarily, so that you can gain perspective, maturity, and a better financial situation. While you are waiting for insight and more certainty, you need something to do, so you need to set some temporary goals.

I have three suggestions. The first is to have fun. The students I know are wound very tightly. They have led stressful, albeit rewarding, lives in high school and college. They can be exhausted by the effort, in need of a break and a chance to recuperate. So, I tell them to go have fun—to find a job in an exciting city, a ski resort, or a sunny island. Will their parents object to their taking a job as a bartender in Aspen or in Tahiti? Absolutely. But if frivolity can help in the long run by helping you, an exhausted college graduate, to recharge your batteries, earn some money, and get a good tan, I say, "Enjoy!"

The second goal can be to experience a new city for the sake of exploration. New York is a great choice, for example, a place designed for the young or the rich—or both, if you are lucky. Having only youth, you will not lack for adventure and appetite if you try new (cheap) foods, get standing-room tickets for the Metropolitan Opera, explore Chinatown, see college buddies, and wait for professional inspiration. There are many great places to live, of course, so what is wrong with sampling them for a while?

Finally, you could set as a short-term goal getting a job that is best done when you are young. Take advantage of your energy, disconnection from family, and willingness to sleep little and on someone's floor. These qualities will fade, but they are a premium for some great jobs that can set a sound foundation for many future careers. These might include marketing or sales jobs that require travel, policy or political jobs that demand late hours for little money, and freelance work as a production assistant or writer. Another great option is in "development," meaning fundraising. Successful fundraisers do not get training in school; they learn on the job, mentored by veterans, and sharpened by countless events, conversations, and phone calls. The work demands travel, long hours, and endless energy. And fundraisers can move up that career path only with experience and success in landing donors. If they go on to something else, they will always have invaluable skills to call upon.

You will notice that none of these suggestions include graduate or professional school. I have excluded these intentionally because it is more challenging to decide what to do when you can't decide. More importantly, *no one should go to graduate or professional school unless he or she has clear professional goals.* In other words, graduate students cannot afford to be lost or to be explorers. College is a great place to explore, to ponder, and to wander. But graduate school is not. Graduate and professional schools are for the serious and the focused—mature students who know what skills and training they need and are intentional and disciplined about getting them.

Too many students have told me that law school is a great idea when you do not know what to do. "A law degree is so flexible!" they argue. If this is true, it is probably because the people who are smart enough to get into and succeed in law school are equally capable of adapting to new needs. Law school, in fact, is a place where lawyers train others to become practicing lawyers—not public servants, or politicians, or real estate developers, or Wall Street brokers.

The same is true for other professional schools, but it is less obviously true for academic graduate schools. I entered a doctoral program in political science at the University of Wisconsin–Madison with about 25 others. The people in that group fell into three categories. The first were students straight out of college. They loved their poli sci classes and thought being a professor might be cool. Most of them did not last through the first year. The second group were more mature, perhaps a year or two out of college, were very bright and less naïve, but were equally likely to use graduate school as an extension of undergraduate life. They did a lot of intellectual exploring, which meant they completed some of the doctoral requirements, but rarely got so far as the dissertation or final thesis.

The final group treated graduate school as a business, and their training as purely professional. Most of us in this small group had graduated several years before and done a variety of interesting jobs in the meantime. One in this group had been a construction foreman and already had a family. We stayed focused. We knew what had to get done. We did it, and we earned our doctorates. Out of the more than two dozen who started, only eight of us did that. And we were all in this last group.

It is always exciting to meet a college student so inspired by her studies that continuing them is tempting. But she should not spend more time in school and more money on tuition unless she has shaped a clear and informed image of the professional life she will lead afterwards. If she is not certain about this, or only almost, she should wait a little while. I know this certainty will vary in intensity; no one can know for sure, and we all make mistakes. But if doubt outweighs determination, recent graduates should have some patience and use some of the suggestions above for teaching and/or travel before coming back to campus.

For the student who struggled in college, there is an added advantage to waiting. Many discouraged pre-meds, carrying weak grades on their transcripts, still harbor the dream of medical school and a successful practice. Others made decisions about a career path late in college, so their backgrounds are incomplete or just uncooked. As determined as they may be, these students probably will not convince anyone, including admissions committees or employers, that they are ready and worthy. Gatekeepers like this do not like risks; they tend to make conservative choices.

So these students need to build a longer resumé beyond a college education. They should do that without apology—regret is for chumps—but with imagination. A student who followed a road full of potholes, many of them of his or her making, needs to be creative to build a distinctive and competitive record. That new post-college record can show the confidence won by working at a newspaper overseas. It can show the humanity of a person who is helping children with Down's syndrome. Such a graduate can show his determination by starting at the bottom of a company with guys who never went to college. As they regain their self-respect, those who struggled in college will earn the respect of others. And that will earn them the chance to get what they deserve.

✤ Put It in Perspective

Life after college is a wonderful and terrifying prospect, like looking down a track at a locomotive making up lost time and coming right at you. The excitement and anxiety of this reality is probably coloring your college life, even now as a freshman, perhaps to the point of distraction and fear. These are worries to be handled head on.

My principal message to the worried student is to be self-aware and intellectually demanding in trying to solve the puzzle of what to do next. Running around aimlessly, throwing up your hands in frustration, or simply being resigned ("I am a philosophy major. Ha, ha, ha. I was expecting to be unemployed!") is lazy and ignorant—two traits a college student should never have. Academically, you know that you have to work hard and get help when you need it. If you apply some of that effort to the question of life after college, you will feel more comfortable and more in command. So, do the research, take the self-

SUSAN MARINE, Ph.D.
ASSISTANT DEAN OF HARVARD COLLEGE and
DIRECTOR OF THE HARVARD COLLEGE WOMEN'S CENTER
HARVARD UNIVERSITY

So you've decided you'd like to play first violin in the Vienna Philharmonic. Or blaze a trail as the world's first translator of the dolphin language into Braille. Somewhere on your campus is a building dedicated to the wholehearted pursuit of the right career for you. The highly skilled people inside will help you determine the best possible course of study, internships, study abroad, winter break shadowing program, and postgraduate fellowships to make these goals into reality. These are the proverbial stepping-stones to securing a livelihood of meaning and purpose, and your planner will soon fill with the minutia of them before your very eyes.

But what about the part of you that wants to perfect the foxtrot? Or to lie on the campus green counting stars? Be sure to tend to that person, too, the one who finds deep solace in throwing a clay pot, in following Kanye West around the country on his summer tour, or in jumping her horse in the show ring. What makes your heart sing won't always be what earns you a paycheck. Finding the job of your dreams sometimes obscures the parts of our waking REM sleep that are purely for enjoyment. Whether you call them hobbies, interests, or guilty pleasures, these are the scaffolding of a lively and surprising life, one filled with learning curves that never end, along with pictures and ticket stubs and other material memories that will make you smile long into your old age. Make sure to save time for them in college, even as you're steadily climbing the ladder up to the top of the career peak. Not only do they make *life* more interesting, they make *you* more interesting. And even if they didn't, the delight they bring will linger on, as you will know when you find yourself at your reunion 20 years hence, smiling and laughing as you think to yourself of the simple, quiet truth: wow, college really was the best four years of my life. (And now, you've got the foxtrot to prove it.)

assessment tests, talk to alumni and family, and use the career counselors. There are people right on campus who can help you build a framework for decision-making that can be used again and again, even as circumstances change and reassessment becomes necessary. This can be done with the knowledge that no plan will ever roll out as expected. But thinking and planning can be two different exercises. If all your thinking and planning fail and you walk across a commencement stage without a specific plan, you can still be useful or at least have fun.

When you make that walk with less anxiety, with the understanding that freedom and uncertainty are twins, and with the confidence that you have spent the previous four years in an enthusiastic pursuit of learning, you will have enjoyed real and lasting success in college.

NOTES

....

Introduction

1. Jennifer Hanson and Friends, *The Real Freshman Handbook: A Totally Honest Guide to Life on Campus*, 2nd ed. (New York: Houghton Mifflin, 2002); Mark W. Bernstein, ed., *How to Survive Your Freshman Year: By Hundreds of College Sophomores, Juniors, and Seniors Who Did* (Atlanta: Hundreds of Heads Books, 2004); Allison Lombardo and Katharine Jackson, *Navigating Your Freshman Year: How to Make the Leap to College Life—and Land on Your Feet* (Upper Saddle River, NJ: Prentice Hall Press, 2005); Grey Gottesman and Daniel Baer, *College Survival: Get the Real Scoop on College Life from Students around the Country*, 7th ed. (New York: Thomson-Peterson's, 2004); Douglas Stone and Elizabeth Tippett, *Real College: The Essential Guide to Student Life—Your Roommate, Your Social Life, Your Grades, Your Parents, Your Self* (New York: Penguin Books, 2004); Laurie Rozakis, *The Complete Idiot's Guide to College Survival* (Indianapolis: Alpha Books, 2001); Michael S. Malone, *The Everything College Survival Book: From Social Life to Studying Skills—All You Need to Know to Fit Right In!* 2nd ed. (Avon, MA: Adams Media, 2005); Ernie Lapore and Sarah-Jane Leslie, *What Every College Student Should Know: How to Find the Best Teachers and Learn the Most from Them* (New Brunswick, NJ: Rutgers University Press, 2002); Sherrie Nist and Jodi Patrick Holschuh, *College Rules! How to Study, Survive, and Succeed in College* (Berkeley, CA: Ten Speed Press, 2002).

2. Sherrie Nist-Olejnik and Jodi Holschuh, *College Success Strategies: Becoming an Effective Learner*, 2nd ed. (New York: Longman, 2006); Lynn F. Jacobs and Jeremy S. Hyman, *Professors' Guide to Getting Good Grades in College* (New York: Collins, 2006); Eric Jensen, *Student Success Secrets*, 5th ed. (Hauppauge, NY: Barron's, 2003); Richard J. Light, *Making the Most of College: Students Speak Their Minds* (Cambridge, MA: Harvard University Press, 2001).

3. Light, *Making the Most of College*, p. 75.

4. Camille Z. Charles et al., *Taming the River: Negotiating the Academic, Financial, and Social Currents in Selective Colleges and Universities* (Princeton: Princeton University Press, 2009).

5. Karen Levin Coburn and Madge Lawrence Treeger, *Letting Go: A Parents' Guide to Understanding the College Years*, 3rd ed. (New York: Harper Perennial, 1997).

6. Frederick Rudolph and John R. Thelin, *The American College and University: A History* (Athens: University of Georgia Press, 1990); John Seiler Brubacher and Willis Rudy, *Higher Education in Transition: A History of American Colleges and Universities, 1636–1976*, 3rd ed. (New York: Harper & Row, 1976); Arthur M. Cohen, *The Shaping of American Higher Education: Emergence and Growth of the Contemporary System* (San Francisco: Jossey-Bass, 1998).

7. G. Lichtenstein et al., "An Engineering Major Does Not (Necessarily) an Engineer Make: Career Decision Making among Undergraduate Engineering Majors," *Journal of Engineering Education* 98, no. 3 (2009): 227–34; M. Firmin, "Frequent Major Changing: Extrinsic and Intrinsic Factors," *NACADA Journal* 28, no. 2 (2008): 5–13.

8. J. McCarthy and L. Anderson, "Active Learning Techniques Versus Traditional Teaching Styles: Two Experiments from History and Political Science," *Innovative Higher Education* 24, no. 4 (2000): 279–94; S. Burns et al., "The Language of Learning Styles," *Techniques: Connecting Education and Careers* 83, no. 2 (2008): 44–48; L. Vaughn et al., "Learning Styles and the Relationship to Attachment Styles and Psychological Symptoms in College Women," *College Student Journal* 43, no. 3 (2009): 723–35.

9. C. White and J. Fantone, "Analysis of Factors That Predict Clinical Performance in Medical School," *Advances in Health Sciences Education* 14, no. 4 (2009): 455–64; M. Albanese et al., "Assessing Personal Qualities in Medical School Admissions," *Academic Medicine* 78, no. 3 (2003): 313–21; E. Siu, "Overview: What's Worked and What Hasn't as a Guide Towards Predictive Admissions Tool Development," *Advances in Health Sciences Education* 14, no. 5 (2009): 759–75; M. Lowe et al., "Is It Possible to Assess the 'Ethics' of Medical School Applicants?" *Journal of Medical Ethics* 27, no. 6 (2001): 404–8.

10. Martin Kramer, Stephen S. Weiner, and Western Association of Schools and Colleges Accrediting Commission for Senior Colleges and Universities, *Dialogues for Diversity: Community and Ethnicity on Campus* (Phoenix: Oryx Press, 1994).

11. M. Dwyer, "Charting the Impact of Studying Abroad," *International Educator* 13, no. 1 (2004): 14–20; E. Norris, J. Gillespie, and J. Gillespie, "How Study Abroad Shapes Global Careers: Evidence from the United States," *Journal of Studies in International Education* 13, no. 3 (2009): 382–97.

12. J. Turner and J. Husman, "Emotional and Cognitive Self-regulation Following Academic Shame," *Journal of Advanced Academics* 20, no. 1 (2009): 138–73; T. Durham, "This Too Shall Pass: Academic Resilience after a Perceived Failure,"

Dissertation Abstracts International, Section A: Humanities and Social Sciences 70, no. 3 (2009): 812.

13. D. Forsyth et al., "What Causes Failure and Success? Students' Perceptions of Their Academic Outcomes," *Social Psychology of Education* 12, no. 2 (2009):157–74; T. Wegner, "Students' with Learning Disabilities Perceptions of Factors That Contribute to or Detract from College Success," *Dissertation Abstracts International, Section A: Humanities and Social Sciences* 70, no. 3 (2009): 843.

14. Gregory Giangrande, *The Liberal Arts Advantage: How to Turn Your Degree into a Great Job* (New York: Avon Books, 1998); Julie DeGalan and Stephen Lambert, *Great Jobs for English Majors*, 3rd ed. (New York: McGraw-Hill, 2006).

15. As always, with gratitude to Marvin Hupart, an inspiring history teacher and teacher of history.

16. A. White and H. Swartzwelder, "Inbound College Students Drink Heavily during the Summer before Their Freshman Year: Implications for Education and Prevention Efforts," *American Journal of Health Education* 40, no. 2 (2009): 90–96; E. Pascarella et al., "College Student Binge Drinking and Academic Achievement: A Longitudinal Replication and Extension," *Journal of College Student Development* 48, no. 6 (2007): 715–27; P. Thacher, "University Students and 'the All-Nighter': Correlates and Patterns of Students' Engagement in a Single Night of Total Sleep Deprivation," *Behavioral Sleep Medicine* 6, no. 1 (2008): 16–31; Walter C. Buboltz et al., "College Student Sleep: Relationship to Health and Academic Performance," pp. 1–39, in *College Students: Mental Health and Coping Strategies*, ed. Mery V. Landow (Hauppauge, NY: Nova, 2006).

17. "Socrates' Defense (Apology)," in *The Collected Dialogues of Plato*, ed. Edith Hamilton and Huntington Cairns (Princeton: Princeton University Press, 1980), p. 23.

18. J. Saults, "A Central Capacity Limit to the Simultaneous Storage of Visual and Auditory Arrays in Working Memory," *Journal of Experimental Psychology: General* 136, no. 4 (2007): 663–84; N. Cowan et al., "Theory and Measurement of Working Memory Capacity Limits," *Psychology of Learning and Motivation* 49 (2008): 49–104.

19. T. Bender, "Updating Higher Education's Past: 1940 to 2005," *Chronicle of Higher Education*, July 11, 2008, p. A24.

Habit #7: Focus on Learning, Not on Grades

1. William N. Hargreaves-Mawdsley, *A History of Academical Dress in Europe until the End of the Eighteenth Century* (Westport, CT: Greenwood Press, 1978).

2. Loren Pope, *Colleges That Change Lives* (New York: Penguin Books, 2006).

Habit #2: Build an Adult Relationship with Your Parents

1. Margo E. Bane Woodacre and Steffany Bane, *I'll Miss You, Too: An Off-to-College Guide for Parents and Students; What Will Change, What Will Not, and How We'll Stay Connected* (Napierville, IL: Sourcebooks, 2006); Robin Raskin, *Parents' Guide to College Life: 181 Straight Answers to Everything You Can Expect over the Next Four Years* (New York: Random House Information Group, 2006).

2. S. Cleaver, "Meet the Micro-Managers," *Instructor* 118, no. 3 (2008): 30–36.

3. W. Pricer, "At Issue: Helicopter Parents and Millennial Students; An Annotated Bibliography," *Community College Enterprise* 14, no. 2 (2008): 93–108.

4. J. Weidman, *Impacts of Campus Experiences and Parental Socialization on Undergraduates' Career Choices*, Final Report, Bureau of Social Science Research Project 549 (Washington, DC: National Institute of Education, 1979).

5. D. Vogel et al., "Parental Attitudes and College Students' Intentions to Seek Therapy," *Journal of Social and Clinical Psychology* 28, no. 6 (2009): 689–713.

6. S. Lipka, "Helicopter Parents Help Students, Survey Finds," *Chronicle of Higher Education* 54, no. 11 (2007): 4; K. Wartman, "Redefining Parental Involvement: Working-Class and Low-Income Students' Relationship to Their Parents during the First Semester of College," *Dissertation Abstracts International, Section A: Humanities and Social Sciences* 70, no. 2 (2009): 502.

7. R. Marom-Tal, "Contributions of Psychological Separation, Attachment, and Ego Identity Development to Dyadic Adjustment in Early Adulthood," *Dissertation Abstracts Internationa, Section B: The Sciences and Engineering* 67, no. 12 (2007): 7383.

8. Karen Levin Coburn and Madge Lawrence Treeger, *Letting Go: A Parents' Guide to Understanding the College Years* (New York: HarperCollins, 1997).

9. E. Hoover and B. Supiano, "Surveys of Students Challenge 'Helicopter Parent' Stereotypes," *Chronicle of Higher Education* 54, no. 21 (2008): A22.

10. A. Trice, "First Semester College Students' Email to Parents, I: Frequency and Content Related to Parenting Style," *College Student Journal* 36, no. 3 (2002): 327–34.

Habit #3: Work the System by Understanding the System

1. Arthur M. Cohen, *The Shaping of American Higher Education: Emergence and Growth of the Contemporary System* (San Francisco: Jossey-Bass, 1998).

2. J. Wellington et al., *Succeeding with Your Doctorate* (London: Sage, 2005).

3. *Graduate and Enrollment Degrees* (Washington DC: Council of Graduate Schools, 2010), as cited in "More Women Than Men Got PhDs Last Year," *Washington Post*, Sept. 14, 2010, p. A1.

4. M. Komarraju, "A Social-Cognitive Approach to Training Teaching Assistants," *Teaching of Psychology* 35, no. 4 (2008): 327–34; C. Jia and A. Bergerson, "Understanding the International Teaching Assistant Training Program: A Case Study at a Northwestern Research University," *International Education* 37, no. 2 (2008): 77–98.

5. Richard Light, *Making the Most of College: Students Speak Their Minds* (Cambridge: Harvard University Press, 2001).

6. R. Kahlenberg, "Cost Remains a Key Obstacle to College Access," *Chronicle of Higher Education*, March 10, 2006, Suppl., B51–52.

Habit #4 : Approach the Curriculum Like a Great Feast

1. A. Yazedjian et al., "'It's a Whole New World': A Qualitative Exploration of College Students' Definitions of and Strategies for College Success," *Journal of College Student Development* 49, no. 2 (2008): 141–54.

2. M. Komarraju, S. Karau, and R. Schmeck, "Role of the Big Five Personality Traits in Predicting College Students' Academic Motivation and Achievement," *Learning and Individual Differences* 19, no. 1 (2009): 47–52; A. Durik, C. Lovejoy, and S. Johnson, "A Longitudinal Study of Achievement Goals for College in General: Predicting Cumulative GPA and Diversity in Course Selection," *Contemporary Educational Psychology* 34, no. 2 (2009): 113–19; M. Balduf, "Underachievement among College Students," *Journal of Advanced Academics* 20, no. 2 (2009): 274–94.

Habit #5 : Understand That Majors and Careers Are Not the Same Thing

1. K. Eyster, "Career Counseling: 101+ Things You Can Do with a Degree in Biology," *Advances in Physiology Education* 31, no. 4 (2007): 323–28.

2. Joyce Curll, *The Best Law Schools' Admission Secrets: The Essential Guide from Harvard's Former Admissions Dean* (Naperville, IL: Sourcebooks, 2008).

Habit #6 : Don't Just Work Hard—Work Smart

1. B. Meyer, A. Talbot, and D. Florencio, "Reading Rate and Prose Retrieval," *Scientific Studies of Reading* 3, no. 4 (1999): 303–29; J. Magliano, T. Trabasso, and A. Graesser, "Strategic Processing during Comprehension," *Journal of Educational Psychology* 91, no. 4 (1999): 615–29.

2. L. Carrier and H. Pashler, "Attentional Limits in Memory Retrieval," *Journal of Experimental Psychology: Learning, Memory, and Cognition* 21, no. 5 (1995): 1339–48.

3. Sherrie Nist-Olejnik and Jodi Holschuh, *College Success Strategies: Becoming an Effective Learner*, 2nd ed. (New York: Longman, 2006); Lynn F. Jacobs and Jeremy S. Hyman, *Professors' Guide to Getting Good Grades in College* (New York: Collins, 2006); Eric Jensen, *Student Success Secrets*, 5th ed. (Hauppauge, NY: Barron's, 2003); Richard J. Light, *Making the Most of College: Students Speak Their Minds* (Cambridge: Harvard University Press, 2001).

4. H. Noland et al., "Adolescents' Sleep Behaviors and Perceptions of Sleep," *Journal of School Health* 79, no. 5 (2009): 224–30.

5. C. Pierce, "An Academic Survey of Engineering Student Athletes at a Division I University," *College Student Journal* 41, no. 4 (2007): 801–12; M. Melendez, "The Influence of Athletic Participation on the College Adjustment of Freshmen and Sophomore Student Athletes," *Journal of College Student Retention: Research, Theory, and Practice* 8, no. 1 (2006): 39–55.

6. C. Choma, G. Sforzo, and B. Keller, "Impact of Rapid Weight Loss on Cognitive Function in Collegiate Wrestlers," *Medicine and Science in Sports and Exercise* 30, no. 5 (1998): 746–49.

Habit #7: Build Integrity to Get into Professional or Graduate School

1. A. Jordan, "College Student Cheating: The Role of Motivation, Perceived Norms, Attitudes, and Knowledge of Institutional Policy," *Ethics & Behavior* 11, no. 3 (2001): 233–47; H. Passow et al., "Factors Influencing Engineering Students' Decisions to Cheat by Type of Assessment," *Research in Higher Education* 47, no. 6 (2006): 643–84.

2. R. Belter and A. du Pré, "A Strategy to Reduce Plagiarism in an Undergraduate Course," *Teaching of Psychology* 36, no. 4 (2009): 257–61; R. Hauptman, "Dishonesty in the Academy," *Academe* 88, no. 6 (2002), 39–44.

3. L. Taylor, M. Pogrebin, and M. Dodge, "Advanced Placement—Advanced Pressures: Academic Dishonesty among Elite High School Students," *Educational Studies* (American Educational Studies Association) 33, no. 4 (2002): 403–21; P. S. Strom and R. D. Strom, "Cheating in Middle School and High School," *Educational Forum* 71, no. 2 (2007): 104–16; E. Anderman and C. Midgley, "Changes in Self-Reported Academic Cheating across the Transition from Middle School to High School," *Contemporary Educational Psychology* 29, no. 4 (2004): 499–517.

4. D. Rettinger and Y. Kramer, "Situational and Personal Causes of Student Cheating," *Research in Higher Education* 50, no. 3 (2009): 293–313.

5. P. Hutton, "Understanding Student Cheating and What Educators Can Do About It," *College Teaching* 54, no. 1 (2006): 171–76; S. Newstead, A. Franklyn-

Stokes, and P. Armstead, "Individual Differences in Student Cheating," *Journal of Educational Psychology* 88, no. 2 (1996): 229–41.

6. A. Miller, C. Shoptaugh, and A. Parkerson, "Under Reporting of Cheating in Research Using Volunteer College Students," *College Student Journal* 42, no. 2 (2008): 326–39; R. Volpe, L. Davidson, and M. Bell, "Faculty Attitudes and Behaviors Concerning Student Cheating," ibid. 42, no. 1 (2008): 164–75.

7. G. Diekhoff, K. Shinohara, and H. Yasukawa, "College Cheating in Japan and the United States," *Research in Higher Education* 40, no. 3 (1999): 343–53; C. Lin and L. Wen, "Academic Dishonesty in Higher Education: A Nationwide Study in Taiwan," *Higher Education* 54, no. 1 (2007): 85–97.

8. John A. Zebala, *Medical School Admissions: The Insider's Guide* (Memphis, TN: Mustang Publishing, 2000).

9. Ibid.

Habit #8: Learn from Diversity at Home and Abroad

1. Thomas L. Friedman, *The World Is Flat: A Brief History of the Twenty-First Century* (New York: Farrar, Straus and Giroux, 2008).

2. See College Board, "Higher Education Landscape: Current Demographic Trends in U.S. Higher Education," at http://professionals.collegeboard.com/data-reports-research/trends/higher-ed-landscape.

3. P. Gurin et al., "Diversity and Higher Education: Theory and Impact on Educational Outcomes," *Harvard Educational Review* 72 (2002): 330–66; N. Bowman, "College Diversity Courses and Cognitive Development among Students from Privileged and Marginalized Groups," *Journal of Diversity in Higher Education* 2, no. 3 (2009): 182–94; P. Schmidt, "The Mixed Benefits of Diversity," *Chronicle of Higher Education* 55, no. 25 (2009): 4.

4. Martin Kramer and Stephen S. Weiner, *Dialogues for Diversity: Community and Ethnicity on Campus* (Phoenix: Oryx Press, 1994).

5. C. Steele and J. Aronson, "Stereotype Threat and the Intellectual Test Performance of African Americans," *Journal of Personality and Social Psychology* 69, no. 5 (1995): 797–811; K. Griffin, "Striving for Success: A Qualitative Exploration of Competing Theories of High-Achieving Black College Students' Academic Motivation," *Journal of College Student Development* 47, no. 4 (2006): 384–400.

6. E. Farrell, "Study Abroad Blossoms into Big Business," *Chronicle of Higher Education* 54, no. 2 (2007): 55; S. Klahr, "Increasing Engineering Student Participation in Study Abroad: A Study of U.S. and European Programs," *Journal of Studies in International Education* 4, no. 1 (2000): 79–102; K. Jenkins, "Educating for the Global Future," *Black Issues in Higher Education* 17, no. 19 (2000): 36; W. Maddux

and A. Galinsky, "Cultural Borders and Mental Barriers: The Relationship between Living Abroad and Creativity," *Journal of Personality and Social Psychology* 96, no. 5 (2009): 1047–61.

7. E. Norris and J. Gillespie, "Study Abroad: Stepping Stone to a Successful International Career," *NACE Journal* 65, no. 3 (2005): 30–36.

8. See the Open Doors Web site, http://opendoors.iienetwork.org.

Habit #9: When You Are Failing, Understand Why

1. D. Forsyth et al., "What Causes Failure and Success? Students' Perceptions of Their Academic Outcomes," *Social Psychology of Education* 12, no. 2 (2009): 157–74; M. Balduf, "Underachievement among College Students," *Journal of Advanced Academics* 20, no. 2 (2009): 274–94; Jennifer Engle and Vincent Tinto, *Moving beyond Access: College Success for Low-Income, First-Generation Students* (Washington, DC: Pell Institute for the Study of Opportunity in Higher Education, 2008).

2. Richard Kadison and Theresa Foy DeGeronimo, *College of the Overwhelmed: The Campus Mental Health Crisis and What to Do about It* (San Francisco: Jossey-Bass, 2004).

3. K. Wimshurst and T. Allard, "Personal and Institutional Characteristics of Student Failure," *Assessment and Evaluation in Higher Education* 33, no. 6 (2008): 687–98; C. Wilkie, "Predictors of Academic Success and Failure of First-Year College Students," *Journal of the Freshman Year Experience and Students in Transition* 8, no. 2 (1996): 17–32.

4. J. Conner, D. Pope, and M. Galloway, "Success with Less Stress," *Educational Leadership* 67, no. 4 (2009): 54–58; J. Peterson and K. Canady, "A Longitudinal Study of Negative Life Events, Stress, and School Experiences of Gifted Youth," *Gifted Child Quarterly* 53, no. 1 (2009): 34–49; S. Suldo et al., "Coping Strategies of High School Students in an International Baccalaureate Program," *Psychology in the Schools* 45, no. 10 (2008): 960–77.

5. Neil Howe and William Strauss, *Millennials Go to College: Strategies for a New Generation on Campus* (Washington, DC: Association of Collegiate Registrars and Admissions Officers, 2003).

6. L. Munday and J. Davis, *Varieties of Accomplishment after College: Perspectives on the Meaning of Academic Talent*, ACT Research Reports, 21 (Iowa City: American College Testing Program, Research and Development Division, 1974); D. Lohman, "An Aptitude Perspective on Talent: Implications for Identification of Academically Gifted Minority Students," *Journal for the Education of the Gifted* 28, no. 3 (2005): 333–60; D. De Sousa, *Promoting Student Success: What Advisors Can Do*, National Survey of Student Engagement, Occasional Paper No. 11 (Bloomington: Indiana University Center for Postsecondary Research, 2005).

7. K. Courtney, "Binge Drinking in Young Adults: Data, Definitions, and Determinants," *Psychological Bulletin* 135, no. 1 (2009): 142–56; M. Mitka, "College Binge Drinking Still on the Rise," *JAMA: Journal of the American Medical Association* 302, no. 8 (2009): 836–37; R. Grucza, K. Norberg, and L. Bierut, "Binge Drinking among Youths and Young Adults in the United States, 1979–2006," *Journal of the American Academy of Child and Adolescent Psychiatry* 48, no. 7 (2009): 692–702.

8. N. Peleg-Oren et al., "Drinking Alcohol before Age 13 and Negative Outcomes in Late Adolescence," *Alcoholism: Clinical and Experimental Research* 33, no. 11 (2009): 1966–72; N. Nasrallah, T. Yang, and I. Bernstein, "Long-term Risk Preference and Suboptimal Decision Making Following Adolescent Alcohol Use," *Proceedings of the National Academy of Sciences of the United States of America* 106, no. 41 (2009): 17600–17604.

9. M. Bruce et al., "Risk Factors for Meningococcal Disease in College Students," *JAMA* 286, no. 6 (2001): 688–93; V. Kak, "Infections in Confined Spaces: Cruise Ships, Military Barracks, and College Dormitories," *Infectious Disease Clinics of North America* 21, no. 3 (2007): 773–84; K. Fromme, W. Corbin, and M. Kruse, "Behavioral Risks during the Transition from High School to College," *Developmental Psychology* 44, no. 5 (2008): 1497–1504.

Habit #10: Cope with Failure by Rebuilding and Forgiving

1. A. Schwartz, "Are College Students More Disturbed Today? Stability in the Acuity and Qualitative Character of Psychopathology of College Counseling Center Clients: 1992–1993 through 2001–2002," *Journal of American College Health* 54, no. 6 (2006): 327–37.

2. B. Sharkin, "Increasing Severity of Presenting Problems in College Counseling Centers: A Closer Look," *Journal of Counseling and Development* 75, no. 4 (1997): 275–81; A. Reynolds and S. Chris, "Improving Practice through Outcomes-Based Planning and Assessment: A Counseling Center Case Study," *Journal of College Student Development* 49, no. 4 (2008): 374–87; J. Bishop, "Emerging Administrative Strategies for College and University Counseling Centers," *Journal of Counseling and Development* 74, no. 1 (1995): 33–38.

3. M. Bigard, "Walking the Labyrinth: An Innovative Approach to Counseling Center Outreach," *Journal of College Counseling* 12, no. 2 (2009): 137–48; T. Russell, "Individual and Familial Influences on Psychological Functioning and Help-Seeking Behavior of Black College Students," *Dissertation Abstracts International, Section B: The Sciences and Engineering* 69, no. 4 (2008): 2640.

4. D. Rabiner et al., "Adjustment to College in Students with ADHD," *Journal of Attention Disorders* 11, no. 6 (2008): 689–99; G. DuPaul, S. O'Dell, and M. Varejao, "College Students with ADHD: Current Status and Future Directions," *Journal*

of *Attention Disorders* 13, no. 3 (2009): 234–50; L. Whitaker, "Forces Pushing Prescription Psychotropic Drugs in College Mental Health," *Journal of College Student Psychotherapy* 21, nos. 3–4 (2007): 1–25.

5. D. Cicero, A. Epler, and K. Sher, "Are There Developmentally Limited Forms of Bipolar Disorder?" *Journal of Abnormal Psychology* 118, no. 3 (2009): 431–47; K. Chang et al., "Management of Bipolar Disorders in Children and Adolescents," pp. 389–424 in *Handbook of Diagnosis and Treatment of Bipolar Disorders*, ed. Terrence A. Ketter (Washington, DC: American Psychiatric Publishing, 2010).

Habit #11: Plan Boldly for Life after College

1. E. Hull-Blanks et al., "Career Goals and Retention-Related Factors among College Freshmen," *Journal of Career Development* 32, no. 1 (2005): 16–30; E. Helm, W. Sedlacek, and D. Prieto, *Career Advising Issues for African American Entering Students*, Research Report #2-97 (College Park, MD: University of Maryland Counseling Center, 1997).

2. Julia Carr et al., *Working Knowledge: 150 Successful Professionals Tell You How to Use College to Get the Job You Want* (New York: Simon and Schuster, 1999); Gerald Bustamente, *From College to Career: Making a Successful Transition to the Corporate World* (Lincoln, NE: iUniverse, 2007); Nancy Pollak, *Getting from College to Career: 90 Things to Do before You Join the Real World* (New York: HarperCollins, 2007); Adele M. Scheele, *Launch Your Career in College: Strategies for Students, Educators, and Parents* (Westport, CT: Praeger Publishers, 2005).

CONTRIBUTORS

....

JOHN B. BADER is Associate Dean for Undergraduate Academic Affairs and National Scholarships Advisor at the Johns Hopkins University, where he has held several positions since 2001 when he became Assistant Dean of Academic Advising. Previously, he was director of Washington Programs and Assistant Professor of Political Science for the UCLA Center for American Politics and Public Policy. His unusual career has also included teaching history in public schools, working in the Political Unit at ABC News, and service as Policy Director to Jon Corzine's successful U.S. Senate campaign in 2000. He earned his B.A. in history from Yale University, and his M.A. and Ph.D. from the University of Wisconsin–Madison. He was a Fulbright Scholar to India and a Governmental Studies Graduate Fellow at the Brookings Institution.

ANYA BERNSTEIN is the Director of Undergraduate Studies on the Committee on Degrees in Social Studies at Harvard University. She earned her B.A. at Barnard College and her Ph.D. in political science at Harvard. She organizes the curriculum and coordinates academic advising and programming in Social Studies, an interdisciplinary undergraduate major, and she works with students from freshmen to seniors. She is also a long-time member of Harvard's Standing Committee on Advising and Counseling.

KAREN BLANK is Dean of Studies at Barnard College. Her office is responsible for pre-major, pre-professional, and fellowship advising, as well as advising international students, monitoring students' academic standing, and directing the College's academic support and enrichment programs. Earlier in her career, she was responsible for pre-major academic advising at Colgate University and Dartmouth College (as Dean of Freshmen at both) and at Columbia University. She earned an Ed.D. at Teachers College, Columbia University.

LEORA BROVMAN has worked in undergraduate advising for many years. She earned her B.A. in social work from the University of the Witwatersrand in Johannesburg, South Africa, her M.S.W. at Columbia University, and an Ed.D. from Teachers' College at Columbia University. She currently advises Undergraduate College and Engineering students in all four years at Columbia University and is the coordinator for transfer students. She also works with students participating in several joint degree opportunities.

SUE BROWN received a B.A. in Russian studies from the University of Virginia and a Ph.D. in Slavic linguistics from Indiana University. She also studied at Middlebury College, Leningrad State University, and the Herzen Pedagogical Institute in St. Petersburg, Russia. She taught Russian for a year at Bucknell University in Lewisburg, Pennsylvania, before coming to Harvard to join the Slavic Department. After eight years teaching theoretical syntax and historical linguistics in the Slavic Department, Dean Brown joined the Freshman Dean's Office in 2005. She is happy to have moved into administration, since it gives her wonderful opportunities to work more closely with students.

MARGARET BRUZELIUS earned her undergraduate degree in English at Harvard and her Ph.D. in comparative literature from Yale. She is the Dean of the Senior Class at Smith College and a lecturer in its Comparative Literature Department; previously, she taught and served as a resident dean at Harvard College. At Smith, she teaches courses on the adventure novel and on pre-twentieth-century theories of language. Her book on the adventure novel, *Romancing the Novel: Adventure from Scott to Sebald*, was published by Bucknell University Press in 2007.

THOMAS N. CHIAROLANZIO earned his B.A. in political science from Gettysburg College and his M.A. from Teachers College, Columbia University. He has worked in both admissions and academic advising. He is currently an Associate Dean at Georgetown College, Georgetown University, where he works with first- and second-year students.

COLE M. CRITTENDEN is the Associate Dean of Undergraduate Students at Princeton University, a position he moved into after serving as the founding Director of Studies of Princeton's Whitman College. Prior to his appointment at Princeton, he served as the Allston Burr Resident Dean of Currier House at Harvard University and was a faculty member in Harvard's Department of Slavic Languages and Literatures. He earned his Ph.D. from Princeton University.

DAVID N. DEVRIES is Associate Dean for Undergraduate Education in the College of Arts and Sciences at Cornell University. He is the director of the Office of Academic Advising, the Office of Admissions, the Registrar's Office, and the college's Career Services Office. After earning his Ph.D. in medieval studies from New York University, he taught for many years at NYU and at Hobart and William Smith Colleges, serving also as Associate Dean of Hobart College. At Cornell, he has taught in the Cornell Prison Education Program, teaching introductory writing and literature courses at the Auburn maximum security prison and at the Cayuga medium security prison.

THOMAS A. DINGMAN has had a career at Harvard spanning more than three decades. It has included interviewing, traveling, and reading for Admissions; directing the Parents Association; coordinating Disability Services; serving as Assistant and Associate Dean of the College; being Resident Dean in Leverett House and Dudley House; and directing the Freshman Dean's Office. He has also taught and coached at the secondary school level, which helps to explain his special interest in issues of transition.

SUZANNE DUKE is a Resident Dean of Freshmen at Harvard University. She received her doctorate in Human Development and Psychology from the Harvard Graduate School of Education, where she studied the intersection of cognitive development and issues in clinical psychopathology (particularly post-traumatic stress disorder). She works with freshmen as an academic advisor and around issues of adjustment to college.

RAIMA EVAN received her B.A. from Radcliffe College, where she studied English and French literature. She went on to receive her M.A. and Ph.D. in English literature from the University of Pennsylvania. She taught part-time in the Department of English Literature at Swarthmore College before joining the Dean's Office at Bryn Mawr College. At Bryn Mawr, she advises students and is in charge of the re-enrollment process for students who want to return to the college after taking a medical leave. She is also responsible for the tutoring program and works with other staff members on the alcohol education program and the party policy.

M. CECILIA GAPOSCHKIN has been the Assistant Dean of Faculty for Pre-Major Advising at Dartmouth College since 2004. She is also a medieval historian and is on the Department of History faculty at Dartmouth. She received her B.A. from the University of Michigan in Ann Arbor (1992) and her Ph.D. in medieval history from the University of California–Berkeley (2001). At Dartmouth, she splits her time between advising and teaching. She believes passionately in the intellectual, ethical, and practical value of a liberal arts education.

BRIAN T. GIBSON is Assistant Dean of Undergraduates and Director of Academic Advising at Rice University. He is currently responsible for campus-wide undergraduate advising and lives on campus at Martel College. He is a published researcher and the recipient of numerous awards for teaching courses related to anatomy, physiology, and exercise science. His unique perspectives are the result of 14 years as a faculty member in residence responsible for cultivating the intellectual, cultural, and social vibrancy of the residential colleges.

LEAH BLATT GLASSER is the Dean of First-Year Studies and a lecturer in English at Mount Holyoke College, where she has been since 1980. Glasser received her Ph.D. from Brown University in American literature. As an academic dean, she works closely with first-year students and their faculty advisers. She develops relevant programs and materials to help students create a web of advising connections early in their college careers. Glasser combines her work as a dean with teaching writing and literature courses. She is the author of *In a Closet Hidden: The Life and Work of Mary E. Wilkins Freeman,* a literary biography of a writer who attended Mount Holyoke in 1870, as well as essays in magazines and journals such as the *Chronicle of Higher Education* and the *Massachusetts Review.*

ADINA GLICKMAN has been Associate Director for Academic Support at Stanford University's Center for Teaching and Learning since 2004. Prior to that, she was an Assistant Director and Learning Skills Specialist in Undergraduate Advising from 2001 to 2004. She oversees the center's peer tutoring program and works with students individually and through residence-based workshops in areas such as time manage-

ment, reading comprehension and retention, test-taking, and procrastination. She has presented workshops across the United States and
in Japan, and is a campus-wide resource for academic skills assessment and coaching. Before coming to Stanford, she was an Educational
Counselor at Keene State College in New Hampshire, where she also
maintained a private psychotherapy practice. She has a special interest
in helping students from diverse backgrounds thrive at Stanford, and
also teaches a course in the Psychology Department entitled "Stereotype Threat."

MAURA GREGORY has worked in student advising roles at Georgetown
University since 1995. She began her university career with a focus
on international education in the Office of International Programs at
Georgetown before moving into a dean's role in the School of Nursing
and Health Studies, followed by her current position as Assistant Dean
in the School of Foreign Service. She has a B.S. from James Madison
University in Spanish and communications. She earned her master's
degree in Latin American studies from the Graduate School of Foreign
Service at Georgetown University.

MARCELLE CHRISTIAN HOLMES is Associate Dean of Students and Dean of
Women at Pomona College, where she coordinates academic and personal support for first- and second-year students, coordinates on-call
crisis support, oversees the Women's Union, conducts training for academic advisors, and serves as the disability coordinator. She is also in
private practice as a licensed clinical psychologist in Claremont, California. She received her B.A. in psychology and French from Vassar
College, where she was inducted into Phi Beta Kappa, and she earned
her Ph.D. in clinical psychology from the University of Michigan–
Ann Arbor. Dr. Holmes has a special interest in college mental health,
women's issues, coping with chronic illness, yoga and mental health,
and cultural diversity issues in counseling. At Pomona she has taught
courses in psychology, women's studies, and black studies.

JOSEPH HOLTGREIVE is Assistant Dean of Undergraduate Engineering and
Director of the McCormick Office of Personal Development for Northwestern University's McCormick School of Engineering. In addition to
counseling undergraduates, he teaches engineering design and communication. He is also a trained mediator who specializes in conflict
management and coaching for corporate clients. He holds a B.S. in in-

dustrial engineering from Northwestern University and an Ed.M. with an emphasis in adult development and counseling from Harvard University. Prior to joining the administration and faculty at Northwestern, he was a change management consultant for Andersen Consulting.

MARCY KRAUS is the Dean of Freshmen and the Director of the College Center for Academic Support at the University of Rochester. Her career in higher education spans more than 20 years, most of them in academic advising. She has also worked in undergraduate admissions at several institutions, co-taught a course for resident advisors, and currently teaches a graduate course on academic advising. She completed her Ph.D. in psychology at the University of New Hampshire, where she studied learning strategies used by college students.

MATTHEW LAZEN is Director of Studies of Butler College at Princeton University, where he has also taught film in the Department of Comparative Literature. Prior to coming to Princeton, he was a lecturer in the History and Literature program at Harvard University. He earned his Ph.D. in French cultural studies and film in the Literature Program at Duke University.

GEORGE LEVESQUE is Assistant Dean of Academics Affairs and a lecturer in the Department of History at Yale. A former residential college dean and Dean of Freshman Affairs at Yale, he oversees freshman year advising and directs the freshman seminar program. He earned his Ph.D. from Columbia University. His teaching and research interests include the history of American colleges and universities.

ABIGAIL LIPSON is the Director of Harvard University's Bureau of Study Counsel. She holds a B.A. from Hampshire College in educational psychology and a Ph.D. from Duke University in clinical psychology. She has been awarded research and training fellowships by Harvard University, the National Institute of Mental Health, and the U.S. Department of Public Health; and she is a licensed clinical psychologist in both Massachusetts and the District of Columbia. She publishes widely in the fields of education and psychology and currently serves as editor of the *Newsletter* of the Association of University and College Counseling Center Directors. She co-facilitates, with Ariel Phillips, the Success/Failure Project at Harvard's Bureau of Study Counsel.

JOHN P. LOGE, JR., is Dean of Timothy Dwight College at Yale University. From southern California and educated at St. Paul's School, Yale, and the University of California–Los Angeles, he has been a schoolteacher and administrator most of his working life. A long-time hiker and camper, he also teaches a writing course on nature writing as a lecturer in the Yale Department of English.

Julie Lythcott-Haims is Dean of Freshmen and Undergraduate Advising at Stanford University, where she takes a keen interest in helping students develop and sustain a strong sense of belonging to the community of scholars at Stanford and to the institution itself. She manages the office of Undergraduate Advising and Research, which oversees pre-major and pre-professional advising, undergraduate research grant administration, freshman and transfer student transition, petitions, and academic standing. University administration is her second career; her first career was law. Her undergraduate degree is from Stanford in American studies, and her law degree is from Harvard University.

Susan Marine is Assistant Dean of Harvard College for Student Life and Director of the Harvard College Women's Center. She has 15 years' experience leading initiatives related to advancing women in higher education, and has expertise in violence prevention, leadership development, and support and development of lesbian, gay, bisexual, and transgender (LGBT) students. She teaches in the Committee on Degrees in Women, Gender and Sexuality at Harvard, as well as at Boston College, where she earned her Ph.D. in higher education.

John T. O'Keefe has been Director of Advising and Academic Support Services at Wellesley College since 2005 and also serves as a class dean. Before coming to Wellesley, he held a number of positions at Harvard College, including Assistant Dean of the College overseeing disciplinary processes and academic procedures, and he was also Allston Burr Senior Tutor in Dunster House at Harvard. He completed his undergraduate work at Columbia University and earned a Ph.D. in the history of American civilization at Harvard University, specializing in colonial American intellectual and religious history.

Ariel Phillips is a Counselor at Harvard University's Bureau of Study Counsel. She holds a B.A. from the University of California (joint major in anthropology, sociology, and psychology), an M.Ed. from the University of California (applied behavioral sciences), and an Ed.D. from Harvard University (human development and psychology). She is a licensed counseling and clinical psychologist in Massachusetts. She has co-authored and co-edited articles on education and on human development in organizations. At Harvard's Bureau of Study Counsel, her roles include working as a counselor to students; consulting to faculty; facilitating groups and workshops on many topics, including leadership and conflict management; and co-facilitating, with Abigail Lipson, the Success/Failure Project.

MICHELE RASMUSSEN was an Associate Dean of Trinity College at Duke University and is now the Director of Duke's Academic Advising Center. She earned her Ph.D. in biological anthropology and anatomy from Duke and a B.A. in history and art history from the University of California–Los Angeles. Over the past decade she has held administrative positions in student and academic affairs at Duke and at Wesleyan University, and currently has an adjunct faculty appointment in the Department of Evolutionary Anthropology at Duke. In addition to advising and serving as an academic dean to Duke students, Dr. Rasmussen teaches undergraduate courses in primate behavioral ecology and is a faculty in residence in one of Duke's first-year residence halls.

ANDREW N. SIMMONS is Director of the Career Development Center at Brown University. He also contributes his efforts to several other advising programs within the College at Brown. Dr. Simmons holds a Ph.D. in higher education administration from Boston College, where his studies focused on college student development as well as the history and philosophy of education.

KATHRYN STUART has served as Oberlin's Dean of Studies since 2002 and Vice President for Strategic Initiatives since 2008. Her previous positions at Oberlin include Associate Dean of Conservatory Academic Affairs, Acting Dean of the Conservatory, and Assistant to the President. She is also Associate Professor of Piano Pedagogy in the Conservatory. Before coming to Oberlin in 1991, Dr. Stuart was a member of the music faculties at the State University of New York in Plattsburgh and Plymouth State College of the University of New Hampshire system. She holds bachelor's and master's degrees in piano performance from the Eastman School of Music and a doctor of musical arts degree in historical performance from Cornell University.

CARL P. THUM is the Director of the Academic Skills Center at Dartmouth College. He received his B.A. in English from Union College, an M.A.

in English literature from Cleveland State University, and a Ph.D. in education from Cornell University. Since 1983, his work at Dartmouth has included helping students learn effectively and efficiently, improving the writing assistance program, expanding peer tutorial services, initiating accessibility services, producing learning strategies videos, and teaching education and writing courses.

JANET A. TIGHE is Dean of Freshmen and Director of Academic Advising in the College of Arts and Sciences of the University of Pennsylvania. Her undergraduate degree is from the Johns Hopkins University and her Ph.D. from the University of Pennsylvania. She plays an active role in the management of the academic advising system at Penn, which involves the coordinated efforts of the faculty, a professional advising staff, and a team of experts in such specialized fields as international programs. She is also a member of the History and Sociology of Science Department and previously co-directed the department's Health and Societies Program. Dr. Tighe has been awarded several teaching awards, and her research has been funded by the Woodrow Wilson National Fellowship Foundation, the Rockefeller Foundation, and the National Institute of Mental Health.

SUE WASIOLEK arrived at Duke University as a freshman 37 years ago and basically never left, except for a nine-month stint practicing law. She holds a B.A. in science education, an M.A. in health and hospital administration, and a L.L.M., all from Duke. She also completed her J.D. at North Carolina Central University and a Ed.D. from the University of Pennsylvania, with her research focusing on intercollegiate athletics. In addition to loving to go to school, Dr. Wasiolek has enormously enjoyed her work in Student Affairs for the past 30 years, currently serving as an Assistant Vice President for Student Affairs and the Dean of Students. She teaches education law, serves as an academic advisor, and just simply loves working with Duke students. She is co-author of *Getting the Best Out of College: A Professor, a Dean and a Student Tell You How to Maximize Your Experience*.

EMILY A. ZENICK has an undergraduate degree in speech communication from Syracuse University. She served as a Peace Corps volunteer in Thailand, where she taught English and developed income-generating projects for local women. Upon her return, she earned a master's degree in applied linguistics with a primary interest in second-language acquisition of third-culture kids. She has worked at Georgetown University since 1999, first in the Business School and now as an Assistant Dean in the School of Foreign Service.

INDEX

···